# ULTIMATE GUIDE TO
# Planting & Growing
# Vegetables at Home

A productive home garden is attainable in any space.

# ULTIMATE GUIDE TO
# Planting & Growing
# Vegetables at Home

## Get High-Yield Results with Expert Advice on Planting, Growing, Composting, and Controlling Pests for Over 80 Vegetable Varieties

By Editors of Creative Homeowner

CREATIVE
HOMEOWNER®

CREATIVE
HOMEOWNER®

*Ultimate Guide to Planting & Growing Vegetables at Home* (2025) contains content first published in *Garden DIY* (CompanionHouse Books 2020); *Organic Gardening Techniques* (New Holland Publishers 2008); *Low-Maintenance Vegetable Gardening* (CompanionHouse Books 2018); *Beginner's Garden* (IMM Lifestyle Books 2018); *You Bet Your Garden Guide to Growing Great Tomatoes, Second Edition* (Fox Chapel Publishing 2020); *Self-Sufficiency: Grow Your Own* (IMM Lifestyle Books 2011); *Homegrown Vegetables, Fruits, and Herbs* (Creative Homeowner 2010); *Fast, Fresh Garden Edibles* (Creative Homeowner 2011); and *Organic Book of Compost, 2nd Revised Edition* (IMM Lifestyle Books 2020).

*Ultimate Guide to Planting & Growing Vegetables at Home*
Managing Editor: Gretchen Bacon
Acquisitions Editor: Lauren Younker
Editor: Sherry Vitolo
Designer: Wendy Reynolds
Indexer: Jay Kreider


Paperback ISBN 978-1-58011-606-0
Hardcover ISBN 978-1-58011-619-0

Library of Congress Control Number: 2024918920


We are always looking for talented authors. To submit an idea, please send a brief inquiry to acquisitions@foxchapelpublishing.com.

Printed in China
First Printing

Creative Homeowner®, *www.creativehomeowner.com*, is an imprint of New Design Originals Corporation and distributed in North America by Fox Chapel Publishing Company, Inc., 800-457-9112, 903 Square Street, Mount Joy, PA 17552.

# About the Contributors

**Ian Cooke** has been a professional horticulturalist for over forty years. He runs his own consultancy, advising, designing, and writing on all matters horticultural, and is the author of six gardening books. He splits his time between the UK and the United States.

**Jane Courtier** has written many gardening books, including *The No-Garden Gardener*, *Patio and Courtyard Gardens*, and *Vegetable Gardening: From Planting to Picking—The Complete Guide to Creating a Bountiful Garden*. She contributes to many magazines, writing on a wide range of gardening topics.

**Nick Hamilton** is the owner of Barnsdale Gardens, Britain's largest collection of individually designed gardens with 39 working gardens on an eight-acre site. He carries on the legacy of his father, the late Geoff Hamilton, legendary host of the *BBC's Gardener's World* TV show. Nick is the author of *The Barnsdale Handy Gardener* and *Geoff Hamilton—A Gardening Legend*. He has a lifelong passion and enthusiasm for organic gardening, principles which he puts into effect at Barnsdale Gardens.

**Daniel Johnson and Samantha Johnson** (Phelps, Wisconsin) are siblings who have collaborated on a number of rural-living guidebooks, including *How to Raise Rabbits* and *Beginner's Guide to Beekeeping*. Both are 4-H alumni and live on the family farm, Fox Hill Farm, in far northern Wisconsin (*www.foxhillphoto.com*). Samantha is a certified horse show judge and raises purebred Welsh Mountain ponies and Dutch, Holland Lop, and Netherland Dwarf rabbits. Daniel is a professional photographer who specializes in imagery of farm life.

**Clare Matthews** runs a successful garden design business. Her own garden has both been filmed by *BBC Gardener's World* and featured in many leading gardening publications. She is the author of several books.

**Mike McGrath** is editor-at-large for *Organic Gardening* and is the former editor-in-chief. He writes a monthly column, "Mike McGrath's Tall Tales," and answers questions on the magazine's website. McGrath's "You Bet Your Garden" airs weekly on National Public Radio. He has made frequent guest appearances on NBC's *Weekend Today* and NPR's "All Things Considered."

**Alex Mitchell** is a journalist, author, and gardener. She has a regular column in *The Sunday Telegraph* where she covers everything from how to deter slugs to the best hand cream to use after a day in the elements. She studied at the Chelsea Physic Garden and grows her own fruits, salad, herbs, and vegetables.

**Pauline Pears** is head of knowledge transfer at Garden Organic Ryton, part of Garden Organic, which is Europe's largest organic membership organization. She and her team answer many thousands of gardening queries a year. She has written six books on organic gardening and is heavily involved with community composting, giving help and advice to members of the public.

**Jim Wilson** was a prolific educator, author, and gardener. He was one of the hosts of PBS's *The Victory Garden*, the national spokesman for the Garden Writers Association's Plant a Row for the Hungry program, and was elected to the Garden Writers Hall of Fame in 1995.

# Contents

## CHAPTER 6:
# Plant Profiles
# 194

**CHAPTER 7:**

## Sowing and Planting, Growing, and Harvesting     257

## CHAPTER 8: Storing and Using Your Produce     293

# Getting Started

The essentials of gardening are sunlight, siting, water, and tools. Once you familiarize yourself with these topics, the nuances of choosing your plants, soil, planning your garden, and more build off this foundational knowledge. It's important to remember that while this book covers general knowledge of planting and harvesting a vegetable garden, it's always key to know the specifics of your region and growing zone.

## Sunlight

Full sun is preferable, by far. No vegetables, fruits, or herbs will grow well in dense, daylong shade, and all but rhubarb will be challenged by light to mottled shade for most of the day. Most kinds will endure either afternoon or morning shade but will produce less than they would in full sun. (Although, afternoon shade can be beneficial where sunlight is extremely intense, such as in deserts and semitropical areas.) Midsummer—when the sun beams straight down at noon—is not the best time for evaluating how shadows might affect food production. Also, keep in mind that shadows from trees and buildings cover more ground during spring and fall months, which are the most enjoyable seasons for working in a food garden.

### Light and Shade

Fruit and vegetable plants like good, bright light; they will struggle to grow well in shade. Most yards are shady only in certain areas or at certain times of the day. On a sunny day, take photographs of your yard or outdoor space every two or three hours so that you have a record of exactly which areas are shaded and for how long. This will help you decide the best position for your vegetables.

If your urban outdoor space is shaded by high walls or fences, you can improve the quality of light by painting their surfaces white or a light color or by propping a reflective or light-colored material against them. Prune back trees and shrubs that are casting shade; however, if a neighbor's tree is causing the shade, first ask for permission.

A white background helps reflect light onto your plants, including those in planters on the wall (like these tomatoes).

### Warmth

Plants need warmth to start photosynthesizing and growing, but the amount of warmth they prefer varies from one species to another. In general, temperatures of 65–80°F (18–27°C) produce the best results but be sure to adjust your planting and sowing dates according to your climate.

You can extend the growing season by starting seeds indoors and planting them outdoors when warm enough, or by using covers. This is especially useful for plants that thrive in heat like tomatoes, squash, and peppers. Start cool-season vegetables, such as radishes, spinach, and turnips, directly outdoors.

Tomatoes are one of the warm-season crops, along with squash and peppers, that love the heat. In most regions, you'll want to start these indoors and wait for warm weather to plant them outside.

When choosing an area for your vegetable garden, pick one that will receive plenty of sunlight.

# Siting

Having little or no outdoor space doesn't mean that you have no room for growing vegetables. In the same way that fast-growing, easy-care vegetables don't require as much of your time as you might have expected, fruits and vegetables also don't need that much space. Don't just look at the obvious areas of ground space for growing your vegetables. You can grow plants in pots on balconies, on windowsills, and at the sides of paths and steps. Walls and fences can support climbers and scramblers, as well as hanging baskets.

If you are planning a roof garden or intend to grow vegetables on your balcony, be sure that the structures will support the weight of the plants and soil in pots, and that hanging baskets and window boxes are safely secured, especially if they are up high.

Once you've decided on a space, the next step is to look at the conditions. You may need to improve or adapt them before you can start growing your own vegetables.

## Small Spaces, Big Ideas

Don't let limited outdoor space make you think you can't grow your own food—there's always space for a vegetable of some kind. Take a look at the many small growing spaces throughout this book to provide inspiration for your own situation.

Your options will depend on your living accommodation. You may have a yard in which you can dedicate a small section for a patch, or you might be able to fit vegetables in with ornamental plantings in a flower bed or border. You can use a patio, deck, balcony, or roof space for growing vegetables. Even if these are not options for you, a window can be enough for fresh herbs, salad greens, and perhaps even a few sweet peppers.

The first step is to look at the space you have with an open mind. Any experienced gardener with a small yard knows that you have to make every inch count. By using some typical gardening techniques and adapting them in innovative ways, you can grow your own vegetables even in small spaces.

## Up On the Roof

A roof garden can be a wonderful oasis, providing the same options as a balcony. However, if you plan to make one, first be sure the roof is strong enough to support the

A vegetable patch doesn't need to be huge. This small, informal plot provides plenty of space for beans, carrots, and beets, among other vegetables.

Urban gardeners are adept at using roof spaces for vegetable gardening, but they need to make sure the structure is strong enough to support the weight of the fully planted pots.

Vertical structures are great solutions to make extra space for growing vegetables.

A courtyard garden is an ideal space for plants. Even if there's no soil, you can build raised beds to grow your vegetables.

weight. Even when using lightweight containers and a soilless mix, freshly watered plants in pots can be heavy. As with a balcony, a structural engineer can advise you whether your roof area is structurally safe.

## At Ground Level

For some homes, the outdoor space is just a small patio area, completely paved over, with no soil in which to grow plants. Often these small plots are courtyards, surrounded with walls or fences. As long as they get some sun for at least part of the day, these can be ideal places to grow plants in containers; tender vegetables, such as peppers and tomatoes, will thrive in the sheltered conditions. Walls and paving absorb heat from the sun during the day and gradually release it over several hours, meaning that a sheltered patio or courtyard can remain several degrees warmer than the surrounding area into the night. It will protect plants from frost and chilling winds, giving you heavier and earlier crops.

It may be possible to lift an area of paving to expose some soil underneath, or you can build a raised bed directly on top of the paving. Raised beds allow you to try a wider range of plants than you can grow in pots. If you do have a yard with ground space, you may want to plan what areas will be reserved for gardening. This helps avoid your entire yard being taken up by your growing vegetables.

## Root Competition

When siting your garden, make sure it is well away from sizeable trees. Tree roots can reach out 1½ times as far as the diameter of the foliage canopy. When trees want water and nutrients, they take them—sucking lesser plants dry and robbing them of nutrients. Cutting invasive tree roots yearly with a spade won't work for long. Roots will retake the moist, porous soil of your vegetable garden in a matter of weeks.

## Drainage

For vegetable gardening, you need to consider both surface and internal drainage. All vegetables and herbs grow best in moderately well-drained soil. Wet soil warms slowly in the spring and is more likely to harbor organisms that cause root rot. Loose, sandy soil drains too rapidly if not modified with organic matter.

Before you select a site for your garden, traverse it like a golfer assessing the best track for a long putt. Look for a good, uniform slope that can carry away heavy rainfall. If the area is level, you will need to build up beds to give your vegetables well-drained root runs. Make sure there are no low spots or swales where runoff from higher areas could create gullies or where water could stand for a day or two. Internal drainage is a function not only of the soil type (clay, loam, silt, or sand), but also of how much you modify your soil with organic matter.

## Choosing the Right Location

Choosing the right location is the best way to start if you want to grow great vegetables with the minimum of effort. Give your vegetable garden the best growing space in your yard or outdoor area. This will save you from the struggle of trying to modify an area that is less than perfect. While it is possible to improve the negative aspects of some sites, it is definitely easier not to. The ideal location is fairly sunny and sheltered with good, well-drained soil that is not prone to flooding, becoming waterlogged, or drying out completely, and where there is no competition from the roots of large trees or vast areas of shade.

Some difficulties can be overcome. A windy site, for instance, can be protected by adding a windbreak in the form of fencing, a trellis, or wires held on posts that are used to support rugged climbers. Poor soil can be improved using organic matter or avoided by building raised beds (see pages 128–136), and shady areas can be opened up with careful pruning. If your garden has to be close to the house, it can be prettied up enough to be proud of. But regardless of the situation, be realistic about what you can achieve.

### THE BASICS
Give your vegetable garden the area with the most favorable growing conditions. The ideal is a sunny, sheltered area with good soil and good drainage.

The siting of this property-line beet garden still allows for prolific vegetable growth despite being in a narrow space.

## Grouping

When creating your vegetable garden, you should always try to avoid grouping all your plants of any one kind in one spot. If, for instance, you have eight tomato plants and eight raised beds, you should place one plant in each bed instead of filling up, say, two of the beds with all your tomato plants.

Grouping all of your plants of the same type together can lead to pests and diseases. Once a bad bug or plant sickness finds one of your vegetable plants, it will spread its negative effects quickly to the adjacent ones. Numerous research studies have found that simply mixing up your plantings greatly limits the spread of disease and discourages garden pests.

You want to avoid planting some plants, like tomatoes, in the same spot season after season. If you do plant them in the same spots, soil-borne diseases like verticillium or fusarium wilt can attack your plants. How long do you have to wait until a spot is safe again? Nobody knows for sure, but a three-year rotation is a safe bet.

If you have a large area for your vegetable garden, you can position your plants perfectly, as well. "Perfect" is where they will get the first possible rays of the morning sun. Vegetables, such as corn and cabbages, do not need the morning sun, but tomato plants need morning rays. If you can't manage to position your garden to get the morning sun, make sure your plants are out in the open, with good air circulation all around. Before you dig holes for your plants, you'll want to make sure:

1. The plants won't be crowded when they reach full size.
2. The plants aren't all grouped together unless you deliberately want to plant them all in one or two large beds with enough room for 1' (30.5cm) of open space between each fully grown plant so you can rotate them to different beds next year. This can be a good strategy—but only if you give each plant lots of room.
3. The plants are in a spot in the garden that gets the most and earliest morning sun, and are out in the open with good air circulation all around. (Don't plant your vegetables up against a wall or where they'll be surrounded by other tall plants.)

Crowding is more of an irreparable issue. If you're short on space, you may have to give away a few of

You'll always get more and better-quality plants from thoughtfully spaced raised beds rather than flat earth.

When digging your holes, make sure each plant has plenty of room and the right amount of light.

Always remove the leaves from the lower half of the plant and plant it deeper than you think you should.

your vegetable plants, grow your extras in a nearby community garden, or use containers, because crowding will hurt your garden. You'll get a lot more from two plants with elbow room than you will from six plants crammed together.

# Water

Water is important for plants. Water pressure within the cells keeps plants firm and upright, preventing them from wilting. All the minerals needed must be dissolved in water before plants can transport and make use of them, and water is essential for photosynthesis, the process by which plants manufacture their energy. The natural source of water for plants is rain, but in some areas, there is not enough rainfall for growing certain vegetables. Urban gardens surrounded by tall buildings often receive a limited amount of rain. For vegetable plants being grown in containers, where the amount of soil is restricted, natural rainfall is rarely sufficient.

Virtually all vegetables have a high water requirement, so keeping your garden irrigated in dry weather is recommended. In particular, containers will need regular

watering. Freshly transplanted vegetables will also need regular watering. Germinating seeds are also very sensitive, and you must avoid damaging delicate seedlings or the soil structure. A heavy sprinkler pounding water onto a seedbed is likely to cap the surface, preventing seedlings from emerging.

Individual plants will, however, have certain peak times in their growth sequence when water is most important. For example, tomatoes must have enough water when the flowers are ready for pollination or they will not set, and potatoes must have generous supplies of water when the tubers are swelling.

In general, the principle should always be to apply liberal quantities of water to allow the soil to become fully charged, then repeating this only when the soil is showing signs of drying. Frequent small applications of water are not recommended as they only dampen the surface and do not penetrate to the roots. You should apply water thoroughly using a hose to get the soil completely moist down to the root level. A good sprinkler with coarse droplets is ideal in the evening or at night rather than in bright sunshine or windy conditions, when a proportion of the water will be lost to evaporation.

Lettuce is just one of the vegetables that will wilt quickly if not provided with adequate amounts of water.

## Water Conservation

In this era of water shortages, storing rainwater is a great option for conserving water in your garden. Various techniques and pieces of equipment are available to divert rainwater into a storage water butt. *Note: This type of stored water is stagnant and may contain plant diseases, so should not be used with any young seedlings.*

It is possible, but not advised to use gray water, which is recycled water from your washing machine, bath, and dishwasher. You can buy diverter kits, which will channel this water into water butts or storage tanks, but this water often contains cleaning agents or other chemicals.

Mulching refers to the spreading of a "blanket" of material over the soil to help retain moisture by reducing evaporation and reduce weed growth. This is often a bulky organic material such as mushroom compost, shredded bark, or leaf mold. For your vegetable garden, you can also use polyethylene sheets or a purpose-made horticultural fabric as a base.

Mulches should always be applied when the soil is already moist so that the water within the soil is trapped.

Organic mulches will slowly break down and act as general soil improvers. They can also be important sources of nutrients, particularly trace elements. A mulch should be applied 3" to 4" (7.6 to 10.2cm) deep to be effective. All mulches also help to regulate soil temperatures, keeping them cool in summer and warm in winter.

## Irrigation

You can economize on water use for your garden by running soaker hoses down rows. The slow drip of water from the porous rubber hoses minimizes evaporation by placing it in the root zone of plants rather than spraying it into the air. Sprinkler irrigation can evaporate or be blown away from your targeted plants. Even if you are not under restrictions on watering, you should consider drip irrigation to save money and ensure optimum growth of your plants. Drip irrigation does have a shortcoming, however; the water spreads horizontally only about 9" (22.9cm) to either side of the leaky hose or drip emitter. The cone of moist soil widens somewhat as the water gravitates down, but you still need to direct-seed or transplant seedlings close enough to the water source to meet your plants' soil moisture needs.

The old saying of "an inch of water per week" won't cut it for vegetable gardens during hot, dry spells, and rarely do summer rains occur weekly. So, plan on irrigating every four to seven days, and providing at least 1" (2.5cm) of water each time. That entails a lot of moving of water hoses, so you should site your garden as near as possible to a faucet. One faucet with a Y adapter can handle two hoses with sprayers or soaker hoses laid down the center of raised beds.

Some homes are equipped with water softeners. Make sure that your outside faucets are not connected to the softener, or you may be irrigating your vegetable garden with sodium-laced water. If water is scarce in your community, consider installing soaker hoses made of porous material down each row to provide drip irrigation. You might also install a catch-barrel for rainwater. Connect it to a downspout from your roof.

## Watering

Watering is one of those jobs that is far more complicated than most people's perception of it. The timing is all-important, and changes based on the season.

### WATERING DURING WINTER AND SPRING

Watering is very important in the late winter and early spring, as slightly too much water will cause your vegetables to rot, while underwatering may cause a delay in your vegetables' growth. If you are ever in doubt about whether you're watering enough during this time, don't be. Even though this may mean that your vegetables grow later in the year, you should always err on the side of caution—a later plant is by far better than one that has rotted in the garden.

To counter this problem during the spring for potted plants, stand all your pots on capillary matting. At least once a day, water the matting to ensure it is kept wet, as the pots will take up the water they require from this matting. It works, as the name suggests, through capillary action, with the drier soil drawing water from the wetter capillary mat. If the soil is not dry, it will not draw up any water, so there is no chance of plants rotting through overwatering using this method. It also limits the amount of overhead watering that is required, minimizing the potential for fungal diseases.

At this time of year, use a watering can with a fine rose to water your garden. Even with a fine rose, there is generally a sudden rush of water out of the can as it

Save water by switching from a sprinkler to soaker hoses.

is tipped forward before it stabilizes into a steady flow. Always start by holding the can away from the garden, and move it over the seedlings once the initial rush of water has passed.

## WATERING DURING WARMER WEATHER

As the weather warms and the light levels increase, the plants' requirement for water becomes greater, so you should switch to a medium rose on the watering can to dispense more water. With warmer weather, there's less of a need for precise watering due to the increased evaporation from the soil surface and loss of water through the plant leaves. This does not mean that water can be applied without thought or care; it simply means that there is a little bit more leeway between watering the right amount and overwatering. This is important because at some point the plants will require feeding, whether to encourage growth or for flowering and fruiting, and this is usually applied as a liquid feed when watering.

In addition to using a watering can, you can also water your vegetable garden with a hose or sprinkler. There will be more evaporation of water from the plant leaves as well as the soil surface, due not only to the summer heat but also to exposure to wind. Underwatering can result in the plants running to seed, producing hard and inedible vegetables, or just ending up with a much-reduced yield, so the need for ample water is vital. The vegetables need to be started in the correct way, and applying water to the bottom of a shallow furrow before sowing will get the seeds germinating quickly and growing properly.

Giving transplanted vegetable plants a good watering after planting will ensure that they do not wilt and continue to grow unchecked, resulting in a bumper yield.

To ensure your vegetables are ready to harvest when planned, the plants must be kept growing at their optimum rate, which is why watering, particularly at stressful times for plants, is so essential. Once your vegetables have been sown or planted, there is no definitive timetable for applying water because each vegetable has different water needs and the weather will not be consistent. It is important to be aware that windy or breezy and sunny days are very drying. It is good to check your garden areas every day.

You have a little more leeway when watering plants in warm weather.

# Tools

You no longer have to do every job by hand to have a productive vegetable garden. Over the years, tools and pieces of equipment have been developed to make every job in the garden that much easier. Most gardeners swear by the tools and equipment they have had for years, but modern developments in certain areas have made gardening much easier, so the best range of tools is a mix between the two.

## Essential Tools

The following tools are the everyday pillars of the home vegetable garden. Depending on the type of garden and the vegetables you're planting, these items are necessary for truly successful planting.

### SPADE

Soil cultivation is one of the most essential parts of the productive process, and the spade is the workhorse most used to satisfy this requirement. There are two basic types, the border spade and the digging or garden spade. Although named for use in other areas of the garden, the border spade does have a place in some growers' sheds, particularly those with bad backs or limited mobility, or who just find a digging spade too heavy to handle when full of soil. The better the quality of the spade, the more expensive it will be, but the longer it will last. For that reason, you should look toward wooden-handled border and digging spades.

There is a spade out there for everyone, as different makes have different lengths of handle. There is no substitute for going to the garden center and trying out prospective spades in person. This will limit the problem of backaches caused by using an inappropriate piece of equipment.

The digging spade has a larger blade and therefore stronger handle than the border spade, as it is made for heavier work. Both types will need to be treated with respect to ensure that the blade is not damaged nor the handle broken. The great advantage of wooden-handled types is that, after many years of use, when the spade has more than fulfilled the promise shown on that first day and the handle finally snaps, you can buy a new handle to replace the broken one. This is not possible with plastic handles.

Border spades are smaller than digging spades, so you can use them in tighter spaces.

A digging spade with a wooden handle can withstand heavy-duty use.

If you are going to be doing a lot of digging, it may be worthwhile investing in a spade that has a foot tread on the blade. It is very easy to get into the digging groove and, without thinking, end up with a hole in the bottom of a good pair of boots because the corner of the spade has pierced it. This generally happens when pushing into heavier ground, but if this may be a problem, then a spade with a foot tread is the answer. It will spread the weight on the underside of the foot and prevent the spade from piercing any quality boot soles.

## FORK

The concerns of quality and handle length apply to forks, as well. A fork is used for many more jobs than a spade, although not usually for such heavy work. It can be used for cultivating, breaking up lumpy soil, harvesting root vegetables, dividing large clumps of herbs and artichokes, and filling wheelbarrows with organic matter, as well as many other jobs in your vegetable garden. There are

The versatile garden fork has a wide range of uses.

digging forks and specialized border forks, with the border forks having a smaller head. These are useful for gardeners who cannot manage the larger digging forks.

### SPORK

A spork is a hybrid between a spade and a fork, hence the name. It does a job that is somewhere between the two, as the tines are wider than a standard fork, without having a complete blade like a spade.

For gardeners confined to a wheelchair or with limited mobility, this tool is easier to use than a spade, while moving more soil than a standard fork.

### TROWEL

Trowels are usually sold in sets with small forks. The trowel is primarily used when planting or transplanting crops outside, although it can also be used to divide

smaller clumps of herbs, where a spade or fork would be too large. Along with the dibble, this is probably the most likely tool to be lost or inadvertently damaged.

Trowels also work well as measuring sticks, so, depending on which vegetable is being planted, using the trowel will very often save on having to fetch the planting board. There are also easy-grip trowels available, with a soft-grip handle angled approximately 90 degrees from the trowel blade.

### DIBBLE

Essentially, the dibble is a tool for making a long hole in which to sow large seeds, such as fava (broad) beans or runner beans, or to plant vegetables. There are types that have markings down their length that are very useful when determining at what depth the appropriate seed is being sown. Although dibbles make excellent presents, if you do not want to go to that expense for yourself, they are cheap and simple to make.

Trowels and small forks work well for more precise work.

A dibble is used to make holes for sowing seeds or transplanting seedlings.

Invaluable for planting seeds, leeks, and onion sets, a calibrated dibble is a garden essential.

## RAKE

The garden rake is a must for leveling ground and preparing seedbeds, but it is also one of the most dangerous tools in the garden shed. It is so easy to lay it down in between jobs, forget where you put it, and then cause severe facial damage to yourself or somebody else when you inadvertently stand on the rake head. When not in use, rakes should always be left with the head up and the end of the handle on the ground. It is better still to hang them up in a toolshed or cupboard.

The head of the rake usually comprises between eight and fifteen prongs. Rakes are available with varying gaps between each prong, with everybody having a particular favorite dependent on their soil type, what they want their rake to achieve, and their past experience. It is possible to buy metal, wooden, or plastic rakes to fit the requirement. When raking soil, the rake head will collect large soil clumps and stones but allow the majority of soil to pass through.

## LONG-HANDLED HOE

There are two main types of long-handled hoe: the draw hoe and the Dutch hoe. It is beneficial to have one of each in your shed, with the Dutch hoe being used for weeding and the draw hoe mainly for making furrows.

In a productive vegetable garden, weeds should usually be small and therefore young and soft when they are hoed off, so the Dutch hoe, which is pushed forward to cut off the top of the weeds where they meet the soil, is very easy and efficient at the job. The draw hoe is very good for chopping through larger, woodier weeds, as a sharp downward action will usually do the job. The draw hoe can move quite a lot of soil around during weeding, while the soil falls through the large central hole of a Dutch hoe, leaving the soil very much in place.

## ONION HOE

The much smaller handheld onion hoe is used where the other types of hoe would be too cumbersome. It is ideal for hoeing weeds growing in between plants growing in rows.

A long-handled draw hoe (bottom) or Dutch hoe (top) will be helpful for weeding.

Wheelbarrows with inflatable tires will make pushing heavier loads much easier.

## WHEELBARROW

There will always be material that has to be moved around the productive areas, and there is no better piece of equipment for this task than the wheelbarrow. For a larger vegetable garden, the wheelbarrow is used to transport mostly soil, compost, or farmyard manure. For tiny vegetable areas, a bucket may suffice, but most people will find a wheelbarrow essential.

As with most tools, there are several different makes, each having good points and bad, with each being preferred by some gardeners. It is beneficial to have a wheelbarrow with an inflatable rubber tire. Although there may be the odd puncture to repair, pushing heavy loads, such as organic matter or soil, will be made much easier with this type of tire. The most satisfying use of a wheelbarrow is when you have to use it to bring the harvest from the productive garden to the house.

## HAMMER

Apart from the obvious hammering in of nails when building structures such as compost bins, a hammer is handy for smashing items, such as brassica stems, before they are put into the compost bin.

## TAPE MEASURE

If you do not have a planting board, then a tape measure is the next best thing to use for ensuring that your row and plant spacing is correct.

## PLANTING BOARD

A planting board is used for measuring the distance between rows and the planting distances of various vegetables and herbs.

## PLANKS

For anybody growing on a heavy clay soil, planks are imperative if work is to be carried out in the winter. The planks will spread the weight of both heavy wheelbarrows and people, thereby reducing compaction. This in turn keeps that excellent soil structure in place that has taken so much work to achieve.

You can buy ready-made planting boards or make your own. Even something as simple as a piece of wood with measurement labels will work.

Garden twine is a great option for keeping your planting lines neat and organized.

## GARDEN TWINE

There can be nothing more exciting than seeing a line of newly sown seeds germinating and nothing more disappointing than that line not being straight. Apart from the aesthetic pleasure gained from seeing a straight line, if a line of seedlings is not straight, it will either be taking up unnecessary space on one side or be too close to a row on the other. You can buy garden twine on a special holder but winding the string onto two 18" (45.7cm) lengths of bamboo is just as good.

When setting out your line, pull it tight and make sure that it is still tight when you are planting along its length and while making any shallow furrows. You need to check it on a regular basis to ensure that it has not moved. The simplest way to check it is to pull it upward, away from the soil, and let it go—it will end up in the same position if it hasn't moved.

## KNIFE

In the average garden, it is generally necessary to have only a pocketknife that can be used for a variety of jobs in the vegetable areas. A blunt knife is more dangerous than a sharp one, so be sure to keep your knife sharp by touching up the blade with a suitable sharpening stone on a regular basis.

## PRUNING SHEARS

In your vegetable garden in particular, pruning shears will be used on a very regular basis, so a good-quality pair is a must. Not only will these last longer, but they will also produce a better cut, and the better-quality blade will require less sharpening. There are two distinct types: anvil pruning shears or bypass pruning shears. The anvil types have the upper blade coming down onto a flat surface, whereas bypass pruning shears have the blade cutting past the usually curved lower section.

Some gardeners feel that the anvil types may bruise the branches and stems that are cut because the blade pushes them against the anvil in the process of cutting. With the bypass type, if the blade is not perfectly sharp, the stem or branch being cut will snag; in other words, it does not make a clean cut, leaving an uneven surface that will be more susceptible to disease. Gardeners are adamant in their opinions about the best type, but both have pros and cons. Some bypass pruning shears can also be taken apart completely, which makes maintenance and blade sharpening very easy.

## PRUNING SAW

This piece of equipment is for cutting branches that are too large to be cut by pruning shears. A lot of pruning saws are now folding types, which makes them much safer to carry around. When making your purchase, ensure that the blade has a good locking system, so that when the blade is open, it cannot suddenly shut onto your fingers.

## SPADE-CLEANING TOOL

Plastic, wooden, and even metal spade-cleaning tools are available, but you can make one yourself. An odd piece of wood lying around can be cut into the correct shape, and the edges then smoothed with a piece of sandpaper. It is worth keeping an edge on the flat cleaning end. This means that the tool does not really need to be too big, so 6" (15.2cm) is generally long enough. It is a simple piece of equipment that is used to keep a spade blade clean of

Bypass-type pruning shears have curved blades.

A watering can with a rose attachment is a must for your vegetable garden.

soil, making digging that much easier. As the soil begins to stick to the blade, run th cleaning tool down the blade's length three or four times before you begin digging again.

### WATERING CAN
A watering can is a must for any productive garden because it will direct water exactly where it is needed. Watering cans come in a range of shapes and sizes, as well as being made from plastic or metal, and available in various colors. Always buy one that has a rose attachment. The most important point to remember is that you must be able to lift it high enough for watering when completely full.

### RAIN BARREL
It is very important with the erratic weather patterns to have a rain barrel at the end of every available downspout to collect water for use on the productive areas. Make sure that the barrel is easily accessible and has an easy-to-use outlet point. Usually, you will need to stand the rain barrel on something, such as stacked bricks, so that

Rain barrels collect valuable water for use on your garden.

you can access the outlet point. As water becomes scarce, the need for collecting your own becomes vital because vegetables and herbs will bolt (send up flower spikes) very quickly if left to go dry.

## HOSES

Used correctly, hoses are not wasteful pieces of garden equipment, although it is essential to check before use whether there is a watering ban in place. In larger vegetable gardens, it is much easier to roll out a long hose and put the same amount of water onto your vegetables than it is to traipse backward and forward with a watering can. When buying a hose, look for a better-quality one that does not kink, and store it on a specially made reel, as it will last longer.

## SOAKER HOSES AND DRIP IRRIGATION

Soaker hoses or drip irrigation are essential for many short-term as well as long-term vegetables. You can lay a soaker hose on the ground next to the vegetable plant, and attach it to a hose that runs to the water faucet. As long as the water is turned on, the hose will constantly drip water exactly where it is required. Soaker hoses are often made from recycled rubber, and the tiny openings in it allow water to easily seep out of the hose. Therefore, not much pressure is needed to force the water droplets out and into the soil. The great advantage of this is that it can be run from a rain barrel and does not need to be attached to a faucet. Drip irrigation is slightly different in that you can bury the pipe just under the ground next to the desired plant.

## POT MAKER

The need to be more environmentally friendly is not going away, and recycling paper is one of the easiest things you can do. With a simple pot maker, you can use surplus newspaper by transforming it into small biodegradable pots that are ideal for starting seedlings. Then, when you are ready, you can transplant the seedlings directly, paper pots and all!

## FIRMING BOARD

Firming boards are used to firm the soil when sowing into seed trays. You can buy them, but they are easy to make.

## SPRAYER

Most vegetable gardeners will find a small hand sprayer sufficient, although some handheld pump-action types

Small holes allow the soaker hose to continually release droplets of water.

A chipper/shredder is a big help in preparing materials for the compost heap.

are worth considering for the ease of use. You need only one sprayer—provided you clean it well after each use—because you will use it only for organically permissible insecticides or fungicides.

### CHIPPER/SHREDDER

A chipper/shredder is an absolute must for the vegetable grower. All types of waste can be passed through a chipper/shredder and recycled into one part of the garden or the another. Tough vegetable waste needs to be shredded before going onto the compost heap. Do not be fooled by very cheap machines that will manage only to squash most of the material. With a chipper/shredder, you get what you pay for.

### LAWN MOWER

If you have grass paths growing in or along your vegetable garden, then a lawn mower is an essential piece of equipment for keeping this grass under control. This piece of machinery is very much like the spade, in that all gardeners seem to have their own personal preference, for no other reason than they like and get along well with the mower they have.

### STRING TRIMMER

String trimmers (commonly known as "weed whackers") are used for tidying up around fruit trees and those areas that mowers cannot reach. It is important always to wear sturdy boots when using one of these, as well as a pair of goggles, to protect against the inevitable flying objects. The bulkier gas string trimmers will come with a string head, used for clearing long grass, weeds, and the like, and a blade head for tougher materials, such as brambles. For gardeners who cannot cope with the weight of gas string trimmers, there is a range of excellent lightweight alternatives. It is also possible to buy a string trimmer with a revolving handle that will cut the lawn edges as well.

### SEED SOWERS

Many gardeners sow seeds with their fingers. Unfortunately, this seed-sowing method, which is taken for granted by most, is not possible for all gardeners, so having a piece of equipment to do the job easily and accurately is important for some. A ball sower uses the suction from a rubber ball to suck the seeds up a needle-like tube, so that they can then be released in the appropriate place. This is an excellent device for all seed sizes, as there are different sizes of tubes for the varying seed sizes.

For gardeners who do not have the use of their hands for sowing, there is also a mouth-operated seed sower available. It looks like a pen connected by a tube to the mouthpiece, and it is the suction created from the mouth that enables the seeds to be picked up and easily dropped

There are many great precision seed-sowing options available.

Gardening gloves protect your hands from soil pathogens, broken materials, and the regular wear and tear of tough jobs.

on the surface of the soil. A filter is provided to prevent inhalation of any dust particles and seeds.

### EASY-GRIP ADD-ON HANDLE

For gardeners with hand or wrist problems, these handles can make their work easier. They fit onto tools with handles up to 16" (40.6cm) long. They are attached with finger-operated wing nuts and come with optional arm support.

### GARDENING GLOVES

You should always have a stout pair of gardening gloves, such as disposable vinyl gloves, to protect your hands when doing tough jobs. Soil can easily contain pathogens, which cause infections, and there is always the risk of broken glass or rusty metal. You can also use a good skin cream on your hands before and after a gardening session.

## Optional Equipment

The tools in this section aren't entirely necessary depending on the space and vegetables you're working with, but they are indispensable in some cases and extremely helpful in most.

### ELECTRIC TILLER

An electric tiller, or rototiller, is a handy piece of machinery. Whether you own, borrow, or rent one, it will cultivate land and prepare areas down to a fine tilth suitable for direct seed sowing. They can be rear-wheel-driven or powered by the rotary blades at the front that churn the soil.

Electric tillers can be used regularly on light soils, but beware of using them too often on heavy clay soils. The blades will smear the clay soil into an almost impenetrable barrier to water (called a pan), which will drastically impair drainage. Most modern machines will cultivate to a depth of between 6" and 9" (15.2 and 22.9cm), so digging is required in most years.

### INTERCHANGEABLE GARDEN TOOL SET

If space is limited for tool storage, or you have problems bending down, then an interchangeable garden tool set can be very helpful to you. These sets come in various sizes with varying handle lengths to suit gardeners of all heights. The vast range of tool heads available includes forks, trowels, rakes, hoes, tillers, edgers, loppers, shears, pruning saws, and more.

### DIY TOOLS

Gardeners who prefer to make instead of buy garden structures (for example, compost bins or hoophouses) will find equipment, such as handsaws and screwdrivers, very useful.

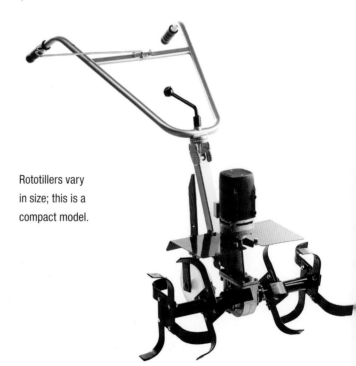

Rototillers vary in size; this is a compact model.

## SLEDGEHAMMER/CLUB HAMMER

Although you can dig holes and refill the soil around supporting stakes, knocking them into the ground using a sledgehammer or smaller club hammer will give a much firmer hold in the ground. Although these hammers are ideal for specific jobs, you might consider borrowing one because their general use in the productive garden is limited and may not warrant the purchase price.

## SPRINKLER

As with the hose, before you invest in a sprinkler, it is prudent to check whether it is possible to use one, or whether they are covered under any water restrictions. Always look for sprinklers that are sturdy and have an adjustable sprinkler head that can be set to water only the areas requiring it. These types are able to water in a full circle or can be adjusted to water partial circles, ensuring that water is not wasted.

## LAWN EDGER

Although a spade can be used to keep the grass edges looking neat and tidy, the blade of a spade is slightly curved, so this straight-edged piece of equipment will do the job much better. For gardeners with back problems, longer-handled versions are available.

## EDGING SHEARS

Edging shears are another piece of equipment designed simply to keep the grass edges looking neat, so that they do not detract from the well-kept productive areas. Also available are lightweight shears, ones with longer or telescopic handles, and shears with geared blades, for gardeners with mobility problems. A great addition to fit most edging shears is the edging-shears grass collector. This does exactly what it says it does by collecting the cut grass at the time of cutting. This saves you the job of having to collect it later.

## FLEECE

Horticultural fleece is a useful white fabric that can be used as a floating mulch, protecting plants from insect pests and frost, or used to warm up the soil early in spring. It gets a little dirty but will last several seasons.

Horticultural fleece provides wamrth and protects against pests.

Chicken wire is an easy solution for keeping animals away from your vegetables.

## CHICKEN WIRE

Chicken wire can be pinned to the soil to keep rodents away from pea and bean seeds, or bent into arched tunnels to keep birds and butterflies off brassicas (cabbages).

## INSECT-PROOF MESH

This mesh is used to protect vegetables from even the smallest insect pest. It's fairly expensive, but can be reused and has the advantage of allowing more air to circulate than fleece.

## PLASTIC BOTTLES

You can make individual cloches out of bottles for small seedlings to protect them from slugs.

## SEED COMPOST

For your vegetable garden, you can use seed compost for planting small seeds.

Modified plastic bottles are excellent, cost-effective cloches to protect your plants.

## Seed-Sowing Tools

For seed sowing, use either small 3" (7.6cm) plastic pots or seed-starting trays—plastic grids of interconnected cells available from any garden center. These are great because, when it's time to transplant the seedlings, you just pop out the cell and plant the whole thing, so you don't have to worry about damaging the roots.

## HOW TO TRANSPLANT SEEDLINGS FROM SEED-STARTING TRAYS

Getting plants out of pots without destroying them is a basic but much overlooked skill. The best way to get your seedlings out intact is to give each cell a gentle squeeze to loosen the roots from the sides, and then poke up through the drainage hole with a stick or the blunt end of a pencil. The whole plant, roots and all, should just pop out, and you can then replant it into a bigger container, handling it by the root ball so you don't damage the plant itself. Also see page 267.

Labels are good for reminding you what you've sown where.

Those gardening in containers can do everything they need with a hand trowel, some nice pots, and a watering can with a rose attachment (a perforated spout).

To make your own raised beds or any of the building projects in the book, you'll need some of the construction tools discussed here.

## Construction Tools:
## A Few Things You'll Need

As a gardener, you may know all about your garden tools, but are you equally adept and knowledgeable about basic construction tools? Here is a quick rundown of the basics you may need when planning and planting your vegetable garden. Many of these tools are common to any household, but some are more specialized and require proper skills to pick up and use safely.

### CIRCULAR SAW

A circular saw is one of the most useful items a DIYer can have on hand in the workshop. Besides its ability to quickly and easily make crosscuts, circular saws are adaptable enough to make miter cuts and rip cuts. You'll find circular saws with a traditional power cord, or you might look into circular saws that run on rechargeable batteries. Battery-powered saws are convenient but may not have quite the strength that a traditionally powered circular saw will have.

### ELECTRIC DRILL

On frequent occasions, a modern cordless electric drill can be used as an electric screwdriver. Coupled with the right bits (you might consider collecting a variety of Phillips, flat, square, and Torx "star" bits in various sizes) and a good selection of screw sizes, an electric drill will allow you to breeze through construction projects, quickly fastening lumber and building large and small items out of wood with minimal effort. You can use cordless drills, but consider your needs and select one with enough voltage to perform at the level you want; at least 12 volts is good, while more might be better. (More voltage may mean a heavier drill.)

### JIGSAW

Perfect for making rounded cuts or for cutting small pieces in tight places, a jigsaw is useful for adding artistic or decorative touches to many woodworking projects. Look for a jigsaw that is powerful enough for what you want it to do, and be sure to purchase the right blade for the right job.

## TABLE SAW

Most of the time when you're making basic cuts to lumber, it's a crosscut—that is, cutting across the grain. But the need often arises to make a rip cut, where you cut along the grain, splitting a piece of lumber lengthwise. A table saw is often the easiest and most accurate way to perform a rip cut, and it can save a lot of time if you frequently need to work this way. Keep in mind that table saws are a large machine and a large investment that you may or may not want to make.

## MITER SAW

Whenever you're faced with a large number of crosscuts to make, a miter saw can greatly simplify and speed up this process. The same job could be performed with a circular saw, but the miter saw is a lot more convenient and more accurate. Another advantage of the miter saw is its ability to quickly and easily make angled cuts; this can come in handy quite a bit whenever you're making multiple cuts that will fit together, like four mitered corners. Again, the circular saw could achieve the same results, but it's a bit more challenging to make an accurate miter cut with a circular saw.

## HAMMER

You probably already have a hammer. It's most likely a claw hammer—the kind with two tapering spikes in the back for prying on things or removing stuck nails. You're probably already familiar with the basics of hammering nails (although not every project requires nailing), and using the hammer to tap or push stuck pieces of lumber

The right jigsaw will be useful for plain cuts or rounded or more detailed cuts.

A miter saw is the most convenient, quick option for making angled cuts.

into place. All in all, you'll want to keep that hammer and those skills nearby during the construction process.

## FINISH NAILER

For any projects that require nailing, a finish nailer powered by an air compressor makes things easy and fast. Even if you don't have access to a finish nailer, keep in mind that you can always nail by hand with a hammer, but consider predrilling your nail holes in this case; it makes the nailing process much smoother.

## TAPE MEASURE

You won't get too far on your DIY projects without a good tape measure to guide you on your way. From measuring lumber to marking your cuts, a quality tape measure with a good locking mechanism is essential to have on hand. A common length is 25' (7.6m), although you could probably get away with a shorter tape measure for vegetable garden projects.

## PENCIL

You'll need a pencil on hand for making cut lines and other marks. Carpentry pencils are the best options. They are thicker (so you get a bolder and easier-to-see mark on your lumber) and usually have a flattened shape so that the pencil won't constantly go rolling off your worktable

or saw horses every time you move a piece of lumber. Also, you can keep your carpentry pencils sharp with a utility knife.

## UTILITY KNIFE

From making minor modifications to wood to cutting plastics or twines, a utility knife can be handy anytime you need to make a small precision cut with a sharp object. Do take care, though—the razor blades used in utility knives are extremely sharp.

## LEVEL

You don't want projects to come out crooked—you want straight, level lines, and the best way to achieve that is with a level. Doubling as handy rulers for marking straight lines, a 1', 2', or 4' (30.5, 61, or 121.9cm) level will help you keep things straight by means of a simple bubble indicator that centers itself when the object on which it sits is perfectly level. You can also do the same thing vertically for verifying the straightness of a vertical line— this is called "plumb" rather than "level."

## FRAMING SQUARE

This handy L-shaped tool is useful to have around any time you're trying to build 90-degree corners or anything else that needs to come out square. Hold the framing

Choose a quality tape measure with a good locking mechanism.

Use a framing square to quickly determine the straightness of your angles.

Use ear protection, dust masks, and safety glasses to keep your project fun.

square up to your corner, and with one quick glance, you can determine the straightness of your angle. It also makes a great ruler for marking straight lines.

### TRIANGLE SQUARE

Triangle squares are smaller and useful for marking both straight and angled cuts—you'll surely want to have one at arm's length (or on your tool belt) anytime you do carpentry work.

### SAWHORSES

Your carpentry work will be much easier if you have a good space to work on, and sawhorses are perfect for this. You can use them when making cuts to lumber, of course, but you can also put a flat surface (like a sheet of plywood) over the top of them to make a temporary workspace.

### SAFETY GEAR

Remember to use your safety glasses, ear protection, and dust mask whenever necessary. You might even keep some extra sets on hand for onlookers or anyone who would like to participate in the project. Also, get help with tools or techniques that are unfamiliar to you. Staying safe keeps your projects fun—and successful.

# CHAPTER 1
# Choosing What to Grow

Choosing what to grow is one of the key factors for a successful and easily managed vegetable garden. Some plants are tolerant and easygoing and will reward little care with a bumper harvest of great-tasting vegetables. Others are more difficult and have particular demands that must be met, often at great effort, for them to produce successfully, and there are plenty that fall in between. One cultivar of a plant may be much easier to grow than another, either in general or specifically because of the conditions in your garden. It is far easier to choose plants that will thrive in your particular circumstances than face the challenge of a relentless battle to provide what a particular plant requires. For example, peppers and eggplants (aubergines) will struggle in colder areas without protection and perhaps artificial heat, so may not be an option if your vegetable garden is cooler and exposed.

## Grow What You Like

Choose plants that give abundant harvests for little care, especially to begin with. Don't try to grow a bit of everything.

Your vegetable garden is all about providing you with great things to eat, so start by listing all the fruits and vegetables that you and your family will enjoy. There is a common vision of vegetable gardens with orderly ranks of parsnips, runner beans, rutabagas (swedes), and leeks and a tendency to think that your patch should include these. The reality is that if you are putting your time into growing something, it should be a vegetable that's a staple in your kitchen.

Once you have made your list, check the ease with which things are grown and the suitability for your garden. Consider how much space you need to dedicate to each vegetable to get a good harvest. Ask yourself if there is space in your garden. If you only want to maintain a small space, then plants with a big space requirement, however easy to grow, may be unsuitable. Statuesque artichokes, for example, may deliver a gourmet crop, but each plant will probably deliver two or three suppers each year and occupy 11' (3.4m) square of your garden, permanently. Also, look at when you can expect to harvest each vegetable; if you are away for long periods, it would be a shame to miss the best of anything.

## HOW EASY ARE THEY TO GROW?

| Very Easy | Easy | | Fairly Easy |
|---|---|---|---|
| • Potatoes | • Kale | • Strawberries | • Carrots |
| • Zucchinis (courgettes) | • Pumpkins and | • Black currants | • Broccoli and calabrese |
| • Onions and shallots | squashes | • Blackberries | • Green beans (French beans) |
| • Rhubarb | • Salad leaves | • Gooseberries | • Cabbage |
| • Runner beans | • Radishes | • Raspberries | • Fava beans (broad beans) |
| • Jerusalem artichokes | • Garlic | • Red currants | • Sweet corn |
| • Leeks | • Artichokes | • Asparagus | • Swiss chard |
| • Spring onions | • Celeriac | • Beets (beetroot) | • Lettuce |
| • Perpetual spinach | • Peas and snow | | • Tomatoes |
| | peas | | • Peppers and chili peppers |
| | | | • Cucumbers |
| | | | • Eggplants (aubergines) |

On page 40, there are three lists detailing which vegetables are "very easy to grow," "easy to grow," and "fairly easy to grow." Those in the first category are forgiving plants that will reward very little care and even neglect with basket-loads of flavorful produce. The second-list plants are a little more demanding of your time or conditions, but certainly not a challenge—in most cases, what makes them more difficult than those in the first list is the need to protect them from pests or their need for water. The second category contains plants that require pruning, but can become permanent fixtures in your garden. The third category will need the most care out of the three lists.

Complete beginners and those really wanting very little to do would do well to grow plenty of things from the "very easy" list and have a really rewarding first season.

# Choosing Which Cultivar to Grow

Growing your own vegetables is all about great flavors, so always go for cultivars known for their great taste. There are a number of characteristics to look for in cultivars that will ensure bumper harvests for your vegetables. Seed catalogs and seed packets are marketing tools, but good ones are also crammed with information about how varieties are likely to perform.

## What to Look For

It is important to look for prolific production over a long period of time. If one plant will give you 10 percent more vegetables than another or will deliver vegetables for several weeks longer, then you are getting better value for your time and money.

Resistance to pests and diseases is also an important factor to consider. A great deal of effort has gone into developing plants that will not suffer attacks from common pests and diseases. Protecting plants from things like carrot flies and cabbage root flies, for example, is time consuming and not always effective, so choose cultivars with built-in resistance, especially if you have experienced a problem before. Unfortunately, resistance does not mean complete and guaranteed immunity.

One of the easiest crops to grow, onions require no care beyond weeding to give a great harvest.

The zucchini cultivar 'Orelia' gives a remarkably bountiful harvest of nutritious yellow fruits.

## Flavor

The exact taste of the produce you grow will depend on many things: the variety, of course, but soil, climate, and watering, as well. Fruits grown in direct sunlight are likely to be sweeter, and the more water some crops receive, the more diluted the flavor is. There can even be a variation between plants. Although a variety is renowned for its superlative flavor, this might not be true in your garden; you may need to experiment to find what works.

## Permanent Productive Planting

Permanent plants in your vegetable garden are the ultimate low-maintenance, productive choice. The most time-economical area would consist just of perennials and fruits. The range is limited, but for the most part the plants will produce year after year with a good layer of mulch in spring and a quick prune. These plants are more expensive and require a bit of extra effort at the outset, but the longevity offsets these concerns. For example, an asparagus bed could last for ten years, so it is worth including at least some permanent occupants in your vegetable garden.

# What Not to Grow

Everyone has their own personal "what not to grow" list based on experience and dislikes. The climate and soil you have will also play a part in determining which plants will flourish and which will take extra work. The following are the vegetable plants that gardeners often have difficulty growing successfully.

### RUTABAGAS (SWEDES)

There is one major reason not to grow rutabagas (swedes): their growing season is long, and they will occupy space from early spring right through to late autumn and winter.

Although they need 11' (3.4m) square of garden space all year round and have a short season, artichokes are really easy to grow.

Planted as container-grown plants or bare-root after the first year, rhubarb provides plenty of tasty stems with just a good layer of mulch once a year.

## CAULIFLOWER

There are some appealing cauliflower cultivars, but to grow a good cauli, you have to be pretty exact with feeding and watering if they aren't to bolt (send up flower spikes).

## SPINACH

The problem with spinach is that it is so prone to bolting if conditions are not right. A much better option is to grow spinach beet, often known as perpetual spinach. The leaves can be cooked, and the young leaves used in salads just like spinach. It will produce for at least a year and maybe more, even lightly through the winter in mild areas.

## CELERY

Growing good celery is very difficult. It requires a constant level of moisture in the soil—the slightest period of drying out and it won't perform. Celery also needs extremely good, fertile soil and regular feeding throughout the growing period. Most cultivars need each plant to be provided with a newspaper or cardboard collar secured with string around its stems, and then the plants need "earthing up" three times to blanch the stems (prevent them from turning green by blocking out light). Moreover, slugs and snails love them. Celeriac offers a similar flavor for much less effort, and it can be grated into salads, roasted, or used in casseroles.

## FLORENCE FENNEL

The delicate flavor of fennel would earn it a place in the vegetable garden were it not for the specific conditions it requires. It is not hard work to grow, but any challenging conditions and it will bolt and, once this has happened, it is inedible. Lack of water, root disturbance, poor soil conditions, changes in temperature, or cold nights could all cause it to bolt. To get tender stems, the plants require "earthing up."

## EGGPLANTS (AUBERGINES) AND PEPPERS IN COLD AREAS

Both of these plants are reasonably straightforward to cultivate if you have the right climate or a greenhouse, as they need a fair amount of heat over a reasonably long summer to produce a worthwhile harvest. If you garden in a cold climate, you may be able to get a decent harvest by growing the plants in pots in a sunny spot sheltered by the house. Eggplants (aubergines) hail from tropical climates, so it is not surprising that they should struggle in a chilly, damp environment.

## SUMMER SQUASH (MARROWS)

Growing a good summer squash (marrow) requires much the same conditions as growing good zucchinis, and they are very straightforward. However, they take up quite a bit of space for the reward and unremarkable flavors. Each plant needs about 11' (3.4m) square and will deliver only two or three summer squash (marrows) (any further flowers have to be removed to get fair-sized fruits).

## VINING (CORDON) TOMATOES

Rather than growing vining or cordon tomatoes (the upright plants that require support and regular tying-in, as well as their side shoots pinched out and trusses removed), it is far simpler to grow outdoor bush tomatoes that require none of the effort and give flavorful tomatoes.

# Dealing with Shade

Choosing what to grow also requires assessing the limitations of your garden. Dealing with shade is one of the toughest problems to face, since most fruits and vegetables will do best in a sunny, sheltered spot. Deep shade is usually impossible to work with, but if your garden is partially shaded, there are plants that will produce reasonably well. Fruiting plants generally need at least six hours of direct sunlight during the growing season. Root plants may tolerate less, but leafy vegetables are the best option for a partially shaded spot as scorching sun can actually damage delicate leaves.

## PLANTS THAT TOLERATE PARTIAL SHADE

- Perpetual spinach
- Summer cabbages
- Spring onions
- Radishes
- Salad greens
- Gooseberries
- Chard
- Jerusalem artichokes (will grow just about anywhere)
- Red and black currants
- Rhubarb
- Peas and beans (only very light shade)

# Buying Seeds

Most vegetable plants are raised annually from seeds, and a good catalog will show an amazing range of varieties. Do not be tempted to buy the cheapest seeds. Many of the best varieties are F1 hybrids and, because of their special breeding, will be more expensive. They are nevertheless worth the extra premium because of their added characteristics, such as vigor, heavier cropping, and disease resistance.

As well as natural seeds, some vegetable seeds may be available in special forms. Some seeds may come pre-treated with a fungicide to protect against diseases. Other tiny seeds, such as lettuce, are available as pellets, which consist of a seed with a coating that makes them bigger and easier to handle.

All seeds should last a full 12 months, but many will last several years if stored carefully. Generally, the larger seeds, such as peas and beans, store the longest, while smaller seeds, such as papery parsnips and carrots, have a shorter storage span. If you have used part of a packet, seal the packet again and store it in a cool, dry place. This is useful for vegetables where you may want just a few plants or a short row each year. Seeds, such as peas and beans, that have been stored for a couple of years can be helped in their germination by soaking them in warm water for 24 hours before sowing.

In general, do not be tempted to save your own seeds. Vegetables do not necessarily breed true, and seeds saved from a successful plant may be mediocre the next year. This is particularly so with F1 hybrids, which never breed true.

Plants designated as AGM (Award of Garden Merit) have been awarded this standard by the Royal Horticultural Society, often following competitive trials at one of their gardens. These plants must have outstanding performance, be easy to grow, be resistant to pests and diseases, and be readily available.

# Choosing the Right Vegetables

As with many things in life, you will be more successful growing your own vegetables (and fruits and herbs) if you take a little time to plan ahead. With so many varieties available through seed catalogs, it's very easy to buy a few dozen packets of seeds, only to find out later that they were not really suitable for your needs.

## Family Matters

Remember to only grow what you—and your family—enjoy eating. This may seem obvious, but many people will grow vegetables simply because they think the plants will do well, will grow quickly, or because vegetables are recommended in books. However, whether it be leeks, tomatoes, zucchini, or another vegetable, there's no point in growing something that you or your family will not eat. Grow small amounts to start so that you don't waste too much precious garden space on failed experiments.

## Sizing up Your Vegetable Garden

If you have a small yard, you will probably never have enough space to grow as much food as you would like, so plan ahead when choosing seeds. Work out roughly where everything will grow, when the plants should be ready for harvesting, and which vegetables can follow after earlier ones are harvested. One good thing about fast-growing vegetables is that you can produce more food in a smaller space.

Where you raise your vegetables will also play a big part in your choices. Climate varies greatly from one region to another. Read the seed packets carefully. (Many are coded so you can see at a glance which areas the varieties will do well in.) Don't forget to contact your local Cooperative Extension Service for information about local gardening conditions.

Individual gardens also have their own microclimates. Conditions in your garden can be different from those in the yard next door—or even from one part of your property to another. A small, sunny patio sheltered by brick walls on all sides will be several degrees warmer than average for the region, while a garden in a low-lying dip at the bottom of a hill can experience frost for days longer than a garden higher up the slope.

## A Question of Time

Nearly all of the vegetables recommended in this book are easy to grow. They don't need a huge amount of fertilizing, watering, or weeding, and they don't demand difficult growing techniques or a lot of time-consuming, painstaking work. Nevertheless, keep in mind how much time you have to devote to your vegetables. If you know you have a hectic schedule, start off by growing small amounts of superfast, easy vegetables. You can always grow more later on if you find you have the time to spare. Growing your own food should be fun. If it starts to turn into a chore, that's when you know you have overextended yourself.

Small, raised beds are ideal for trying out new vegetables you haven't grown before. It's easier to provide care for plants confined to a smaller area.

# CHAPTER 2
# Soil

Soil influences the health and productivity of any vegetable garden, so the most important element in making your vegetable garden easy to manage and productive is getting the soil right. Healthy soil provides the necessary nutrients, water, and support for vegetable plants to thrive. Many gardens start with soil that is depleted, compacted, or contaminated in some way, so soil remediation is an essential step of the process. This chapter breaks down the types of soil you might encounter and the various issues with each.

Good, healthy soil is rich in nutrients and contains plenty of organic matter. It has an open structure, can hold onto moisture, and yet lets any excess drain away. It will also be home to a whole host of creatures beneficial to the soil—bacteria, mites, worms, fungi, and centipedes are just a few—all of which help in the process of

breaking down organic matter into humus. Worms are great for the soil, aerating it as they drag down organic matter and help to break it down. Ideally, 18" (45.7cm) of great soil is perfect for a vegetable garden. A healthy soil is easy to cultivate and produces robust plants that will survive a little damage from pests and put up a good fight against disease. Walking on the soil, especially when it is wet, can compact it and ruin its structure.

## Types of Soil

A plant needs a firm base in which to anchor itself so that it can grow. This growing medium needs to be the right texture for the roots to penetrate and spread through it easily, and it must hold enough moisture for the roots to absorb. In most cases, the growing medium is soil,

Rows of cabbages and shallots grow beautifully in garden soil made rich with plant nutrients and organic amendments.

## THE CONFUSING BUSINESS OF SOILS

Beginners are often advised to add compost to improve the fertility of soil. This means adding the rotted down contents of your compost pile—the heap of kitchen scraps, prunings, lawn cuttings, and old leaves in the corner of your garden. When rotted down, this mixture (sometimes called "garden compost" or "kitchen compost") is full of nutrients that will improve the soil fertility and improve drainage, too. If you don't yet have a compost pile, then buy premade compost or composted manure from the garden center.

On the other hand, if you are advised to fill a pot with all-purpose potting mix (also known as "multipurpose compost"), do not head to your compost pile. Instead, buy a bag of potting or all-purpose mix from the garden center and use that. This is great for starting seeds and seedlings in but only has enough fertility in it to sustain a plant for around a month. It will do little to improve garden soil.

Topsoil is the uppermost layer of garden soil—around the top 12" (30.5cm). This is where all the fertility and organic matter lies. Under this is the subsoil, low in nutrients and high in rocks and minerals. You don't want to grow vegetables in subsoil, so if you're preparing a new planting area, make sure you leave the topsoil in position. If you're making raised beds, you can buy bags of topsoil from garden centers and this, mixed half and half with compost, makes the ideal starting mix.

either natural soil from the garden or a packaged product. Potting mix available from garden centers is usually a soilless mix based on peat or a peat substitute, plus plant nutrients. You can also buy soil-based mixes made from sterilized garden soil.

By investing a little time up front on thorough soil preparation for your vegetables, you can prevent a plethora of problems and disappointments later on. This is true whether you are growing your plants in beds of soil already in your yard, or if you are filling raised beds or containers with store-bought soil or potting mix.

Soil is composed of two types of particles: mineral and organic. (Forget about rocks since those will be raked out.)

**Mineral particles** range from the smallest (clay), to the largest (sand). In between clay and sand are very fine, gritty particles called silt. The soil texture is the feel of soil particles when you rub them between your thumb and fingers.

**Organic particles** come in several sizes and various stages of decomposition. In a healthy soil, microorganisms help to glue together (the technical term is flocculate) mineral and organic particles into clusters that are separated by air spaces. This arrangement allows good internal drainage and permits air to penetrate into the root zone. The combination of mineral and organic particles, along with the degree of clustering, determine the "structure" of the soil.

From one garden to the next, the quality of the soil varies greatly, so check how your garden soil measures up before you start sowing and planting. Take a good look at what is already growing there. Is the existing plant growth

Sand (left) is composed of large particles. Clay (right) is made of smaller particles. Loam (center) contains sand and clay and is ideal.

**<0.004 mm** **0.004–0.06 mm** **0.06–2 mm** Soil particle size

**Sandy soil:** Sandy soils have large particles and, like sand on a beach, allow water to drain through quickly. This means that they warm up quickly in the spring, so you can start planting earlier than those with other soils. They are also easy to dig. On the downside, nutrients get washed out of them, so you need to add organic matter to slow this down and to prevent them from drying out in hot weather. Generally, though, this is one of the easiest soils to deal with. Because sandy soils are easy to work, they might seem ideal for growing vegetables and small fruits. However, they dry out rapidly and can't hold many nutrients or much moisture in reserve. When soil nutrients are added, they tend to drain down through sandy soils to lower layers. Also, organic amendments can decay more rapidly during the summer when the sun heats up the soil. Consequently, organic amendments need to be added to sandy soils more frequently, about every year or two.

**Silty soil:** If your soil is silty, it will contain more nutrients than sandy soil but will still drain well. When dry, silty soils are smooth and look like dark sand. They are easy to work with when moist and hold moisture well, but benefit from the addition of gravel or pebbles (grit) and organic matter. Detecting a silty soil is more difficult because you have to gauge by feel the relative size of gritty particles. If they're small, around the same size, and gritty, yet don't have the sharp-edged feel of play sand, you may have silt. Because silts are usually deposited by floodwaters or by the drying up of ancient lakes, they're usually found in isolated areas and are often mixed with clay or sand. Silt tends to fill up the air spaces in soil and make it slow to absorb water and to drain. Silty soils tend to dry hard and resist water penetration. They need to be amended with organic matter in order to be most productive.

**Clay soil:** Clay soil is often described as a "challenge." However, if treated properly, it can be the most fertile of all soils, so persevere and you'll be rewarded. To understand why clay soil has this rather fearsome reputation, imagine digging a lump of sticky, wet clay with a trowel. It's the tiny particles that make up clay soil that make it so heavy since there is very little room for air pockets. When wet, it is very sticky; when dry it forms rock-hard clods. Clay soils naturally contain high levels of nutrients, however, so if you can improve the drainage, you are onto a winner. Add lots of organic matter—manure or compost.

lush, deep green, and healthy, or does it seem stunted, pale, and starved? Strong, healthy plant growth—even if it's only weeds—shows that you shouldn't have to worry about much. However, if the plants seem less than perfect to you, some soil improvements will probably be needed.

Start by taking a handful of moist soil and rubbing a pinch of it between your fingertips, adding a splash of water if it's dry. A gritty feeling indicates sandy soil, while a smooth, slippery, or sticky feeling indicates there is some clay content. Now, squeeze the rest of the handful of soil and roll it between your palms; sandy soil falls apart, but clay soil is easy to mold into a ball that holds together.

Sandy soil warms up quickly and drains freely, but it is often low in nutrients and has trouble retaining water for plants. Soil that contains a lot of clay is usually fertile, with a good supply of plant nutrients. However, it can easily become waterlogged, can be difficult to work, and warms up slowly in spring.

Sandy, silty, and clay soils are the most common types encountered by home gardeners, but you might also find chalky soil or loamy combination soil.

Even a challenging soil can produce a bountiful harvest.

**Chalky soil:** Soil that is chalky is alkaline, light brown, and contains large quantities of stones. Basically, chalky soils aren't great, but also aren't irredeemable. They dry out quickly and tend to stop elements, such as iron and manganese, from getting to plants, which can cause poor growth and yellow leaves. Add a lot of organic matter to make the soil slightly more acidic over time. Most fruits and vegetables prefer a neutral to slightly acidic soil with the exception of the cabbage family, which prefers it slightly alkaline. If your troubles persist, it might be worth investing in raised beds with imported topsoil. Chalky "caliche" soils are common in the Southwest, as are dense "desert floor" soils. Gardening on caliche soils is complicated by the fact that water rising through the soil by capillary action can become saturated with calcium, magnesium, or other minerals that are deposited in the root zone. Desert floor soils are so dense that heavy iron rods shaped like javelins have to be driven into the soil to break it up enough for a tiller to finish the job. Local garden centers can tell you how to prepare and manage these difficult soils.

**Loamy soil:** This is the most desirable soil type as it has a combination of sand, silt, and clay. Loamy soil combines good drainage with an ability to hold on to nutrients well. If you have been working your garden soil for years, adding well-rotted manure and compost regularly, you may well have this type of soil. A silt loam soil that includes fractional amounts of clay and sand is the first choice of most commercial vegetable growers; only highly organic "muck" soils are more valued by gardeners who sell their produce.

## SOIL SOLUTIONS

There are a variety of ways to fix problem soil. Some methods improve the structure of the soil; others feed the plants directly by providing nutrients. Here are the most common.

**Soil conditioners and amendments.** Usually organic materials, such as compost, that improve soil texture by aerating the soil and feeding microorganisms.

**Fertilizers.** A variety of organic or inorganic materials deliver nutrients to plant roots. By-products of fish processing and bottled liquid concentrates are common types.

**Green manures.** These plants are grown and then turned under to supply nutrients to the soil. They include alfalfa and common grasses.

**Mulches.** Spread on the surface, mulches suppress weeds and limit evaporation of moisture from the soil. When they decompose, they feed microorganisms. Common mulches include woodchips and compost.

## TESTING FOR SOIL TYPES: TEXTURE AND STRUCTURE

A few simple steps can tell you a great deal about the texture of your soil. Do this test when the soil is damp, not wet. Dry soil will fall apart, and soggy soil may not crumble.

**1.** Make a ball of soil, pressing just hard enough to make it stick together.

**2.** Gently bounce the ball up and down in your hands with a rocking motion.

**3.** Loamy soils crumble partially, sandy soils fall apart, and clay soils stick together.

**4.** Feel the texture. Sand is gritty, silt feels silky, and clay is slippery.

# Soil pH

Soils can be acidic or alkaline and are measured on the pH scale. In the middle of the scale at pH7, the soil is considered neutral—neither acidic nor alkaline. Above pH7, soils are alkaline and below, they are acidic. The ideal pH for many plants is pH6.5, just slightly acidic. Some plants are very sensitive to pH and will only grow at certain levels. For example, vegetables in the brassica family, such as cabbages, Brussels sprouts, and turnips, need a high pH to grow successfully. Potatoes, however, prefer slightly acidic soil. The availability of certain plant nutrients may also be controlled by the pH level. If the pH level is not properly adjusted, nutrient deficiencies and other problems can occur.

The pH of a soil does not remain constant. The very action of rain and natural cycles within the soil slowly make it more acidic. From time to time, it may be necessary to add lime or chalk to your soil to neutralize the acidity. Liming should be linked to crop rotation so that lime is applied just before a brassica crop is planted.

It is important to know the pH of the soil in your garden. Garden centers sell home testing kits in which you'll mix small soil samples from various areas in your garden to create an average. You shake the soil with a testing reagent and water in a small tube. The reagent changes color according to the pH level, which you check against the color chart supplied with the kit. There are also mail-order kits you can use to send a sample to a laboratory for analysis.

Soil testing kits will usually also contain information on how much lime to use, and the laboratories that test mail-order kits will also provide advice as needed. Lime should ideally be added to the soil in the autumn, as the response is slow and may not be fully effective until the next spring. It is difficult to reverse the effects of liming, so you should use small quantities at first and monitor the effects before adding more. Always wear rubber gloves, a dust mask, and eye protection when applying lime, as it can be an irritant. Never apply lime at the same time as farmyard manure—the two will react, resulting in the release of excess ammonia, which will scorch roots and wastes the effect of both additives.

Most soil testing kits don't include your soil's nitrogen levels because they fluctuate a lot (some tests will reveal your soil's "organic matter content," which is similar), but all will list the levels of phosphorus and potassium, the pH of your soil, and more. It's good to know what you have before you start adding things (especially lime). Keep in mind that soil tests for most West Coast states are either unavailable or prohibitively expensive compared to the rest of the country. If that's the case, check some out-of-state listings. Many state labs accept out-of-state samples.

# Water in the Soil

An adequate supply of water is essential for healthy plant growth. A good, well-structured soil will have plenty of open spaces within it, which not only allow for air to penetrate but are also capable of absorbing water. Good soils act as a sponge, holding water in reserve ready for use by plants. Clay soils with tiny particles and tiny air spaces hold the greatest amount of water. Sandy soils have larger pores and, although they fill up easily with water, this drains away quickly and is therefore not held in reserve for the plants. In general, you will have to water a sandy soil more often than a clay soil.

When it rains or when you water soil, all the spaces become filled up with water, and the soil becomes saturated. When the rain or irrigation stops, the excess water runs away, leaving the soil holding water within its pore spaces. This stage, where there is both air and plenty of water within the soil, is the ideal condition in which

roots function, but eventually a stage is reached where they can remove no more and the plant starts to wilt.

If the excess moisture cannot drain away after rain or irrigation, the soil remains waterlogged. It may seem contradictory, but under waterlogged conditions, plants will wilt. The roots do not thrive since there is no air present, and they'll eventually die. With dead roots, the plant cannot take up water and wilts.

# Life in the Soil

Good soil is a living, thriving community all of its own. There are many small beneficial creatures, some visible like earthworms, wood lice, and centipedes, and others microscopic like bacteria and fungi, which live within the soil and contribute to a healthy condition. One of the main activities of soil organisms is breaking down dead materials within the soil and converting them to organic matter. This is vitally important, and the reason that adding extra organic matter is one of the best ways to improve almost any type of soil. There are many different sources of organic matter, but they are all derived from living materials.

## Microbiota

The term "microbiota" is an all-inclusive name for the microscopic critters in your soil. It includes a great variety of soil organisms: bacterial, fungal, and others with names you may have never heard before. We now know that establishing and maintaining a healthy balance

In this microscopic image, a beneficial nematode is investigating a mite to determine if it is good enough to devour.

between the many species that make up microbiota, more than fertilizing or watering, is the single most important factor in gardening.

Bacteria, fungi, and nematodes are only a few of the great variety of species at work in the top 8" (20.3cm) of your soil. Some species live in colonies and work together in what scientists call "symbiotic activity" to nourish plants. These microorganisms are commonly called mycorrhiza and vary according to the genus of the plant. Not all plant species require specific mycorrhiza for optimum growth.

Some species of microbiota could be called "grazers." They extract the energy they need to live and reproduce by snacking on dead organic matter in the soil, including the carcasses of microorganisms. Predatory species, on the other hand, get their energy by consuming living organisms. Working together, grazers and predators release essential minerals into the soil or the fertilizer. Some of these organisms surround rootlets the way gloves surround fingers. They absorb nutrients and pass them on to the rootlets for passage into the vascular (circulatory) system of the plant.

## Macrobiota

Without a microscope, you can't see the teeming mass of microscopic animal and vegetable organisms that keep your soil "alive." However, you can see the mass of larger organisms that are called macrobiota. Included are the many wriggling or crawling species that live in the soil, and some that spend part of their life cycle as flying insects. Earthworms, beetles, bugs, millipedes, pill bugs, springtails, and spiders are only a few of the species included in macrobiota. Most of these species are predatory, but some graze on succulent fungi and decaying organic matter. In turn, species of microbiota graze on the leftovers.

## Well-Aerated, Well-Drained Soil

Beneficial bacteria and several other microorganisms require good levels of oxygen in the soil and are described as aerobic. To keep them healthy, garden soil needs to be well aerated and porous enough to allow moderately fast drainage. When soil remains soggy for extended periods, anaerobic fungi—which function best when oxygen levels are low—take over, and garden plants can suffer

## SOURCES OF ORGANIC MATTER

Organic matter is very important in producing a well-structured and naturally fertile soil. Before soil was actively cultivated to produce food, the organic matter that went into it came from vegetation that was naturally shed, such as leaves, and any animals that died. These would rot down and be taken into the soil by organisms and insects, which is how topsoil was created, long before it was bagged and sold in the garden center. It is the organic matter that is the vital constituent of soil when creating a good structure. Organic matter enables good drainage in heavy soils, conserves moisture in lighter soils, and produces a perfect environment for roots to grow.

The following materials are all valuable and vary in price according to whether there is a local source. Farmyard or chicken manure must be well rotted before use, or it can damage the roots. Mushroom compost is good but is quite often alkaline, so should be used with crops that need lime.

- Garden compost
- Recycled green waste (from your local authority)
- Farmyard manure
- Chicken manure
- Spent mushroom compost
- Leaf mold
- Composted seaweed
- Spent hops or brewers' grains

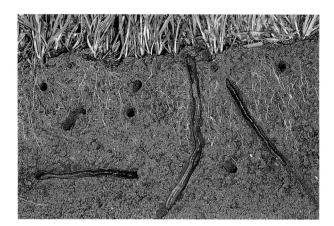

The channels that earthworms create remain in place after the earthworms have moved on. These channels provide an easy path for both air and water.

and die. Soil turns sour, and you can actually smell the fermentation that is taking place.

It is indeed possible to modify your soil so that it drains well and supplies good levels of oxygen while still retaining sufficient water to sustain plants for several days. You need to add certain things to the soil to reach this near-optimum level of drainage and aeration, and it will not occur right away. Your particular soil may need at least two or three years to rebuild itself once you have completed the initial cultivation.

# Soil Cultivation

Your garden has a few different layers of soil, each of which provides different benefits to your plants. Topsoil is the rich, well cultivated uppermost layer of soil, in which most plant roots grow. This is generally around 12" (30.5cm) deep, although it may vary considerably according to whether it has been cultivated or neglected. Subsoil is the material below topsoil, which is generally poorer, more compacted, and less rich. By cultivating

Marigolds planted alongside asparagus and other crops help control nematodes.

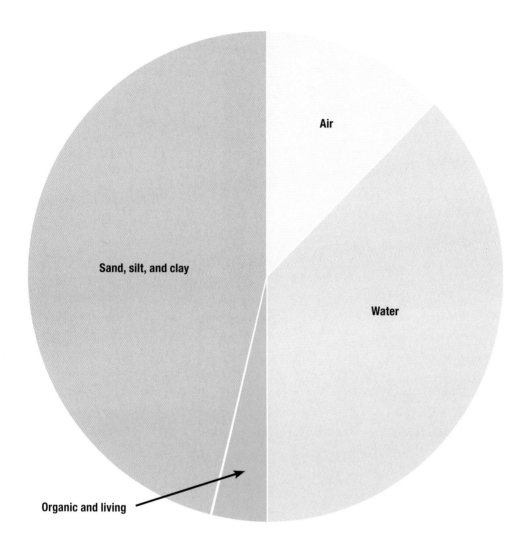

Air

Sand, silt, and clay

Water

Organic and living

A good soil will contain mineral solids, organic matter, air, and water.

your soil deeply and adding soil improvers, you should be able to increase the topsoil depth in your garden. This in turn will result in increased cropping potential.

A good soil will contain mineral solids, organic matter, air, and water. The space for air and water is very important and when a soil is compacted, say with heavy wear or vehicles driving over it, the spaces for air and water are squashed out. This makes it much more difficult for plants to grow adequately. Cultivating soil opens it up for air and water to penetrate.

Soil cultivation is at the heart of most growing techniques, and particularly so with vegetable growing. These will include digging, forking, hoeing, and raking. You should avoid cultivating your soil when it is wet.

This is particularly important for clay soils, which are sticky and can easily be damaged if cultivated wet. The most valuable technique is digging, which is the basis for preparing soils for almost any type of growing. The whole process improves drainage and aeration of the top layer of soil. Digging can be done at any time, although it is particularly valuable to dig clay soils before the winter, as cold, wind, and frost will help break up the surface and make it more friable for spring plantings.

In existing beds, break up the soil and remove all weeds; be sure to remove their roots, too. Dig as deeply as you can; using a garden fork is often easier than using a spade. Turn the soil over and strike any lumps with the fork to break them up. The object is to break the soil down to a fine,

## RAISED BED KITS

If you don't want to prepare your soil for planting, there is a way out. Most garden equipment suppliers sell raised bed kits, basically shallow wooden or plastic squares that you fill with potting mix or topsoil. They work like giant containers and mean you don't have to be so vigilant about your garden soil since you're raising the level a few inches. Just break up the earth at soil level before you put the raised bed on top so you don't compromise drainage.

Raised bed kits are popular because they give the impression of instant gardening and look very neat and tidy. However, you will have to construct them, so make sure to factor in some time to build them while constructing your garden.

Raised bed kits are almost like an instant garden—things look well organized with little work.

Fill a raised bed with good-quality topsoil to make sure you grow healthy vegetables.

The best time to dig is in late fall, when the plot is bare. Cold weather during the winter months will help break up the soil.

crumbly texture that plant roots can easily explore, as well as to break up any consolidated layers below the surface.

A bed should never be more than 4' (1.2m) wide, raised or not; you need to be able to reach everything in the bed without stepping on your nice loose soil and making it poor again. Compacted soil is the second largest human cause of plant death—overwatering is number one. The lanes around such beds should always be 2' (61cm) wide, so you can walk around the beds without stepping in them.

### Single Digging

The basic cultivation method is single digging using a spade. To do this, you need to take out a small trench the width of the area to be cultivated and transport the

Lazy gardeners often avoid making a trench when single digging, but you should not—it will only muddle the digging process!

surplus soil to the far end of the plot. Then proceed with digging, inverting the soil into the open trench, burying weeds, and leaving a fresh layer of soil on the surface. You should work backward to the end, where the surplus soil goes into the final trench. You can add compost or other organic matter to the open trench you cover it with soil.

## Double Digging

Double digging is a traditional and laborious technique that breaks up the soil to twice a spade's depth. It is very valuable on land that is compacted or has not been previously cultivated. The process is started with a trench about 2' (61cm) wide. You take the soil out and move it to the end of the plot. Then you break up the base of the trench with a fork, down to another spade's depth. You can add organic matter before the topsoil is inverted into this trench, creating a second trench, and so on.

## Using A Rotary Tiller

The use of a rotary tiller to quickly cultivate large areas seems very attractive, particularly to those with limited

# NO-DIG GARDEN

A no-dig garden technique involves minimal disturbance to the soil. Instead, you apply a thick dressing of fresh garden compost each year and allow worms and other organisms to incorporate it into the soil. You sow vegetables directly into the new layer of compost. For this to work, the basic soil must be well cultivated and free from any drainage problems, and it is essential not to compact the soil by walking on it. This, therefore, works best with small beds that can be tended from either side. The compost must be well rotted and weed free.

time, and such machines can be very valuable, but they do have problems. These are heavy pieces of equipment and handling them to cultivate a neglected plot can be hard, shoulder-wrenching work. Rotary tillers also smash through the soil and can quickly turn good soils into either dust or a sticky mess. They should only be used when the soil is moist but not wet.

The double digging starting trench is double the width of a single digging starting trench.

## IMPROVING CLAY AND CLAY-LOAM SOILS

**1.** Wait until your soil is dry enough to crumble, but not dust-dry, before you turn it overusing a spade or tiller. Working clay while it is wet or parched is self-defeating; you end up with big, hard clods or dust that puddles and runs together when wet.

**2.** Work up one small area at a time. Budget for adding at least 2" to 3" (5.1 to 7.6cm) of organic soil amendment (see page 61) before tillage. Soil conditioners can be expensive but are necessary for good drainage, aeration, and biological activity. Consider buying them in bulk quantities to save money.

**3.** Spread fertilizer and lime according to your soil test recommendations before tilling your soil.

When improving clay or clay loam soil, work up one small area at a time.

**4.** In your initial soil preparation, use soil excavated from aisles to raise the level of beds for planting. Raised beds will give your plants a moist but not soggy root run.

**5.** Every year after, add a 2" to 3" (5.1 to 7.6cm) layer of organic soil conditioner to beds at the end of the fall or winter gardening season. Cut furrows or planting holes through it for planting seeds or setting out plants, and you won't need to till your soil again.

## Combating Weed Growth

It is important to note that both tilling and double digging will expose lots of buried weed seeds to the germinating power of sunshine, and then covers them with soil, essentially planting weeds. The best solution is to create a stale seed bed. Level out the tilled soil, water it, wait ten days, and then use a sharp hoe to slice off all the weeds at the soil line. If you can't do that, be prepared to hoe them as they pop up and use a good mulch to smother any existing weeds.

In future years, don't till or double dig. Keep your feet off the growing area and the soil will stay nice and loose. Whatever you do, don't till *every* year—even if you really enjoy doing it; repeated tilling depletes soil nutrients.

## "Grit" is Useful

You can add grit and coarse sand to heavy soils, such as clay, to let water drain through better and not waterlog the roots of plants. Coarse sand is used because the coarse grains allow water to run through better than finer varieties. Don't use beach or children's sandpit sand because they contain salts that damage plants. Horticultural gravel or grit works in a similar way, opening up the soil and letting water drain through. If you have a heavy clay garden soil, it's worth a trip to a garden center or DIY superstore to get a bag or two of either.

Perlite, which looks like little polystyrene balls although it's actually made of volcanic rock, does the same thing but is used when planting in pots. It's worth adding a handful to the potting mix when you're planting things you want to avoid being waterlogged, such as Mediterranean herbs or those that will stay in the same pot.

Grit and coarse sand are added to heavy soils for better water drainage and to avoid waterlogging the roots of plants.

## MAKING YOUR OWN SEED AND POTTING MIXES

**Seed sow mixes.** Try using sifted well-rotted leaf mold (see page 98) on its own, or mix it with up to 25 percent coarse sand or perlite to improve drainage. Seed sowing mixes do not need lots of nutrients, in fact, high nutrient levels can inhibit germination of small seeds.

**Potting mixes.** On its own, compost is too rich for most plants and does not have the right structure for use in pots. However, it is valuable if mixed with other ingredients. Try combining equal proportions of compost, loam, and leaf mold, or use three parts leaf mold to one part worm compost. Coarse sand or perlite can be added for extra drainage, and you can add organic fertilizers for a richer mixture. Experiment with your own mixes until you find one that suits your needs.

Measure out the appropriate volume of each ingredient for your potting mixture.

# Soil Conditioners

Soil conditioners, or amendments, are either organic or mineral and are worked into soil to open its structure to improve drainage and aeration. Organic conditioners, like some composts, improve soil structure by increasing the activity of microorganisms that glue together small particles into clusters. Technical terms for this process are aggregation and flocculation. The "gluing" promotes aeration and the movement of water both in and out of the soil. Organic conditioners also provide food for microorganisms that thrive on the energy produced as they break it down.

Particles of organic amendments should range from thumbnail-sized down to the consistency of coffee grounds. Particles that are too fine, such as dust, tend to filter down through soil and collect in layers that impede drainage. Particles that are too large, such as woodchips, can open the soil too much, causing it to dry out. They can also create "nitrogen drawdown," in which microorganisms draw on nitrogen in the soil for nourishment while they are breaking down the chips.

## CONDITIONERS VERSUS FERTILIZERS

Soil conditioners, unlike fertilizers, are not a primary source of concentrated plant nutrients. All organic conditioners do contribute a significant amount of nitrogen (if slowly) and minor amounts of phosphate, potash, and micronutrients. Conditioners do not require an analysis of nutrients or a "derived from" statement on labels.

Plants growing on such soils can suffer obvious yellowing, a sign of nitrogen deficiency. Yellowing can be alleviated with nitrogen fertilizer, but can recur until the large particles are decomposed.

## Types of Soil Conditioners

Soil conditioners are available at garden centers in plastic bags and bales and can also be purchased at municipal composting centers. If you are purchasing large quantities, it makes sense to use a local source, because long-distance shipping can be expensive. This is one

Piles of yard waste obtained at the municipal dump won't work as a soil conditioner, but they do make good, inexpensive mulch for your garden (see page 62).

reason why peat moss is frequently used in Northeast gardens. (Major peat bogs are nearby, in Canada's maritime provinces.) Peat moss is also shipped to West Coast and northern Great Plains states from bogs in the central Canadian provinces.

Double-ground pine bark, produced from southern yellow pine, and ground and composted cotton bolls are popular soil conditioners in the South. Pulverized pine and fir bark, produced from western tree species, are often used as conditioners in West Coast and Intermountain states. Rice hulls composted with chicken manure are available in the South and West. Bagged cattle manure—dry, virtually odorless, and nearly weed-free—is widely available. Remember, cattle manure is not a fertilizer; it is a soil conditioner.

Shredded municipal yard waste, while inexpensive, is usually too coarse for use as a soil conditioner. Consider it for mulching instead. Occasionally, double-ground yard waste—passed twice through a grinder—is available. It makes an excellent soil conditioner, especially after a few months of composting.

## Mineral Soil Conditioners

Technically speaking, minerals, such as limestone, sulfur, and aluminum sulfate, are also soil conditioners. Primarily, they are worked into the soil to raise or lower soil pH. Gypsum (calcium sulfate) is occasionally touted as a soil conditioner for breaking up clay. It works on

Many farmers use gypsum to correct soil acidity and break up clay, but it is not as reliable as organic matter.

some types of clay but not on others. Overall, organic matter makes a more dependable soil conditioner.

The relative permanence of mineral soil conditioners, such as Permatill, which is slate expanded under heat and pressure, make them attractive, but they can be expensive because of shipping costs. Consequently, Permatill is rarely used in food gardens outside of the Southeast where it is mined and processed. A similar material, Haydite, is available in the Midwest.

**Why sand is not a good soil conditioner.** Clay is composed of so many fine particles that it tends to overpower any mineral additive. Its effect is so dominant that even if clay amended with sand contains only 25 percent clay, it will act much like pure clay. This is why organic soil conditioners, rather than sand, are preferred for modifying clay. The action of soil organisms opens clay by "gluing" particles together into clusters rather than by mechanical means. As the clusters form, they leave open spaces throughout the soil for the passage of air and moisture.

You can fill aisles using gravel or crushed rock, providing you grade your garden site so that excess rainfall can drain away rather than collect beneath the gravel or rock. You will also want to box in your planting beds using treated wood timbers or concrete blocks 6" to 8" (15.2 to 20.3cm) in height. The boxing will keep gravel out of your planting beds and soil out of the graveled

---

## TONICS

There are numerous elixirs promoted as a means to improve soil health and to increase productivity. These are neither fertilizers nor soil conditioners, and none can cause a major or lasting improvement in soil. Some of them work—some don't. Some were developed before scientists used electron microscopy to study soil microorganisms.

Older tonic formulations include vitamins, enzymes, and seaweed extracts. Vitamins and enzymes are composed of relatively large molecules that are too big to be absorbed intact by plant roots. They have to be broken down by soil organisms before they become "available" to plant rootlets.

pathways. One of the continuing problems with gravel aisles is the unavoidable spillage of soil onto the gravel walks, where it tends to provide a seedbed for weeds.

## Economic, Cosmetic, and Olfactory Considerations

When you calculate the cost of adding a significant amount of soil conditioner to your soil, you may suffer from sticker shock. For example, if you wish to improve the soil in a 500' (152.4m) square garden by mixing in 3" (7.6cm) of soil conditioner; a simple way to figure it would be to calculate 500 x 0.25 = 125' (38.1m) cubic, or a little more than four cubic yards. One cubic yard equals 27' (8.2m) cubic. Most bags contain 3' (91cm) cubic of conditioner, so you would need about 42 bags to cover the soil to 3" (7.6cm) deep. Three cubic yards of conditioner would fit into a long-bed pickup truck. Most garden centers offer delivery service on bulk amounts. Be aware that they may require a minimum order larger than your immediate needs, so you might wish to over-order and stockpile the surplus for improving the soil in ornamental borders or lawns. Whoever does the transport should plan on lashing a tarp tightly over the load, or wind could suck much of the conditioner out during the delivery run.

Peat moss is so dry when bagged or baled that it should be moistened while it is still in the plastic packaging. If you try to work dry peat moss into the soil, you may create pockets of bone-dry matter that will persist throughout the growing season and beyond. Small bales of compressed peat moss contain about 4' (1.2m) cubic. When fluffed, they expand to about twice that volume.

Finding a place to dump a load of soil conditioner can be a problem in developed properties. Fences, hedges, and mushy lawns may prevent dumping the load where it's needed. Be prepared to wheelbarrow it to your garden site before it blows around or starts getting tracked into the house.

Compost and sand are used to modify soils.

# NUTRIENT COMBINATIONS OF COMMON SOIL AMENDMENTS AND FERTILIZERS

Soil amendments and fertilizers derived from natural sources often contain much more than simply mineral nutrients. The table below lists some of their other benefits, as well as giving application rates.

| Material | Primary Benefits | Analysis (N-P-K, plus minor & trace nutrients) | Average Application Rate per 1,000 sq. ft. when Soils Test: | | | Notes |
|---|---|---|---|---|---|---|
| | | | Low | Moderate | Adequate | |
| Alfalfa meal | Organic matter, nitrogen | 5-1-2 | 50 lbs. | 35 lbs. | 25 lbs. | Contains a natural growth stimulant plus trace elements |
| Aragonite | Calcium | 96% calcium carbonate | 100 lbs. | 50 lbs. | 25 lbs. | Can replace limestone |
| Calcitic lime | | 65-80% calcium carbonate 3-15% magnesium carbonate | Use soil test; quantity depends on soil type as well as pH | | | Use in soils with adequate magnesium and low calcium |
| Colloidal phosphate | Phosphate | 0-2-2 | 60 lbs. | 25 lbs. | 10 lbs. | Adds to soil reserves as well as available quantity |
| Compost | Organic matter, soil life | 0.5-0.5-0.5 to 3-3-3 | 200 lbs. | 100 lbs. | 50 lbs. | Adds balanced nutrients & the microbiota to make them available |
| Dolomitic lime | Calcium, magnesium | 51% calcium carbonate 40% magnesium carbonate | Use soil test; quantity depends on soil type as well as pH | | | Use in soils with low magnesium and low calcium |
| Epsom salts | Magnesium, sulfur | 10% magnesium, 13% sulfur | 5 lbs. | 3 lbs. | 1 lb. | Use when magnesium is so low that other sources won't work |
| Fish emulsion | Nitrogen | 4-1-1; 5% sulfur | 2 oz. | 1 oz. | 1 oz. | Can be used as a foliar feed too, mix 50/50 with liquid seaweed, and dilute to half the recommended strength |
| Granite meal | Potash, trace elements | 4% total potash; 67% silicas, 19 trace elements | 100 lbs. | 50 lbs. | 25 lbs. | Rock powders add to long-term soil fertility and health |
| Greensand | Potash, trace elements | 7% potash, 32 trace minerals | 100 lbs. | 50 lbs. | 25 lbs. | Excellent potash source |
| Kelp meal | Potash, trace elements | 1.5-0.5-2.5 | 20 lbs. | 10 lbs. | 5 lbs. | Best for spot applications where extra potash is needed |
| Rock phosphate | Phosphate | 0-3-3; 32% calcium, 11 trace elements | 60 lbs. | 25 lbs. | 10 lbs. | Apply when you start the garden and every four years once soil phosphate levels are adequate |
| Soybean meal | Nitrogen | 7-0.5-2.3 | 50 lbs. | 25 lbs. | 10 lbs. | Excellent soil amendment during the second half of the season |
| Sul-Po-Mag | Sulfur, potash, magnesium | 0-0-22; 11% magnesium, 22% sulfur | 10 lbs. | 7 lbs. | 5 lbs. | Use only if magnesium levels are low & never with dolomitic lime |
| Worm castings | Organic matter | 0.5-0.5-0.3 | n/a | n/a | n/a | Use in potting soils and for spot fertilizing |

Organic soil amendments provide mineral nutrients and other benefits to promote lush growth and production.

# CHAPTER 3

# Compost, Fertilizer, Manure, and Mulch

You are pretty much stuck with the mineral content of your soil—it is down to the geology of your area—but the depth, structure, and fertility can be improved by the addition of plenty of organic matter, such as well-rotted manure, garden compost, and leaf mold. Whether you are working on heavy or light soils, organic matter is the key because it opens the structure of heavy soils, prevents it from clogging together, improves drainage and the fertility of light soils, adds bulk, and makes the soil more moisture-retentive. Protecting light soils with a layer of mulch can also stop nutrients from being washed away. Heavy clay soils can be improved with the addition of plenty of grit to improve drainage. There are no quick fixes; your first efforts will make a difference, but each year that the soil is cultivated and improved, it will become better and healthier, and this is an ongoing task. No-dig gardening protects the soil's structure and promotes fertility, and over several years, will really improve any soil.

## What Is Compost?

Composting is a natural biological process carried out by millions of tiny creatures. Some of them, such as worms, you can see with the naked eye, but the majority are microscopic. Suitable creatures will arrive in your compost heap of their own accord if the conditions are right. They will eat their way through the organic material you have put in the bin, breaking it down further and further until all that remains is a dark brown earthy substance—compost.

Composting takes place constantly in nature. Think about all those leaves that fall from the trees and plants that die. Have you ever wondered where they go? They are all consumed by worms and myriad smaller "decomposers"—and the goodness they contain is recycled back into the soil to help more plants grow.

## NUTRITION IN A NUTSHELL

Here are a few quick nutrition tips from this chapter to keep in mind during your gardening journey:

- Compost supplies all the nutrients your plants need in a form that plants can use easily. Feed your plants with compost, and you won't have to worry nearly as much about "NPK," (see page 101) if you have to worry at all.
- If your plants are small, stunted, or otherwise don't seem to be growing, give them some nitrogen, but don't overdo it. And don't add nitrogen alone if your plants are already big and strong.
- Enhance your garden soil with a little rock phosphate and greensand the season before, or add them to your fall compost piles and then feed your plants the finished compost.
- If you buy fertilizer, make sure it's balanced. That doesn't mean equal numbers, like 10-10-10. The ideal ratio is 3-1-2. If you can't find that, look for something close, like 4-2-3. Fertilizer that's 6-2-4 or 9-4-6 would also be close to perfect. Don't buy anything with numbers much higher than that—a nitrogen number over 11 or 12 is a good indication that the fertilizer is not organic. Also, chemical fertilizers contain concentrated chemical salts that are bad for plants and for the environment.
- Don't overfeed. If you're using a packaged fertilizer, work it into the soil when you put your plants in the ground, and then mulch over it with a thin layer of compost. In a normal year in a normal climate, you should be set for the season. If needed, give your plants a boost of compost tea or a diluted fish and seaweed fertilizer mid-season. If you're growing in a place with a long, hot season, you can do two or three boosts.

Nature is continually at work, decomposing and recycling living materials, including the leaves on the forest floor.

## The Stages of the Natural Composting Process

The decomposition of organic (living) materials in compost has five main stages. Each stage involves the work of different organisms that are adapted to the specific conditions in the compost heap at that point. They come and go of their own accord.

### STAGE 1

Weeds, grass, kitchen scraps, and other organic materials you put in a compost bin will already have plenty of bacteria living on them. These bacteria start the decomposing process.

### STAGE 2

The bacteria and other microorganisms multiply rapidly as they feed. Larger creatures, such as insects and worms, move in and start to feed on the decomposing organic material, breaking it into smaller and smaller pieces. All this activity releases energy as heat and the heap may begin to feel warm if a lot of material has been added at once. If the heap becomes too hot, then the worms and other larger creatures will move out until it cools down once again.

All you are doing as a home composter is managing this natural process in a tidier, more efficient fashion to give you the end product you want. You don't have to understand every detail of the process to make compost, but if you have some idea of what it consists of, you are more likely to be successful and be able to adjust the conditions in your compost heap to get a good end product. All types of soil can be vastly improved by adding garden compost or manure—anything that contains organic matter. Well-rotted organic matter acts like a sponge in sandy soil: it absorbs water and nutrients so that they are always available to plants. Organic matter breaks up sticky, clinging clay, improving soil texture and making it easier for plant roots to penetrate (and for gardeners to dig).

Worms are some of the larger creatures involved in the composting process.

The number of worms in your compost heap can sometimes fluctuate, depending on the stage it is at.

Woodlice break down cellulose fibers in woody material, making it easier for other creatures to work on it.

## STAGE 3

This stage sees the most intense microbial activity, and the heap may get hot as activity increases. The bacteria involved at this stage are specially adapted to work at high temperatures. The heat generated may be enough to kill weed seeds, pests, and disease organisms. Even if the heap does not heat up noticeably, the microbial activity can kill off many plant disease organisms that may have been added to the compost bin. At this stage, the volume of the material you've put in the bin will be consumed and disappear at a dramatic rate.

## STAGE 4

All the creatures involved in composting need air to survive. At this stage, air supplies within the heap may have been used up and suitable food supplies may be running low, so the composting activity slows down. A hot heap will cool down, allowing other bacteria and fungi to move in to take over from the heat-loving species and continue the work.

## STAGE 5

The compost will continue to decay slowly, and after a period of time, it will be ready to use. Don't worry if you find your compost bin full of earthworms, woodlice, ants, and so on at this stage. They are part of the process and will continue working until there is nothing left—but you should have used the compost on your garden long before that.

# How to Make Compost

After tilling and double digging, the compost you make yourself from shredded leaves, coffee grounds, and small amounts of other nonmeat kitchen garbage is the best possible amendment you can add to your soil. (Too much kitchen waste in the mix will make things nasty, though, so "dry browns," like shredded fall leaves, should always be in the majority.) Next best is municipal compost made from collected fall leaves and other yard waste, which many municipalities provide free to their residents. If your city or township has a place to take yard waste for recycling, you can probably get free compost there since that's what they recycle the stuff into. Take home lots of this "black gold" for your garden.

Making compost is a fundamental part of any vegetable gardening project, but especially in a no-dig plot. Garden compost is one of the most valuable commodities in your vegetable garden for improving the soil and providing replenishing levels of nutrients in the soil, and making it isn't hard. For the most part, it is a by-product of the gardening process, costs nothing, and takes very little work to achieve the best results. Garden compost improves the soil's ability to hold moisture and at the same time helps create air pockets in the soil, allowing water to work its way through. This helps create a good medium for healthy root growth while encouraging biodiversity in the soil. Not only is garden compost a readily available and inexpensive way to improve the soil's fertility, but it is also very effective, providing a whole array of nutrients and trace elements. In a warm summer, a "hot" heap can produce usable compost in just three to four months.

How you actually make your own compost will depend on your circumstances: how much time you want to spend, the size and style of your garden, how fit you are, how much you have to compost, and how quickly you want to produce and use the end product. Don't be surprised if your homemade compost is lumpy, coarse, and quite unlike anything you might buy or have seen pictures of in books. It is also likely that it will contain some partially rotted material that can be put back into the bin. As long as the composting process has taken place, however, your compost is fine and will do wonders for your soil.

## THE BASICS

- Add a good balance of lush green waste and coarser brown waste to the heap in alternating layers.
- Never add too much of one thing in a single layer—no more than 6" (15.2cm).
- Keep the heap warm by covering it.
- Retain moisture levels by covering the compost and add more soft green waste if it seems too dry.
- If the heap seems too wet, mix in scrunched-up newspaper or coarse waste and add a rainproof cover.

Homemade compost bins can be made from free wood pallets.

## HOW COMPOST HEAPS BECOME HOT

As plant wastes are broken down, the energy that went into making them is released in the form of heat. The heat build-up is a result of the oxidation of organic substances and the manufacture of carbon dioxide and water. Energy is released as molecular bonds are broken and reformed. Temperatures in the middle of a heap can reach up to 176°F (80°C)!

There is an initial phase of rapid microbial growth on the most readily available sugars and amino acids. This phase is initiated by mesophilic organisms, which generate heat by their metabolism and raise the temperature to a point where their own activities are suppressed. Then a few thermophilic (heat-loving) fungi and bacteria continue the process, raising the temperature of the material within a few days.

Adding browns as well as greens will make your hot heap work more efficiently.

## Quick Or Slow Composting?

A well-managed "hot heap" can produce compost in as little as 12 weeks. This requires you to fill your compost bin in one go with the appropriate mix of ingredients, having chopped or shredded any larger items first. You will also need to turn the heap several times. This can be very satisfying if you have the time, the space, and volume of ingredients.

At the other end of the scale is "cool composting," which may take 12–18 months to produce usable compost.

In this case, ingredients are added as and when they are available (still aiming to keep the balance of greens and browns). No other action is necessary.

Both methods can produce equally valuable compost. In practice, most heaps are sometimes hot and sometimes cool.

## How To Make A "Cool" Compost Heap

**1.** Put a 6" (15.2cm) layer of twigs or branches at the bottom of the bin if you have them available. This is not vital if you don't have any to hand.

**2.** Start adding compostable materials to the bin. A successful compost heap needs a roughly balanced mix of green and brown materials.

**3.** When you put in fruit and vegetable waste from the kitchen, try to add roughly the same volume of "browns." This could be cereal boxes or toilet paper tubes, for example. Remember to scrunch up the cardboard to help maintain air gaps in the composting material. You may not be able to balance each "offering" you add to the bin, but try and average it out generally. You will learn by

## HOT AND COOL COMPOSTING COMPARED

| Hot Heaps | Cool Heaps |
| --- | --- |
| Relatively quick process | Relatively slow process |
| More likely to kill weed seeds | Less likely to kill weed seeds |
| Many diseases killed | Some plant diseases killed |
| Requires large volume of materials to be | Materials can be added as and when available at once available |
| Heap must be turned several times | Requires minimal management |

A cone-shaped compost bin is simple to use and suits many garden situations.

## COMPOST ACTIVATORS

A compost activator is simply something that gets the compost heap working. In general, if you add a good mix of green and brown materials, there should be no need to add a specific activator.

Tender, quick-to-decompose materials, such as grass clippings or comfrey leaves, are natural, cost-free activators. Comfrey is a vigorous herbaceous perennial with leaves rich in nitrogen and potassium that can be cut several times a year to make a compost activator. Comfrey also makes a good liquid feed and can be mixed with leaf mold to make a rich potting mix. Comfrey 'Bocking 14' is the best variety to grow for garden use.

Human urine can also be used as an activator in a compost heap; as it has a high salt content, so it must be diluted by at least 1:10 and not applied in excess.

You can also buy activators, which are watered on or sprinkled on as a powder as the bin is filled. Some types supply nitrogen in an easily accessible form to get the bacteria started, some supply enzymes and microorganisms, while others claim to stimulate bacterial activity.

Some people feel that activators do make a real difference but the choice, ultimately, is yours. Organic gardeners would not use any activators that contain a chemical nitrogen fertilizer.

experience what works. The same applies to weeds, grass clippings, and other compostable items from the garden. Balance grass clippings with cardboard, autumn leaves, or tougher plant material.

**4.** Spread the ingredients out over the whole area of the bin. A garden fork is useful for this, or a long-handled hand fork if you don't add much to the bin at once.

**5.** As the composting process gets going, the level in the bin will go down. Compost will begin to form from the bottom up.

**6.** Keep filling your compost bin with material from the garden and kitchen as and when it is available.

**7.** After 6–12 months, you have several courses of action available. You could just keep on adding to this bin. If your compost bin has a door at the base, you may be able to scoop out ready compost. Alternatively, you could start a new bin, leaving the first one to finish composting. Or you could lift the bin off the heap to see how things are going. The upper layers should consist of material in various stages of breakdown. Put this back into the bin. At this stage, you can adjust the mixture. If it is rather wet and slimy, mix in more browns. If everything is rather dry, add more greens or water it.

**8.** The remaining compost that is ready for use can be employed immediately, or you can cover it up and store until you need it.

## How To Make A "Hot" Compost Heap

**1.** Start with a compost bin that is about 3' (91cm) high, wide, and long.

**2.** Gather together sufficient compostable materials to fill the container. Aim for roughly equal volumes of green and brown materials.

**3.** Chop up or shred larger items, such as cabbage stalks, prunings, and large plants. Smaller pieces are easier for the composting creatures to work on.

**4.** Add alternating layers of greens and browns that are 12" (30.5cm) or so deep. You can just mix everything up together, but layering makes it easier to gauge green to brown proportions. Water the layers as you go if the materials are too dry.

**5.** Spread the ingredients out evenly to the edges of the container and press down gently, but do not compact them down.

**6.** Put the lid on or cover the heap. A compost "blanket," such as some wool sweaters, a black plastic sack full of leaves, or some polystyrene packaging, will help to keep the heat in.

**7.** After a few days (times will vary), you should feel warmth if you put your hand on the heap. If you stick an iron bar into a hot heap for a few minutes, it can be too hot to handle when you pull it out. The heap may continue to heat up over a period of days and then will gradually begin to cool down.

Hot compost zaps weed seeds.

**8.** Once the heap has cooled down, turn it to incorporate more air. At this stage, you can also adjust the proportion of greens and browns or add water if necessary.

**9.** At this point, the heap may heat up again, to a lesser extent. If it does, repeat step 8 to incorporate more air into the heap.

**10.** Leave your hot compost heap to mature before use. It is possible to produce finished compost in as little as 12 weeks, but it may take up to six months, depending on how fine a product you are aiming for.

# What Is Needed for Effective Composting

If you fill your compost bin with roughly equal amounts of "green" and "brown" raw materials, maintain the right moisture balance, and allow for good air flow and temperature control, the result should be good-quality compost. There is no need to be very precise, however, and you will soon learn from experience what makes good compost.

## Raw Materials

What you regard as kitchen and garden "waste" provides a healthy diet to the creatures that make compost, keeping the composting process going and producing the best compost. Tender young materials, such as grass clippings,

Kitchen waste as shown here is considered to be "green" waste, and rots down quickly.

kitchen waste, and young weeds, provide nitrogen and speed the process along. These are known as "greens" in compost-speak.

At the other end of the scale are "browns"—tougher items, such as older plant material and cardboard. Slower to decompose, these give the heap structure, maintain air pockets, and give body to the end product, compost. Many things you compost will be somewhere between the two, known as "green/browns."

### Water

Composting creatures need moisture to live and work, but not too much of it. Too much water drives air out of the heap, and the air-loving composting creatures will drown. The bin will begin to smell and turn slimy and unpleasant. However, if there is too little moisture, then very little noticeable composting will occur.

Green materials contain a high proportion of water, and brown materials contain very little, so a mixture of the two is important. Some materials have a good balance on their own.

When adding dry, tougher ingredients to a compost bin, try to mix them with greens or water them before

Material that is this dry will be very slow to compost. Add greens when adding dry material to your heap and water, if necessary.

Ideally, compost should feel damp to the touch but should not ooze water when squeezed in the hand.

Compost that is this wet will tend to be airless and may smell unpleasant.

putting them into the bin. A good tip is to add weeds and spent plants collected after a good shower of rain. Once the composting process has got going, you can test the water content. Squeeze a handful of the decomposing material in your fist; it should feel similar in dampness to a wrung-out sponge.

Use the lid of your compost bin to help manage the moisture content. In very wet weather, leaving the lid on will stop rain soaking the compost; in dry conditions, keeping the lid on will stop it from drying out.

A compost bin must drain well so water cannot build up in it. Most bins don't have a base, so this is not a problem. If you are thinking of converting a garbage can or barrel for use as a compost bin, cut off the base or make plenty of drainage holes in it. The drainage aspect is important, but you also need to allow access and exits for all the useful creatures that will inhabit your bin and make it work.

## Air

Air is another essential ingredient for making good compost. The composting creatures, large and small, need air to live (these are known as aerobic organisms). If a heap is very wet, air is excluded. Decomposition will occur, but it will be done by bacteria that don't need air (anaerobic organisms). The result will be a smelly, slimy mass (not compost), and methane (one of the greenhouse gases responsible for global warming) will be produced.

Build air into a compost heap by adding browns among the green materials to create air spaces. Egg cartons, toilet paper tubes, crumpled corrugated cardboard, and scrunched-up paper are useful if you are short of browns from the garden. It helps if you start your compost heap with a layer of twigs or branches in the bottom of your container so that the air can flow upward from the base.

If a compost heap has slowed down due to lack of air, you can kick-start it again by "aerating" it in various ways:

- Make holes in the heap with a broom handle, right down to the bottom, if possible. Alternatively, use a purchased aerating tool, which works in a similar way to a broom handle.
- Mix the whole heap up again (this is known as "turning").

You can use a purpose-made aerating tool or broom handle to get more air into your compost heap, or you could try turning it over.

## Warmth

Composting activity is also affected by the temperature outside. It will slow down as the temperature drops, and will almost come to a standstill when the weather is very cold. In warm weather, the process will speed up.

You can regulate the temperature of a heap to some extent by placing the bin in a sunny spot, but it will still work (albeit more slowly) in the shade. You can also make a compost heap that retains the heat released by the various composting organisms, speeding up the process considerably (see How to Make a "Hot" Compost Heap on page 72).

## What to Compost

- Green garden waste (but not growth that shows any signs of disease since this may survive the composting process and spread across your plot as you spread the compost)
- Kitchen waste (excluding cooked food waste and animal or dairy products)
- Cut grass
- Leaves (although these are better used as leaf mold)
- Annual weeds and nettle tops (but no flower heads)
- Tea bags and coffee grounds
- Shredded woody prunings (left unshredded, they will take too long to rot down)
- Animal manure
- Egg boxes, newspaper, and unglazed cardboard

## What Not to Compost

- Animal feces
- Diseased vegetation, as this may do more harm than good to your vegetable plot if the disease survives the composting process
- Weeds that have gone to seed or the roots of perennial weeds, such as bindweed, creeping buttercup, or ground elder, as these likely will not be killed during the composting process; as you spread your compost, you will be planting weeds

*Note: You can safely add weeds that have gone to seed or the roots of perennial weeds to the heap if you process them properly. Put them into a sealed black plastic sack or bucket of water for a couple of months, and only add them to the heap once they have become an unrecognizable sludge.*

# Collecting Materials for Your Compost Heap

It is possible to compost a number of different materials generated by everyday life, some from the kitchen, from the household generally, and from your garden. Do not use biosolids or other forms of sewage sludge from water treatment plants. Some municipalities try to pass it off as compost, but it is not. It is human waste and contains shockingly high amounts of prescription medication residue and potentially toxic waste that was flushed into the sewers instead of being disposed of properly.

Aged mushroom soil (also known as mushroom compost, spent mushroom soil, etc.) purchased in bulk can be good compost, but it has to be aged (cool to the touch and with an agreeable odor), not fresh (hot and stinky). In a pinch, packaged (bagged) composts can also be good, but look for a premium, branded product with details about its contents and origins. Don't buy the generic bag that just says "Compost," or composted manure.

If you are tilling or turning your dirt, mix lots of that fine compost into your loosened-up soil as you go. If you've got an existing bed where the soil is already nice and loose, just layer 1" or 2" (2.5 or 5.1cm) of fresh compost on the surface of your enviable soil. Applying your compost to the surface is never a bad idea; it never needs to be tilled in, and doing so year after year would invite endless weed woes.

*Note: If you have sandy soil, you're in luck. Just mix an equal amount of compost or screened black high-quality topsoil in with your sand, and you'll create the perfect growing medium—a soil that holds moisture and nutrients, but also drains well during wet times.*

---

## GET SMART ABOUT COMPOST

Don't use compost made with treated sewage sludge (also known as biosolids). Compost in a bag is acceptable, but not nearly as good as homemade, municipal, or aged mushroom soil. Here's how to tell for sure if the compost is okay to use:

- It should look like rich, black "super-soil."
- It should have no "off" or foul odors; it can smell a little sweet or earthy, but nothing that makes you turn up your nose.
- It should not contain any recognizable woodchips or other "original ingredients."
- When you pick some up in your hand and squeeze it, it should have the consistency of a damp, wrung-out sponge.
- Lots of worms living in it is a very good sign.

---

## SOME COMPOSTING DOS AND DON'TS

- **DO** compost uncooked vegetable peelings and scraps.
- **DO** compost coffee grounds and tea bags (but take the tea leaves out first if you don't want to see the bag intact years later—they don't rot down).
- **DO** compost lawn clippings, but try to add them in small quantities interspersed with cardboard torn up into hand-sized pieces to avoid sliminess.
- **DO** compost leafy garden prunings.
- **DO** compost cardboard and newspaper in small quantities torn up into pieces. You don't want to create a "mat" that will keep water from getting down to the contents below. Beware cardboard with a thin plastic film since this won't rot down and will come back to haunt you when you're digging.
- **DON'T** compost cooked vegetable waste, meat, fish, or eggs.
- **DON'T** compost flowering weeds and perennial weeds, such as nettles, unless you want to reintroduce them to the garden. Instead, either throw them away, or soak them in a bucket of water for a week to kill them before adding them to the compost bin.
- **DON'T** compost eggshells unless you are prepared to wash them first and risk attracting rats.
- **DON'T** add avocado skins or pits (stones)—they take years to rot down.
- **DON'T** compost large branches—they'll still be there decades later.

## Kitchen Materials

Collect vegetable peelings, coffee grounds, fruit cores, and other kitchen waste in a container in the kitchen.

A related type of product, called "kitchen compost" or "green compost" is a product of recycling the green trash you discard. The recycling plant removes all the materials that will not biodegrade quickly, with the remainder being composted in big heaps. Once ready, it is bagged and sold back to gardeners at a greatly inflated price. Due to the complete lack of control over what is discarded and the amounts of each item included, however, the end result is a compost that can have variable nutrient levels, making it suitable only as a soil conditioner.

Empty your kitchen container into the compost bin every day or so. There are many types of small kitchen caddies on the market, but you can also use a plastic tub or just a simple bowl with a lid.

A purchased caddy used with a compostable liner is a good choice for a neat and tidy look. If you use a compostable starch-based plastic-like liner, empty the contents out into the compost bin first before adding in the liner rather than throwing in a full liner with the top tied up. Sturdy brown paper liners are also available and will rot more quickly than the plastic-like ones.

A sturdy brown paper liner keeps the can clean, and you can deposit the liner in the compost bin, too!

## TIPS FOR NO-SMELL, NO-FLIES BIN/CADDY USE

- Empty the kitchen can every day or two in order to deter fruit flies and avoid smells.
- If you don't produce much kitchen waste, choose a small can so you have to empty it regularly.
- Add paper towels, tissues, toilet paper rolls, and the like to soak up excess moisture generated by the kitchen scraps.
- Don't empty liquids into the can.
- Consider using a brown paper or newspaper liner. Simply remove the full paper liner and deposit the whole thing in your compost bin, where the paper liner will provide useful brown material to the heap.

You can make your own kitchen compost for free instead of purchasing it.

Add shredded paper to your kitchen can to soak up excess moisture.

With so many different designs of bin to choose from, you are sure to find a suitable home for your kitchen waste.

## Household Materials

Low-grade cardboard (such as cereal boxes), cardboard boxes, toilet paper rolls, and shredded paper can all be used in a compost heap to balance out the moisture content of fruit and vegetable peelings, grass clippings, and other greens. Store these in a box or bag, then add them to the compost bin as required.

## Garden Material

Garden compost is the most common organic matter put into the soil, as it is the easiest to come by, generally being produced on site. Most garden "greens" should be added straight to the compost bin, as they will start to rot if stored.

As far as organic lawn care goes, it is best to leave the clippings on the lawn; worms will soon take these back down into the soil. If you prefer to compost your lawn clippings, and have large quantities to deal with, try leaving these on the lawn to dry out before raking them up. Once they're dry, you can store them for a while, if necessary, in an open plastic bin or bag, for use as required in your compost heap.

Store dry autumn leaves for use later as browns to balance your compost heap.

You can produce garden compost easily, creating a nutrient-rich soil amendment.

You can also heap autumn leaves on their own to make leaf mold (see page 97).

Deciduous leaves that fall in the autumn are also worth collecting and storing for later use. Large quantities are best made into leaf mold (see page 97), but you should also store some dry leaves in a bin or bag for use in your compost over the coming year.

The great thing about using garden material is that the quality of the final product is controllable. If you manage the compost heap correctly, the nutrient levels should be balanced and create finished compost almost like loam. Good-quality garden compost adds bulk to the soil, improves drainage where required, and conserves moisture on lighter soils. It also adds vital nutrients to the soil. By putting material into the bin in thin layers and turning the compost once a month, you can convert raw compostable material to friable compost in three months during the warmer weather, and six months in winter. The most important factor to take into consideration when choosing garden compost, however, is that it is free.

## Materials Sourced from the Locality

Once you get started with compost-making, you may find that your garden or yard does not provide sufficient ingredients for your compost heaps. It makes sense to try and find other materials locally that you could use for compost, particularly from an environmental viewpoint, if this saves the materials from being transported to other sites to be recycled or taken to a landfill.

Local public works may deliver autumn leaves to a designated area—or you may get permission to collect leaves locally. Go for leaves from parks and cemeteries rather than those on the roadside. Shredded tree and shrub prunings are another useful resource that landscape contractors are often keen to give away.

# What can I compost?

The following charts outline what you can and can't (or shouldn't) put in your compost bin. For ease of reference, the chart has been divided into groups of materials: plant materials; animal products; kitchen waste; animal waste; packaging and paper; and miscellaneous items. The chart will also help you decide which type of composting method to use as well as providing further information and cautions in the notes.

**C** = Compost      ✓ Yes      ☐ Green – quick to rot
**W** = Worm composting      ✗ No      ◨ Green/brown
                          ! Caution      ■ Brown – slow to rot

## PLANT MATERIALS

| Item | C | W | Notes |
|---|---|---|---|
| ☐ Apple windfalls | ! | ✗ | Large amounts of apples will stop a traditional compost heap working well. Instead of composting, store apples to feed birds through the winter. Other methods: Apple worm heap; compost trench. |
| ◨ Carrot tops | ✓ | ✓ | These will not attract carrot root flies. |
| ◨ Citrus peels | ✓ | ! | Citrus peel is very acidic, and can upset a worm compost system if it makes up a high proportion of the material added. |
| ◨ Potato and tomato plants | ✓ | ✗ | Blight-infected potato and tomato foliage can be composted safely. Add straight to the bin, cover with other materials, and close the lid. Do not compost infected potato tubers or tomato fruits. |
| ◨ Potato peelings and tubers | ! | ! | Do not compost potato tubers and peelings that include an "eye" that may be blight infected. New shoots may grow from these and could also carry potato blight, spreading the disease. Peelings from healthy tubers can be added to a compost bin and a worm bin. Whole potato tubers are quite resistant to decay and are not suitable for a worm bin. |
| ◨ Rhubarb leaves | ✓ | ✗ | Although poisonous to eat, rhubarb leaves will not harm a compost heap; the compost produced will not harm plants. |
| ■ Sweetcorn cobs | ✓ | ! | May have to go through two or three compost heaps before they decay fully. |
| ☐◨ Vegetable and fruit waste from garden | ✓ | ✓ | |
| ☐◨ Vegetable and fruit waste from kitchen | ✓ | ✓ | Mix with low-grade paper to soak up excess liquid. Chop up tough stems of Brussels sprouts, cabbages, etc. Other methods: High-fiber heap. |
| ☐◨■ Plant debris and waste flowers, leaves, old bedding plants, etc. | ✓ | ! | Chop up tough stems. Other methods: Compost trench. |

# PLANT MATERIALS

| Item | C | W | Notes |
|------|---|---|-------|
| ◧ Fern | ✓ | ✗ | Good source of potash; makes compost more suitable for acid-loving plants. |
| ☐ Comfrey leaves | ✓ | ✗ | Good activator, rich in potash and nitrogen. |
| ☐ Seaweed | ! | ✗ | Composts well and is a traditional source of fertility, but collecting it can remove valuable wildlife habitats. Only use seaweed from your locality, that has been recently washed up, and then only in small quantities. |
| ☐ Flowers *Purchased bunches* | ✓ | ✓ | Chop up tough stems; compost paper wrappings. |
| ◧ Houseplants | ✓ | ✓ | Root ball and compost can also be added if broken up first (though it will not compost any further). Check for white vine weevil grubs in the root ball. These pests should be squashed or fed to the birds. |
| ■ Leaves *Autumn deciduous* | ! | ✗ | Store drier leaves in sacks and use to balance excess greens next season. Make the rest into leaf mold. Other methods: Leaf mold. |
| Leaves *Evergreen* | ! | ✗ | Mix well with other ingredients as these take a long time to break down. |
| ■ Moss | ✓ | ✗ | Slow to rot; mix with other ingredients. Do not use if taken from a lawn recently treated with weed killer. |
| ☐ Nettles | ✓ | ✗ | Young leaves are a good compost activator. Roots may not rot in a single composting. Other methods: Weed bag; "nasty weed" heap. |
| ☐ Grass clippings | ✓ | ✗ | Very quick to decay, these make a good activator, but particularly need to be balanced with "browns." Don't compost clippings from the first two cuts after treating a lawn with weed killer. Other methods: Grass boarding; mulching; leave on lawn. |
| ◧ Hay | ! | ✗ | Hay should be soaked well before adding to the compost heap; spoiled hay is best for this purpose. Other methods: Mulching. |
| ■ Straw | ✓ | ✗ | Old, weathered straw is best. Fresh straw is very dry and must be well soaked or mixed with wetter ingredients. |
| ☐◧■ Pest-infested plant material | ! | ✗ | Pests that only live on living plant material will not survive a compost heap. Pests that live on dead and decaying plant material or have a resistant stage are more likely to survive. Other methods: Weed bag; compost trench. |
| ☐◧■ Diseased plant material | ! | ! | Plants with soil-borne diseases, such as white rot on onions, brown rots on fruits, wilts of tomatoes and cucurbits, and clubroot of brassicas, are best not added to a compost heap. These types of disease can survive for many years in the soil and are unlikely to be killed off. Many other common diseases, such as mildew, only survive on living plant material, so infected plants can be composted safely. |

## PLANT MATERIALS

| Item | C | W | Notes |
|------|---|---|-------|
| **Poisonous plants** | ✓ | ✗ | Plants that are poisonous to eat will not harm a compost heap; the compost produced will not harm plants. Take care not to inhale dust or fumes when shredding poisonous plants. |
| **Weeds** *annual* | ✓ | ! | Try to pull up weeds before seeds form. Some weed seeds will be killed in the composting process, particularly if it heats up. Keep compost covered to prevent weed seeds blowing in. |
| **Weeds** *perennial, roots, and tops* | ! | ✗ | Including bindweed, lambsquarters, pigweed, buckhorn plantain, and crabgrass. Other methods: Weed bag; and "nasty weed" heap. |
| **Japanese knotweed** | ! | ✗ | This is a very invasive weed. There are best practices for its disposal. |
| **Christmas trees** | ! | ✗ | Shred before adding to a compost heap. Be cautious when adding large quantities of this material. Other methods: Composting woody waste. |
| **Pruning and hedge clippings** *evergreen, conifer, and deciduous* | ! | ✗ | Young, supple items can be added to a compost heap. Take care when using compost if you have added thorny prunings. Thorns take a long time to compost and may still be sharp. Other methods: Shredding compost. |
| **Sawdust and wood shavings** | ! | ✗ | Very dry, high in carbon, and tend to exclude air. Mix well with wet greens, and only use in relatively small amounts. |
| **Dead wood** *branches, twigs, and shrubs* | ! | ✗ | Dead wood is much harder to shred than recently cut living wood. Other methods: Wildlife heap; plant supports. |

## KITCHEN WASTE

| Item | C | W | Notes |
|------|---|---|-------|
| **Bread** | ✗ | ✗ | Tends to grow molds rather than compost. If you do want to try composting bread, crumble it up and mix with moist ingredients. Other methods: Bokashi. |
| **Tea leaves and bags** | ✓ | ✓ | Some tea bags have a very small amount of plastic in them, which is not immediately obvious. If the packaging doesn't say "tea bags compostable," then don't put the bag itself into the compost. The contents can be emptied, or even better use loose-leaf where possible. |
| **Coffee grounds** | ✓ | ✓ | Paper coffee filters can be composted. |
| **Food** *cooked leftovers* | ! | ✗ | Cooked food does not compost particularly well. Mix with uncooked materials and items that will allow air into it. May attract bluebottles and vermin, such as foxes and rats. Can make heap smell. Other methods: Bokashi; Green Cone. |
| **Oil** *olive oil, vegetable oils, etc.* | ! | ✗ | Composting is not a good way to dispose of cooking oils. Oil-soaked paper or cardboard can be composted. |

Any garden trimmings can be used in the compost heap.

A healthy garden has an abundance of companion plantings to encourage pollinators.

## ANIMAL PRODUCTS

| Item | C | W | Notes |
|---|---|---|---|
| **Bones—meat and fish** | ✗ | ✗ | May attract bluebottles and vermin, such as foxes and rats. Can make heap smell unpleasant. Other methods: Bokashi; Green Cone. |
| **Meat and fish scraps** | ✗ | ✗ | May attract bluebottles and vermin, such as foxes and rats. Can make heap smell unpleasant. Other methods: Bokashi; Green Cone. |
| **Dairy products** *milk, cheese, yogurt, etc.* | ✗ | ✗ | May attract vermin, such as bluebottles, foxes, and rats. Can make heap smell unpleasant. Other methods: Bokashi; Green Cone. |
| **Eggshells** | ✓ | ✓ | Eggshells do not compost as such, but will eventually break down into tiny pieces. They may remain visible in finished compost, but this is not a problem. Baking shells in the oven will make them more brittle and therefore easier to break down into tiny bits. |

## ANIMAL WASTE

| Item | C | W | Notes |
|---|---|---|---|
| **Cat litter** | ✗ | ✗ | Although some brands of cat litter say they can be composted, once it has been used, there is a health risk to anyone handling it. |
| **Dog feces** | ✗ | ✗ | Toxocara is a dangerous disease that can be found in dog and cat waste and can be passed on to humans if handled. |
| ■ **Hair,** *human and pet* | ✓ | ✗ | Very slow to compost, but adds useful nutrients. |
| ◨ **Manure** *from livestock and pets with straw, hay, or paper bedding* | ✓ | ✗ | Only compost manures from vegetarian or omnivorous animals and pets. |
| ■◨ **Manure** *from livestock and pets with wood shavings bedding* | ! | ✗ | Use only as a small proportion of the compost heap. Risk of nitrogen robbery. |
| ■ **Diapers** *disposable* | ✗ | ✗ | Not generally recommended to compost disposable diapers. Some types claim to be biodegradable and may produce compost when balanced with a high number of "greens." Use urine-soaked diapers only. |
| ☐ **Urine** | ✓ | ✓ | Dilute first, approximately 1:10 with water. Research (limited) indicates that there appears to be no need to be concerned about pharmaceuticals and hormones excreted with the urine. |

# PACKAGING AND PAPER

| Item | C | W | Notes |
|---|---|---|---|
| ◼ **Cardboard boxes** *(see also cardboard packages)* | ✓ | ✗ | Plain and color-printed cardboard can be composted. Crumple it up into rough balls—flat sheets will exclude air. A good counterbalance to excess "greens." Remove any packing tape and staples. A large box can make a good short-term compost bin. Other methods: Grass boarding. |
| ◼ **Cardboard food packages** *cereal boxes, tubes from paper towel and toilet paper rolls* | ✓ | ✓ | Plain and color-printed cardboard can be composted. Check juice and other cartons that may include a layer of plastic. Other methods: High-fiber heap. |
| ◼ **Egg cartons** | ✓ | ✓ | Their shape helps keep air in the heap; a good counterbalance to kitchen waste. Other methods: High-fiber heap. |
| ◼ **Food and drink cartons** | ! | ✗ | Do not compost cartons that have an aluminium foil lining. Other cartons may have a plastic lining, but this can always be removed once the composting process is complete. |
| ◼ **Newspaper** | ! | ! | Large quantities are best sent for recycling. Newspaper is good for absorbing excess moisture, particularly in a worm bin. It can also be used as a weed-control mulch in the garden. Other methods: Garden mulch. |
| ◼ **Paper** *high quality* | ! | ! | Environmentally, this is best sent for recycling, but it can be added to a compost heap. Scrunch it up into balls first. Flat sheets don't allow air movement in the heap. Shredded paper can be added, but scrunched is better. |
| ◼ **Paper** *low-quality, including paper bags, paper towels (see also newspaper)* | ✓ | ✓ | Good for absorbing excess moisture. Scrunch up before adding to allow air movement in the heap. Do not add paper towels if it has been used to mop up bleach or other chemical products. Other methods: High-fiber heap. |
| ◼ **Junk mail** | ! | ! | Some leaflets contain plastic. Tear a page to check before composting. Both black-and-white and colored printing can be composted. Scrunch it up rather than adding as flat sheets. |
| ◼ **Plastic-style carrier bags and packaging** *labelled biodegradable and compostable* | ! | ✗ | The whole area of compostable and recyclable "plastic" packaging is complex, and the current terminology is misleading or at least confusing, so it is best to avoid adding plastic-style materials to your heap. |
| ◼ **Plastic bottles** | ✗ | ✗ | Will not compost; recycle with other household waste. |
| ◼ **Plastic wrap** | ✗ | ✗ | Not biodegradable. |
| ◼ **Chip bags** | ✗ | ✗ | Not biodegradable. |
| ◼ **Glass** | ✗ | ✗ | Not biodegradable. Recycle. |
| ◼ **Beverage cans** | ✗ | ✗ | Not biodegradable. Recycle. |
| ◼ **Tin cans** | ✗ | ✗ | Not biodegradable. Recycle. |

## MISCELLANEOUS ITEMS

| Item | C | W | Notes |
|------|---|---|-------|
| **Wool, cotton, and other natural fiber clothing** | ✓ | ✓ | All natural fiber materials can be composted, although care should be taken if a garment has a printed logo on it. |
| **Ashes** *coal and coke* | ✗ | ✗ | Coal ash does not compost, and it contains high levels of sulphur and other impurities. Small quantities that may be mixed with wood ash can be put in a compost bin. |
| **Ashes** *wood* | ✓ | ✓ | A good source of minerals, wood ash (and unburned charcoal) from lumpwood barbecue charcoal is fine; do not use ash from briquettes. |
| **Soil** | ! | ! | There is no need to add soil to a heap. Soil on roots of weeds and plants is fine, but avoid adding large clumps and clods. |
| **Stones and pebbles** | ✗ | ✗ | These are not compostable since they are nonliving materials. |

Any extra garden waste from adjacent meadows or plantings can be useful compost additions.

## Adding Material to Your Heap

The key to good compost is to build your heap in layers of material with different characteristics, with no single layer being too thick. Luckily, this normally happens as a matter of course as the heap grows out of the varied activities around the garden. The ideal heap consists of equal amounts of nitrogen-rich and carbon-rich material. You can also think of it in terms of a good balance between green material (grass clippings, plant waste, and peelings) that provide nitrogen and brown material (coarser things like woody plant remains, dead leaves, and newspaper) that provide carbon. The ideal is to follow a green layer with a brown layer, to keep the heap's structure open, allowing air and water to permeate the heap. You will likely have too much green material, especially from grass clippings—a dense layer of grass clippings forms a black slime rather than wholesome compost, so keep a pile of cardboard, straw, or scrunched-up newspapers handy, and add some of this every time you have an overabundance of green material. Chopping or cutting the material on the heap into small pieces makes decomposition faster, as it gives the microbes that cause decomposition more surface area to get stuck into.

## Problems Solved

If a heap is becoming slimy, smelly, and sludgy rather than decomposing properly, it is too wet, and there is insufficient air in the heap. Mix the contents of the bin with chopped straw, scrunched-up newspaper, or coarser brown waste, ensure that the bottom layer of the bin allows drainage, and cover the bin with a tarp to keep the rain out.

If the material heap is not decomposing, it is probably because the heap is too dry. The best solution is to turn the heap out, mix in plenty of soft green waste, and return it to the bin. If this isn't available, watering the heap and adding a covering to keep the moisture in will both help.

# Buying a Compost Bin

There are numerous kinds of compost bins made of plastic or wood on the market, at a wide range of prices. The type of compost bins you choose will depend on your space and budget. If possible, try before you buy to be sure that you like what you are getting, and that the bin meets the criteria listed here. However, as the greatest range of composting bins is available via mail order or online this isn't always possible. Also, ask your local public

Perhaps the ultimate in home compost, a three-bin system allows for one bin to be filled while another is maturing and the third is in use—ideal in a large plot.

There are many types of compost bins available. Choose one you like.

works; these days many local governments are keen to help promote composting and often offer their residents compost bins at low prices.

As a newcomer to composting, it is probably best to buy or make your own simple no-frills plastic or wooden bin. No matter what type you use, you should ideally have at least two bins so that one can be filled while the other is working.

## Features of a Good Compost Bin

Whether bought or homemade, there are features that make some compost bins better than others—for example, durability or ease of use. Ultimately though, it is what you do that makes the biggest difference to the quality of the compost produced. The most important feature is that you like the bin and that it suits you, your lifestyle, and your garden. If you don't like your compost bin, you will be less inclined to use it, and more likely to hide it away in an inaccessible spot.

### WHAT IS IT MADE OF?

A compost container can take quite a battering when being filled and emptied, and a full load of compost is quite a weight, so make sure your container is sturdy enough to stand up to constant use.

Wood is an appropriate material for a compost bin, as it is itself a natural product. It is a renewable resource and will, in time, decay back into the soil. Wood is strong, provides some insulation, and it "breathes," so the compost is less likely to get too wet.

There are a few wooden boxes on the market, but you can also make your own. You can be creative with the design, and you can even stain the wood a color of your choice as long as you use a non-toxic product. It makes sense to use recycled wood if possible—old pallets, for example, or whatever you can find locally.

Wood preservatives may be an issue here. Even though some preservatives are more "environmentally friendly" than others, none really fit in with the ethos of organic gardening. It is best to use untreated wood, accepting that the bin will rot eventually.

While wooden bins tend to be square and on the large side, plastic bins (usually made from recycled plastic) come in a wider range of shapes and sizes, to suit all sorts of gardens. You can also construct homemade compost containers from straw bales, wire mesh fixed around four

A double-bay wooden compost box—the front slats can be removed for easy access.

posts and lined with cardboard, sheets of corrugated metal, and many other reused materials, including plastic garbage cans with the bottoms cut off.

## HOW HEAVY IS IT?

If your compost bin needs to be lifted up to access the compost, then make sure you get one that you can lift. In a windy spot, a heavier bin is less likely to blow over when it is relatively empty.

## SOLID OR SLATTED SIDES

Air is an essential component of good composting, but this is built into the heap as you make it. A compost bin does not need any holes or gaps in the sides. Large gaps allow the material to dry out and heat to escape; they are not particularly effective at getting air into the center of the heap where it is needed. If you have a wire mesh container, line it with flattened-out cardboard boxes.

## VOLUME AND DIMENSIONS

The size of bin you choose will depend on how much material you have to compost, rather than the size of your garden or of your family (although these elements may be linked). About 200 gallons (757L) or 1 cubic yard/meter is the traditional size recommended as a minimum for fast, hot composting. This is a good size for a large garden. Most bins on the market average 50–90 gallons (189–340L) and are appropriate for most households and gardens of today. Models smaller than this are unlikely to make compost satisfactorily.

## KEEPING IT COVERED

A lid or some sort of cover is useful as it can help regulate the moisture content in the bin. A cover also prevents weed seeds from blowing in. The lids on some models are much easier to get off than others. It helps if it doesn't blow away easily.

## BASE

It is important that excess moisture can drain from a compost heap—so most compost bins do not have or need a base. If there is a base, it must have good drainage to allow excess moisture to seep away, and worms should be able to get into the heap from below.

### RAT-PROOFING

Rats can eat their way into a plastic or wooden compost bin if they feel so inclined. To make a bin rat-proof, you need to line it (including the base) with wire mesh.

### STATIC OR MOBILE

Some bins are free-standing and easy to move. Others have stakes in the ground for support, so are not easy to move. Choose the style that best suits your circumstances.

### FILLING THE BIN

A reasonable-sized opening at the top is important. Trying to deposit a forkful of compost material through a narrow opening is not easy.

### GETTING IT OUT

Some compost bins have a small access door at ground level, so you can scoop out the finished compost. This is only practical for small quantities, so a bin without an access door is fine. You just lift it off. Wooden bins may have one side that is removable, which makes it very easy to empty the bin.

## Using Plastic Bins

If you have a pocket-sized patch, then two of the plastic composting bins available from garden centers should work well. These are light, their fabric is maintenance-free, and they can be easily moved if needed. Choose bins of at least 44 gallons (167L) in volume, as smaller bins are likely to make the composting process less efficient. If possible, select bins with a hatch near the base, so any compost that is ready can easily be removed from the heap.

## Using Wooden Bins

If you have space, large purpose-made wooden bins in various styles are available. A thrifty option is to put together a bin from old pallets, either wired together or wired to posts on three sides and with an opening in the front to make it easy to remove the finished compost. Add a tarp covering to conserve heat and moisture.

This compost bin constructed from old pallets is a lovely piece of pragmatic recycling and will make compost just as well as fancier models at a fraction of the cost.

## Using Worm Bins

Hungry brandling worms will munch their way through their own body weight in kitchen waste per day to produce very rich compost and a liquid feed. This means more kitchen waste can be recycled than what could be added to a standard compost heap. Purpose-made worm bins are available, and worms can be bought by mail order. The bins need to be well sealed to avoid letting vermin in, but everything except onion and citrus fruit waste can be added daily. The liquid needs to be drained off regularly to avoid the bin flooding.

## Open Heap

This is simply waste heaped in a hidden corner and turned occasionally. You will wait and burrow in at points to find compost ready for use. For this method, you must periodically turn the edges in toward the center. It is simple, and there are no structures to buy or build, but the frequent turning of the heap is backbreaking work, and the rotting process can take a long time.

# Using Compost

Depending on your current garden situation, you will need to determine what type of compost will work best for your vegetable garden. Below are a number of suggestions for the use of various types of compost in a variety of gardening situations.

Hungry plants, such as potatoes and members of the brassica (cabbage) family, make the best use of compost or worm compost. Apply before sowing or planting in spring and early summer.

Winter brassicas, such as Brussels sprouts and sprouting broccoli, can benefit from a second application in July or August. In poorer soils, vegetables, such as squash, Swiss chard, onions, beans, and beets, will also benefit from the application of compost.

If you use crop rotation in your planting scheme, carrots, peas, and parsnips will generally thrive on leftover nutrients from a previously fed crop. Use leaf mold where you plan to grow these crops to improve the structure and water-holding capabilities of poorer soils.

Worms might not be the most beautiful of creatures, but they are exceptionally effective at producing rich compost.

If you only have minimal supplies of compost, put it to best use in your vegetable plot to provide nutrients for your crops.

You will find the compost that is ready to use at the bottom of the heap.

## When Is It Ready?

Compost is ready to use when it is dark brown and soil-like and has a pleasant earthy smell. It does not matter if it isn't just like the fine "multipurpose" compost that you buy in bags for sowing and potting. Even if it is a bit lumpy and stringy, and there are twigs and eggshells still visible, you can use it as it is, or sieve it to make a finer product.

However, unless you are using a compost tumbler or have turned the heap several times, the compost won't be ready all at once. Some material at the top of the bin will be only partly decomposed when there is "finished" compost at the bottom.

To get the best from your finished compost, use it within a few months. It is much more valuable when it is on the garden, rather than taking up space in your compost bin!

All garden compost can be put to good use—on vegetables, fruits, and ornamental plants, and on lawns and containers, too. It can be an ingredient in homemade potting mixes. It is a good source of potassium and trace elements, and gives a reasonable supply of phosphate.

## When To Apply

Compost is best applied in spring and early summer when plants are growing and can take up the nutrients. Don't apply compost in late summer as this can encourage soft, sappy growth that may not harden properly in time for the winter, leading to winter injury. As compost is quite stable and is slow to break down in cold weather, you can also apply it later in the year with little risk of nutrients being washed out. It's helpful to mix some compost in with your soil when you are loosening it up or spreading some compost on the surface of your previously prepared soil. If you only loosen up your soil or just plunged your plants into unamended rock-hard clay or super-porous sand, then you need to add some compost sooner rather than later. If you don't expect disease to be a significant problem, then you can go ahead and mix some of the compost into the soil before you start planting.

Spread compost on the surface of the soil or fork it into the top 6" (15.2cm) of soil.

Roses thrive on a mulch of compost every year or two.

## How Much Compost

There is no need to be precise in the quantities you use. Concentrate on soils and plants that need feeding, but don't overdo it. As a rough guide, use no more than one 12-gallon (45L) wheelbarrow load for every 16' (4.9m) square of growing area per year, about ½" (1.3cm) deep.

An ideal amount would equal a 1"-2" (2.5-5.1cm) layer on top of about a 2' x 2' (61 x 61cm) plot of soil. If you feel the need to measure something, spread out 1" or 2" (2.5 or 5.1cm) of compost on top of a 2' x 2' (61 x 61cm) area in the center of where you will plant. Then mix it up with the soil that's already there (minus rocks and clay clods, of course).

If the plant is already in the ground, spread 2" (5.1cm) of compost all around it, covering a 2' x 2' (61 x 61cm) area (feel free to extend it out even further for really big plants). If you've already mixed some compost into the soil, spread another 1"–2" (2.5–5.1cm) on top. Compost used as a mulch prevents weeds just as well as shredded bark or woodchips (both of which may breed disease in the vegetable garden), provides all the foods our growing plants need, and prevents disease spores from breeding on the surface of the soil (wood and bark mulches encourage these spores).

## Where Should It Go?

The best use for garden compost will depend on how rough or fine it is and whether it contains viable weed seeds.

### ROUGH COMPOST

Rough compost that still contains woody bits, eggshells, fruit pits, and other material that has not fully decomposed is best applied as a mulch around fruit trees and bushes, roses, and other shrubby plants. Earthworms and other soil-dwelling creatures will gradually incorporate it into the soil.

Some nutrients will be released from the compost during the first growing season, but plants will still be getting some benefit from it a year or two after application. Alternatively, you can sift rough compost, and use it as you would finer compost (see page 95).

### "WEEDY" COMPOST

If your compost tends to produce a flush of weed seedlings when spread on the soil, it will cause less work if you incorporate it into the soil—for example, when you are planting fruit trees or bushes, or potatoes in your vegetable plot. Fork it into the top 6"–8" (15.2–20.3cm) of soil, no deeper. Alternatively, apply the compost in a

# BURYING YOUR PLANTS WITH GARBAGE

Plants that grow auxiliary roots along any part of their stem that is buried, like tomatoes, can reach much more water and nutrients than the roots of an unburied plant. Bury the bottom three-quarters of your plant starts underground; just the top 4" (10.2cm) or so should be left above the soil line. There are two different methods, which have benefits depending on your climate:

- **In really cold climates:** Bury your stems "trench-style." Dig your hole, fill it halfway back up with your loosened soil mixed with compost, add some crushed-up eggshells, lay the plant stem down horizontally on top of the soil, and then gently bend the last 4" (10.2cm) or so straight up. Cover the to-be-buried section with at least 2" (5.1cm)—4" (10.2cm) would be ideal—of your soil mix. By placing the rooted section close to the surface, you keep it in the warmest possible soil while still getting the benefits of the buried stem. This also helps your cold soil warm up faster in the spring, especially down deep.
- **In warm to normal climates:** You should not trench. The warmer your region gets in the summer, the more your vegetables' roots will wiggle around in deep, cool soil. So, fill in your hole with loosened soil and compost until you can place the root ball of your plant against the bottom of the hole and have just a few inches of the top of the plant poking out into the world. Remove any leaves that would otherwise be underground, put the plant in the hole, and then fill the hole with more soil and compost and some eggshells, tamping it down lightly. Remember, no plant likes compacted soil.

*Note: To get your plants safely out of their containers (like plastic nursery six-packs), squeeze the outside of each container gently all around until the plant and its soil slide or pop out easily. Try not to disturb that big clump of soil around the roots.*

Generally, you don't need to sieve compost, but it is worthwhile if you are making potting mixes or top-dressing plants in containers.

situation where you can easily hoe off any weed seedlings that appear.

## FINE CRUMBLY COMPOST

Compost that is reasonably free from lumps, twigs, and weed seeds can be used in any of the ways already mentioned, and others, too.

Fork or hoe it into the soil (no deeper than 6"–8" [15.2–20.3cm] as this is where most of the plant's feeding roots are), or spread it on the surface for the worms to take under. It can also be used to feed and improve a lawn or mixed with other ingredients to fill large pots, window boxes, and troughs.

## SIFTED COMPOST

Compost can be sifted to create a very fine product, which is ideal if you want to use it in potting mixes or for top-dressing plants in pots. Many of the fibrous bits and lumps in the compost will break up in the sifting process; others can be returned to the compost heap or used as a mulch around trees and shrubs. You can buy a simple garden sieve or improvise—for example, by attaching a piece of wire mesh (about ⅖" [10.2mm] grid size) to a wooden frame.

To make it easier on your back, try fitting the sieve into the top of a large plastic tub. Rocking the tub back and forth is less hard work than holding a sieve full of heavy compost. If you are producing large amounts of compost, you might want to invest in a rotary sieve.

## Compost Tea

A safe way to feed and nurture your plants throughout the season without overfeeding your plants is by brewing up some compost tea once a month or so during the season. Place some nice, finished compost into a porous cloth container (an old sock for a gallon [4L] of water; a tied-up old T-shirt for a five-gallon [19-liter] bucket of water; or an old pillowcase for a big and clean trash can full of water). Place this "tea bag" in the container of your choice, fill it with cool water, and then let it steep in the shade for 24 hours to create compost tea.

When it's done steeping, remove the bag and return the contents of the bag to your compost pile. Thin the liquid with water until it's the color of tea, and then use it to immediately water your plants. Compost tea is

Making a nutrient-rich compost tea at least once a month is a safe option to avoid overfeeding.

full of living beneficial organisms, and they're using up the limited amount of oxygen in that water. So, make only what you'll need within an hour or so of tea-bag removal time.

Since morning is the best time to water your plants, start your tea brewing around 10 a.m. on Saturday morning and use it around 10 or 11 a.m. Sunday morning; you'll deliver the maximum number of beneficial soil helpers to the roots of your plants.

# Manure for Composting

For your vegetable garden, the manure you want is from horses or cows and is mixed in with straw and left to rot down for at least a year, preferably two or three. If the manure doesn't smell, it's well-rotted and is ideal to use. When you add it to the soil, it helps water drain through and adds nutrients, particularly nitrogen, which promotes healthy green growth, as well as phosphorus and potassium, which stimulate root growth and fruit production. If you don't let it rot down first, it'll burn the plants and smell awful. Well-rotted manure can be bought from garden centers in nice, clean plastic bags. There are also online companies that will deliver manure, but you must make sure to order from responsible companies.

Manure essentially adds the same things to the soil as compost. The main problems with any farmyard manure are that it is much harder to come by if you live in the city than if you live in the country, and it can upset close neighbors because of the inevitable smell. An overriding problem for the organic gardener, however, is to ensure that any farmyard manure is obtained from a clean farm. The cleaner and more well kept the farm, the less likelihood the manure will be infected with weed seeds.

## The Realities of Manure

While most people believe manure is good, it often isn't. And there is no single thing known as "manure." Here are some manure rules and realities:

1. Never put "raw" or "fresh" manure on your garden. It smells bad, can be full of pathogens, can be full of weed seeds just waiting to sprout (especially horse manure), and it could "burn" your plants with its excess nitrogen.

Cow manure is gentler than other animal manures, but you must still be sure to use only composted cow manure.

6. Llama poop, sheep poop, gerbil poop, rabbit poop—any poop from an animal that doesn't eat meat and that isn't routinely medicated makes great food for your garden.

7. Waste from dogs and cats should not be used anywhere near a garden. Even indoor-only animals can harbor worms or parasites, and their waste should be carefully disposed of in the trash.

8. Elephant dung is fine. Circuses often give it away. The "pellets" are the size of footballs, so it's a little slow to break down, but it's very effective.

# Using Autumn Leaves and Leaf Mold

These materials have slightly different uses to conventional composts. Leaf mold is low in readily available plant nutrients, so it can be used at any time of year and in larger quantities than compost. It is excellent for protecting and improving the soil structure, and is a useful ingredient in homemade sowing and potting mixes. It is also a good autumn top-dressing for lawns. Leaf mold is a free commodity depending on how many trees you have in your garden or whether you live close to a park or public woods. Leaves make an excellent soil conditioner, but they can take between one and three years to break down, depending on the types of leaves. It is the amount of lignin contained in leaves that dictates how long decomposition will take, as some leaves have much more of this fibrous tissue than others. Leaf mold makes an excellent soil conditioner, and you can use the result as a seed or potting soil, as it has an excellent structure and consistent nutrient levels.

## Newly Fallen Leaves

Newly fallen leaves can be spread over bare soil to protect it over winter. Rake the leaves back before sowing into the soil in the following spring.

## Young Leaf Mold

Leaf mold can be used on your garden as soon as the leaves begin to break up and crumble easily in your hand. This will take about a year, though more resistant species, such as oak or chestnut, may have to be left longer. Spread it as a

2. Composted manures may be good to use. Composted manure—the result of piling up the stuff the animal was done with and the bedding they made—has no objectionable odor, is cool to the touch, and looks like dark soil or compost.

3. Composted horse manure and poultry manure are excellent for feeding non-fruiting plants, like sweet corn and lawns, but are a poor choice for flowers and other garden crops we grow for their fruit—like tomatoes, peppers, eggplants, zucchini, etc. If a crop you want to eat from the vegetable replaces a flower on the plant, don't feed the plant horse or poultry manure. Horse and poultry manures are excessively rich in nitrogen, the nutrient that makes plants grow larger in a shorter amount of time. But nitrogen can also inhibit flowering, which is why you can end up with huge plants with only two tomatoes on them.

4. Composted cow manure is theoretically much safer. It's a "cold" manure (not a lot of nitrogen), and its (relatively weak) nutrients are balanced.

5. If you have access to manure from animals raised without hormones, continuous antibiotics, or extensive confinement, you can use it. Mix some horse or poultry manure into your compost piles—or even into big piles of shredded fall leaves—and you'll make hot compost, which is the type that best fights diseases.

To make the nutrient-rich potting medium known as comfrey leaf compost, mix equal volumes of comfrey leaves and leaf mold. Leave to rot for several months.

mulch, or incorporate it into the top 6"–8" (15.2–20.3cm) of soil almost anywhere in your garden. It is particularly valuable as a soil improver for crops, such as carrots, and annual flowers that don't like lots of nutrients. In this case, spread a thin layer of ½" (1.3cm) over the soil surface (the autumn before sowing if possible), and hoe it in lightly before sowing any seeds into it.

## Well-Rotted Leaf Mold

After another year or so, you will have what is called "well-rotted" leaf mold. This is dark brown and crumbly, with no real trace of the original leaves. This product can also be valuable in seed and potting composts. You can sift it, if necessary.

## Comfrey Leaf Compost

Comfrey leaf compost is a nutrient-rich potting mix that contains levels of available nitrogen and potassium in proportions particularly suitable for growing tomato plants. It can also be diluted with extra leaf mold for raising other young plants.

Leaves make excellent compost, but take a long time to break down.

To make comfrey leaf compost, mix well-rotted leaf mold with chopped fresh comfrey leaves in equal proportions by volume. Put the mixture into a plastic lidded bucket or garbage can, and leave for a few months or over winter until the comfrey has completely decomposed.

# Using Composted Woodchips and Shreds

Woodchips and shredded woody prunings are very slow to break down, and do not immediately provide nutrients or improve the soil structure in the same way as compost. Even after they have been composted separately for a year or more, they will still be decomposing. Don't dig them into the soil as they can use up nitrogen that could otherwise be feeding your plants (this is known as nitrogen robbery). Wood is the ultimate carbon source, and carbon seeks out nitrogen in an attempt to merge and decompose. Wood ashes are highly alkaline and will dry out the average vegetable garden.

Woodchips will gradually rot down when used in a pathway.

However, woodchips and shreddings can be useful as a mulch around established trees and shrubs to keep down weeds and retain moisture, and they will very gradually add organic matter to the soil. Spread them in a layer 2"–4" (5.1–10.2cm) thick, starting about 4" (10.2cm) out from the trunk. You can do this at any time of year provided that the ground is not frozen and that you make sure the soil is thoroughly moist first.

Woodchips and shreddings can also be used, fresh or composted, to mulch informal paths. Dig out the pathway to a depth of 6" (15.2cm) or so, line with a permeable weed-proof membrane if weeds are likely to grow up from below, then cover with woodchips. After a year or so, you can dig out the partially rotted woodchips for use on the garden, replacing them with a fresh batch.

# Fertilizers and Plant Nutrients

Plants manufacture their own food from sunlight. However, to keep that process in action, they need some other supplies, which they generally get from the soil. In a well-run, organic, no-dig garden with a good mulching regimen, very little extra feeding is necessary as your soil should contain all a plant needs to thrive. With the constant introduction of organic matter into the soil, you are feeding the soil using natural products and natural processes, which then feeds the plant. The nutrients removed with every plant you grow, or leached away through the soil, are replaced by the rotting organic matter.

However, there are some circumstances, especially in new gardens, in which feeding may be required to get a good, healthy crop, or where well-judged feeding can significantly increase the yield. The vegetable plot is the area of the garden where the most is asked of the soil and keeping it fertile is vital. Routine feeding, however, can

> **THE BASICS**
> In an established, organic, no-dig garden, very little extra feeding is required.

A steaming pile of compost for making raised beds.

## SHOPPING FOR FOOD GARDEN FERTILIZERS

Visit any major garden center, and you will find a bewildering array of brands and formulations of fertilizers. Here's how to find what you need.

- Avoid lawn fertilizers; they are too high in nitrogen for tomatoes and peppers.
- Consider the granular inorganic fertilizers such as 10-10-10 or 13-13-13, often called "corn fertilizers"—but only for the first time you prepare the soil. Thereafter, switch to granular organic fertilizers for maintaining soil fertility. They are easier on soil organisms than the harsh chemical compounds in processed fertilizers.
- You won't find many brands of granular organic fertilizers, and they will be considerably more expensive than granular processed or inorganic fertilizers. When you compare, you will be paying even more per pound of actual nutrients than you would with inorganic fertilizers. But don't despair—processed chicken manures are coming on the market; they combine a relatively high analysis with more attractive price levels.
- If your plants are yellowing, and you want them to green up, consider a water-soluble liquid fertilizer. Buy the crystals and dilute them per the directions. Avoid pre-diluted brands: the water in them is as expensive as the bottled water in an airport.
- Don't rely on liquid fertilizers for your basic nutrient supply; their effect lasts only a few days. Some of the liquid fertilizers are labeled "organic," but may be spiked with chemicals to raise the nitrogen and phosphate content. Use granular organic fertilizers with the "no-till" garden method to decrease having to resort to liquid plant foods.

be a waste of valuable time and money; in fact, it can be detrimental, encouraging the wrong type of growth, too much leaf instead of fruit, or soft growth that is more prone to disease.

As a regular measure in new gardens, you could use a little broad-spectrum organic fertilizer developed for the vegetable garden when you plant or sow seed. A general fertilizer will probably contain roughly similar quantities of nitrogen, phosphates, and potassium. In bald terms, nitrogen promotes leafy growth, phosphates are good for roots, and potassium promotes flowering and fruits. There is a whole range of fertilizers developed for the vegetable patch and each has a different make-up of nutrients tailored to the requirements of different plants— you could quite easily buy a specific fertilizer for every crop. It is reassuring to imagine that you have exactly the right product for each crop, but for the most part, it is unnecessary because soil in good condition will do the work for you.

A number of products and processes must work together to create a successful first garden and to build productivity over the years. Understanding the various factors involved is a continuing challenge for gardeners. The following sections explain in a bit more detail how fertilizers and plant nutrients fit into the big picture.

## Solving The NPK Mystery!

**Fertilizers and plant nutrients are not the same.** Think of fertilizers as the vehicles for delivering nutrients to the soil. The soil then delivers these nutrients to plants in forms that can be absorbed by their roots. Plant nutrients are either major (essential) or micro (trace elements). The three major plant nutrients are nitrogen, phosphate, and potash. These are listed by percentage and weight on all fertilizer packaging. Micronutrients are usually added to fertilizer sold in liquid forms. Laws do not require their percentages to be listed in fertilizer analyses, but they are usually mentioned as a sales advantage.

On any packaged fertilizer, such as organic or chemical, powdered, granular, or liquid, there will be a set of three numbers displayed prominently on the label, like 10-10-10 (bad), 5-3-5 (better, but far from ideal), or 3-1-2 (perfect). Those numbers are that fertilizer's NPK ratio— the relative amounts of Nitrogen (N), Phosphorus (P), and Potassium (K) the fertilizer contains. Based on all the available evidence, it appears that a ratio of 3-1-2 is ideal for most garden plants. Here's a little NPK 101:

- **Nitrogen (N):** Nitrogen is the basic plant food—it helps grow a big, strong "body" and lots of leaves. Although, feeding plants that you want to produce lots of flowers and/or fruits too much of this nutrient can limit the number of flowers and fruits because the plant is putting too much energy into making lush, leafy green growth instead of producing fruit. You will note that in the ideal 3-1-2 ratio, nitrogen is still the dominant nutrient. That's because nitrogen is ephemeral; it moves around so much in the soil, and is so quickly taken up and used by plants that it needs to be replaced more often than the other nutrients.

- **Phosphorus (P):** This is the key nutrient for top tomato production. It helps plants put down strong roots and encourages them to produce more flowers, which on tomato plants turn into tomatoes. Because it is essential to strong root growth, you want this nutrient to be in the soil right away. It's OK to add a little nitrogen later in the season if you suffer from smaller and weaker plants; you need your phosphorous to be there from day one. It also has to be right where the roots can reach it—phosphorus doesn't travel in the soil like nitrogen. You can toss a handful of bonemeal into each planting hole—right on top of old eggshells if you're using them. Rock phosphate is the best source of phosphorus, but your soil has to be nice and acidic and alive for it to work its best. A product called colloidal rock phosphate is almost as rich in phosphorus, but a lot less needy, and it's especially good for use in sandy soils—it's a little "clayey," and it helps hold the sand particles together better. Either way, a little goes a long way, and it needs a fairly long time to become active and available to your plants. But it also lasts a long time; you should only add rock phosphates to your soil once every three to five years.

- **Potassium/potash (K):** This nutrient essentially helps plants do everything better. It helps the flow of all the other nutrients throughout the plant, improves fruit quality, and helps the plant better resist stress. There are two good standalone potassium sources. One is greensand, which contains only a small amount of potassium but has a big effect, perhaps due to all the micronutrients it also provides. Greensand also takes a while to break down, so you should add it to your soil the fall before planting. Organic matter speeds its release, so some gardeners like to add greensand to their fall-built compost piles to supercharge the results. The other is Sul-Po-Mag, which is organic,

mined, and contains magnesium (the "mag" part) as well, so you wouldn't ever want to use more than a pinch on tomatoes—it can interfere with calcium absorption, which the plants need and love more than the magnesium.

## Other Required Nutrients

In addition to nitrogen, phosporous, and potassium, plants require a range of other elements in differing levels. Magnesium (Mg), calcium (Ca), and sulphur (S) are the next most important. Then there are those required in minute quantities, usually called trace elements. These include iron (Fe), manganese (Mn), copper (Cu), zinc (Zn), boron (Bo), molybdenum (Mb), and chlorine (Cl).

Sufficient amounts are usually present in most soils because only tiny quantities are needed by plants. However, deficiencies do occur and can cause striking symptoms. Leaves with distinct yellow margins or bright green veins standing out against a yellow background signal that some of these minor nutrients are in short supply. Look for a fertilizer, such as a foliar fertilizer, with "trace elements" to rectify the problem.

There is a bewildering range of fertilizers available for use, and products will be described in many different ways. Chemical or inorganic fertilizers are factory produced, generally cheap, and the type of fertilizers widely used in agriculture, for vegetable and fruit production or for fertilizing lawns. Organic fertilizers originate from some sort of natural product and include fertilizers, such as bonemeal or dried blood. They will

## GARDENING ORGANICALLY

Some gardeners may choose to produce crops on an organic basis, and this means growing as naturally as possible, without the use of any chemical fertilizers, pesticides, or weed killers. This is quite possible and, for many people, a matter of strong personal belief. All gardeners should respect the wildlife within the garden and the living aspects of the soil in particular. For those who feel less strongly, a moderated approach using a mix of organic principles and modern fertilizers, together with a minimum of pesticides, is often an acceptable compromise.

generally be more expensive and slower in reaction than chemical fertilizers, as the material has to break down in the soil to release the nutrients.

## Packaged Fertilizers

If it's organic (says "approved for use in organic agriculture" or "certified organic" or "Organic Materials Review Institute [OMRI] approved" somewhere on the package), it's likely to be good to use.

Compound or balanced fertilizers have a blend of different nutrients within them, supplying all the plant's needs in one go. One of the most common would be Growmore, a cheap chemical fertilizer, widely used for vegetable production. Straight fertilizers are simple chemicals providing only one or two nutrients, for example superphosphate or sulphate of potash.

Liquid mixtures of fish and seaweed are good mid-season boost fertilizers. They provide a great balance of the big essential nutrients, and the seaweed (or kelp; the terms are used interchangeably) component is full of trace elements and other hard-to-find nutrients that help plants better resist stress. Seaweed/kelp can even give plants a couple extra degrees of frost/cold weather endurance! Be wary of fish emulsion alone; these products are traditionally very high in nitrogen, and some contain way too much chlorine.

Liquid feeds are fertilizers in a soluble form that have the advantage of giving a rapid response. They may be

sold as a concentrated liquid that is diluted or as a soluble powder. In both cases, they must be mixed with the correct amount of water before using. Liquid feeds should never be applied to a plant that is dry, as root scorch may occur. Some suppliers of liquid feeds produce their own diluters, which connect to a hose and make application an easy job.

Granulated fertilizers (organically approved ones) are fine, but use them sparingly, don't let the granules

Granular organic fertilizers should always be covered with some soil or compost to become active. Conventional ones too—but it's best to stick with organic.

## TYPES OF FERTILIZERS AT A GLANCE

There are different ways to apply fertilizers—the choice you make usually depends on the reason for using them.

- **Liquids:** Fertilizers in liquid form are usually quickly absorbed by plants. Liquid fertilizers are almost always concentrated and need to be diluted with water before application. Check the directions on the label.
- **Powders:** You need to apply powdered fertilizer either straight from the package to the soil or dissolved in water before application; check the instructions carefully. Dry powdered fertilizers can scorch the young leaves and growing tips of plants, so apply them carefully on a still day. Don't spread them right up against plant stems. Lightly rake the fertilizer into the soil surface after application.
- **Granules:** Granular fertilizers are usually spread on the soil surface. They are easier to handle and, therefore, quicker to apply than powders. They are also less likely to scorch plants or to be blown around by the wind.
- **Foliar fertilizers:** Plants can absorb nutrients through their leaves as well as their roots, and foliar fertilizers produce a rapid response. Choose a specially formulated foliar fertilizer where normal fertilizers are not suitable.

Bonemeal, rich in phosphorus, is a fertilizer that encourages flowering; and more flowers equals more fruits.

touch the stem of any plants, and always cover granular fertilizers with a little soil or compost after you apply them (it activates the nutrients faster). Slow-release fertilizers are generally the "Rolls Royce" of fertilizers and will have all the nutrients required bound up into a small pill shape, which breaks down slowly within the soil, feeding the plants over a predictable span of time. Such fertilizers are very useful in providing a whole season's nutrients in one application.

Avoid overly strong fertilizers—and unbalanced ones like the popular 10-10-10 fertilizer, which is both too strong and unbalanced. The numbers may be equal, but no plant on the planet uses the "big three" nutrients in equal amounts. Like it says in "Solving the NPK Mystery!" on page 101, the ideal ratio of nutrients for fruiting plants like tomatoes is 3-1-2.

Now, if you want to try and induce a little more flowering (and thus fruit), bonemeal is the best source of immediate phosphorus (the P in NPK—the middle number on a bag of fertilizer), which is the essential nutrient for getting lots of flowers and fruits. Bonemeal makes its phosphorus available faster than any other P source, so it would be the bloom booster you'd use at the beginning of the season. Rock phosphate (a mined mineral product) is much better but takes much longer to become available—you'd have to apply rock phosphate (just a little; it's highly concentrated) the fall before. Whatever you use, spread some soil or compost over top to get it working a little faster.

Many of the above explanatory terms can be used together because they describe different aspects of a fertilizer. So, for example, we could have a slow-release, inorganic fertilizer, like many modern commercial products, or an organic balanced fertilizer, such as blood, fish, and bone—a very smelly mixture of traditional constituents.

### Organic Fertilizers

Organic fertilizers fulfill the age-old wisdom to "feed the soil rather than the plants." Although this advice came long before scientists understood why it is sound practice to do so, many now agree that feeding the soil is valid. If you keep soil healthy by "feeding" it organic soil conditioners and organic fertilizers, it will in turn feed your plants. However, some technicians, and many home gardeners, still prefer to apply processed fertilizers because of their predictability and efficiency.

Organic fertilizers are usually derived from the waste stream produced by food production facilities, animal feedlots, and stables. But supplies of the raw materials that are available to fertilizer manufacturers are drying up. Canning and freezing facilities for fish, shellfish, and mollusks are converting more of their waste into food for the very species they process, and more by-products, such as beef, pork, and chicken trimmings, are going into pet foods. Asian countries are purchasing some of the meats that are not marketed here. Cottonseed and soybean meals, both excellent fertilizers, are becoming prohibitively expensive.

### AVAILABLE ORGANIC FERTILIZER TYPES

**Organic fertilizers come in three basic forms:** dry granular, liquid concentrate, and ready-to-use liquid nutrient sources. The ready-to-use sources are the most expensive by far. Why pay for shipping water from a manufacturing plant to your garden when you can dissolve concentrated sources using tap water?

Many brands of concentrated liquid organic fertilizers are by-products of fish processing. They offer the benefit of complex organic compounds as well as moderate, but adequate, levels of nitrogen, phosphate, potash, and micronutrients. A processor of farm-raised catfish in Mississippi hydrolyzes fish scraps to produce a product that's effective, yet virtually free of the fishy odor that often follows the application of many of the better-known fish fertilizers.

### READ THE LABEL

It is worth repeating that the analysis of granular organic fertilizers on labels is misleading, and not by intent. Organic fertilizers require the action of soil microorganisms for the breakdown and release of nitrogen, phosphate, and potash, along with beneficial, complex organic compounds. Most organic fertilizers are rather slow and gentle in reaction, but chicken and sheep manure are exceptions. Unless mixed with an organic carrier, chicken or sheep manure can be so "hot" that it can burn plant roots. The term "hot" refers to the quick release of ammonia and salts during breakdown.

On the plus side, methods are being refined to process poultry manure into safe-to-use, nonodoriferous fertilizer. Sheep manure has long been used as a mild fertilizer despite its lingering odor. Dried cattle manure, while too weak to be considered a fertilizer, does work well when used as a soil conditioner.

If you are determined to use strictly organic fertilizers, you should read the "derived from" information on labels. Some formulations are "juiced up" using di-ammonium phosphate to boost the nitrogen and phosphate numbers on the analysis. Three of the best-known sources of brand-name organic fertilizers are Bradfield Organics, Espoma, and Milorganite.

Certain mail-order catalogs and independent garden centers in large cities specialize in organic fertilizers and pest control. Large, independent garden centers often have organic fertilizers packaged for their customers under a private label.

## Mineral Fertilizers

Mineral fertilizers are usually processed to boost their percentage of major nutrient elements. This processing consumes much more energy, as does the grinding and pelletizing of raw or processed materials to simplify mixing or handling. Such fertilizers are maligned by some organic gardeners and are blamed for poisoning soil. That situation exists in only a miniscule number of fields owned by commercial growers, and in most cases, can be rectified by flooding the field to leach away accumulated salts. A more serious problem with processed fertilizers, especially those applied to lawns, commercial turf, and row-crop farmland is their tendency to wash into ponds and waterways along with valuable topsoil.

Many societies have to burn most of the available organic matter to cook meals and heat homes. Growing and turning under green manure crops (see page 108) is out of the question; they need to grow food crops on every square inch of arable land to produce enough to stay alive. They require mineral fertilizer to maintain productivity in their soil, even when it has to be shipped in.

Acorn squash thrives in a nutrient-rich, well-drained soil.

## Granular, Processed Fertilizers

More packaged fertilizers than any other are the granular, processed type, and lawn fertilizers dominate. Most of these fertilizers are too high in nitrogen content for feeding vegetables. Unless they are side-dressed into the soil, meaning trickled into furrows alongside rows of plants and covered over with soil, the release of ammonia and salts can burn the roots.

Some include herbicides in their formulation and should not be used on food crops or ornamental plants. Other fertilizers mention "acid forming" in their promotional copy. These are suitable for blueberries, currants, and gooseberries, but not for general use on food crops.

Magnesium sulfate, sold as Epsom salts, is often used but seldom recommended as a booster for tomatoes, peppers, eggplant, and roses. Epsom salts works on some soils but not on others. This may explain why Epsom salts are rarely recommended in state extension service bulletins on growing vegetables. Magnesium is a secondary nutrient and is not usually deficient in soils, unless they are acidic. Epsom salts are usually used at a concentration of ½ cup (112g) dissolved in 8 quarts (7.6L) of warm water.

## CHEMICAL VERSUS ORGANIC

Both chemical and organic fertilizers are needed, and home gardeners should be encouraged to use in moderation whichever works best for them without being subjected to criticism. Laws are in place to limit the environmental impact of fertilizer manufacturing processes, and the industry is one of the most heavily regulated and monitored in the USA. The goal of most manufacturers is to think globally and reduce the number of people suffering from malnutrition. The energy used in producing mineral fertilizers is much the same as the energy used in grinding and hauling organic soil conditioners and mulches. It is extremely difficult to raise or maintain levels of organic matter in the soil using just the output of a home compost heap fed with trimmings, clippings, and leaves. Supplementary sources of organic matter are often needed.

# DO THE MATH

Soil test results are often stated in terms developed for farmers, not for home gardeners. For example, the amounts of nitrogen, phosphate, and potash needed to reach optimum productivity may be listed at "pounds (kg) per 1,000' (304.8m) square." The easy way to convert these figures for your home garden is to divide the pounds by 10, which will give you the amount per 100' (30.5m) square, (10' x 10' [3 x 3m]), roughly the size of a small room.

Soil labs will ask you what you will be planting in your soil—for example, a food garden, flowers, or a lawn—then make their fertilizer recommendations accordingly. But you will need to get out your calculator. **After deciding which kind and analysis of fertilizer you want to use, you will need to figure how much to apply in order to meet the amounts suggested by the lab.** For example, the lab may tell you that your proposed food garden will need 10 pounds (4.5kg) each of nitrogen, phosphate, and potash, per 1,000' (304.8m) square. That converts to 1 pound (453.6g) each of nitrogen, phosphate, and potash per 100' (30.5m) square.

Organic fertilizers are typically low in analysis. Let's consider one with an analysis of 2-3-3, for example. How much would you need to apply per 100' (30.5m) square to meet the recommendations listed above? The answer isn't precise because the numbers in the analysis are unequal. You would need to apply approximately 5 ounces (141.7g) per 100' (30.5m) square. This would be spot-on for the phosphate and potash. But you have shorted the nitrogen somewhat. You would need to bump up the amount to 8 ounces (226.8g) of organic fertilizer per 100' (30.5m) square. You will be adding a bit too much phosphate and potash, but plants have some capacity for luxury consumption beyond their need for healthy growth. Because it is organic, the slight excess won't burn plant roots.

An urban community garden in Spain.

## Crystalline and Liquid Concentrates of Processed Fertilizers

Some of the most familiar brands of fertilizers are crystalline or liquid. Scott's Miracle-Gro 15-30-15 is probably the best-known water-soluble, crystalline fertilizer formulation. Schultz and Peters make different liquid or crystalline formulations for various specialty plants, including vegetables. Numerous regional processors package proprietary, liquid-feeding products. All produce a quick but short-lived result. You could liquid-feed vegetables twice weekly, using recommended concentrations, and not overstimulate your plants, but much of the nutrient value would be wasted.

## Plastic-Coated, Controlled-Release Fertilizers (CRF)

Used for many years by commercial growers of containerized nursery stock, plastic-coated, controlled-release fertilizers (CRF) eventually became widely available to home gardeners. When mixed with potting soils, they can feed for three to nine months, depending on the thickness of the plastic coating and the prevailing soil temperature. Given normal watering frequency, plants in containers will be fed at a rate consistent with their seasonal needs, meaning at a low rate during cool months and a higher rate during warm months.

Another benefit of CRFs is their efficiency—relatively little of their nutrient content is lost in drainage water. However, CRFs are simply too expensive to use on most food crops growing in the ground. The one exception is with sandy soil, where granular or water-soluble fertilizers leach away quickly. High-value food crops, such as strawberries and blueberries, can also justify their use.

Osmocote was the first CRF to be introduced. Since its introduction, several competitive coated fertilizers have been put on the market. All of them work well for feeding plants in containers.

## Using Fertilizers

When planting fruit trees or bushes during the winter months, a fertilizer with a high phosphate content, such as bonemeal, should be used to encourage root growth. Growmore can be used as a top dressing during the summer months to encourage balanced growth. This

should be sprinkled along the rows, hoed in lightly and then watered in.

Crops such as tomatoes, courgettes, or runner beans, that you will want to go on producing over an extended period of time, respond well to regular liquid feeding. In general, do not feed in the autumn, as any overwintering vegetables do not do well with soft lush growth that would be damaged by the winter cold. The following are a few examples of common plants that respond well to specific types of fertilizers or plant foods:

- **Zucchinis (courgettes):** Feed with diluted high-potash tomato food only if production is slow.
- **Brassicas:** Nitrogen should be fixed by companion planting of peas rather than feeding by the gardener.
- **Peppers:** Feed with high-potash tomato food once a week when the fruits form.
- **Eggplants (aubergines):** Feed with high-potash tomato food once a week when the fruits form.
- **Tomatoes:** Feed with high-potash tomato food once a week.
- **Cucumbers:** Provide balanced feed once a week once harvesting begins.
- **Beans (all types):** Feed with high-potash tomato food a couple of times once harvesting begins to prolong production.

# Green Manures

Green manures are special crops grown expressly for chopping and turning under, serving the same purpose as animal manure. They are especially valuable for enhancing the population of animal manures, as they are not alkaline in reaction and do not release ammonia. Green manure crops should be annuals since annuals will not regrow strongly when mowed and turned under. They can be grown on a portion of your food garden that can be spared from production for an entire season; they

# COVER CROPS AND GREEN MANURES

| CROP | Lifecycle | Primary Purpose | Seeding Rate lb./1,000 sq. ft.* | Planting Time | Time to Turn Under | Soil Type |
|---|---|---|---|---|---|---|
| **Alfalfa** *Medicago sativa* | Perennial | Contributes nitrogen | 3 | Spring | After 2 years | pH 6.5–7; well-drained |
| **Buckwheat** *Fagopyrum esculentum* | Annual | Contributes phosphorus/ smothers weeds | 3 | Early–mid summer | Late summer– early fall | Widely adaptable |
| **Clover, Dutch white** *Trifolium repens* | Perennial | Contributes nitrogen | 0.25 | Spring–late summer | Fall or following year if at all | pH 6.5–7; well-drained |
| **Clover, Mammoth red** *Trifolium pratense* | Biennial | Contributes nitrogen | 0.5 | Spring–fall | After 1–2 years | Well-drained, tolerates pH of 6.0 if limed at seeding |
| **Clover, Crimson** *Trifolium incarnatum* | Annual | Contributes nitrogen | 0.5–0.66 | Late summer in South/spring in North | Late spring in South/ midsummer in North | Well-drained, pH 6.5–7 |
| **Marigold, 'Sparky'** *Tagetes erecta* | Annual | Controls nematodes | 2–3 oz. | Mid–late spring | After flowering | Adaptable |
| **Oats** *Avena sativa* | Annual | Prevents erosion | 3–4 | Early spring or fall | At flowering; winter-kills in North | Adaptable |
| **Peas, field, 'Trapper'** *Pisum sativum* | Annual | Contributes nitrogen/ smothers weeds | 3 | Early spring | After pods form | Well-drained |
| **Rapeseed** *Brassica napus* | Annual | Alkalizes soil | 3 oz. | Mid–spring | After flowering | Adaptable |
| **Ryegrass** *Lolium multiflorum* | Annual | Adds organic matter | 2 | Early spring– late summer | At flowering; winterkills in North | Adaptable |
| **Sweetclover** *Melilotus officinalis* | Biennial | Contributes nitrogen; breaks up hardpan | 0.5 | Mid spring– summer | After flowering or following spring | pH close to 7, well-drained |
| **Vetch, Hairy** *Vicia villosa* | Annual | Contributes nitrogen | 1–3 | Spring–late summer | After flowering or early following spring | Adaptable |
| **Winter Rye** *Lolium* | Annual | Adds organic matter; phytotoxic to weeds | 4–6 | Spring through mid-fall | At flowering or early following spring | Adaptable |

*Decrease seeding rate appropriately when using the seed in a mix.

Winter rye is used as a green manure crop.

# Mulching

To keep vegetable, herb, and fruit crops growing and returning as much produce as possible, you must ensure they do not have competition from other plants or suffer from a lack of water. Mulch is a term used to describe anything that is used to cover the soil; this might be rich in nutrients, or just a sheet of black plastic to suppress weeds. The term "floating mulch" is even used to describe a layer of horticultural fleece draped over salad leaves to protect them from aphids or flea beetle. Mulches have three main functions—some achieve all three while others are more restricted: mulches feed the soil, suppress weeds, and help retain moisture. Applying them is quick and simple, and can be as easy as tipping your grass cuttings onto a vegetable bed instead of the compost heap. There are plenty of materials, most without cost, that make excellent mulches and help fight against weeds. Mulching is quicker and easier than weeding, and plants generally thrive in the conditions suitable mulch creates.

In a busy, productive garden, it is often not possible to hoe as often as is required, so preventing weed growth in the first place is the answer. The weeds, if left to grow, will compete for water with any productive crop, as well as taking vital nutrients out of the soil. With the global need to conserve water as much as possible, as well as the extra costs involved in applying unnecessary water to the productive areas, anything that prevents gardeners from applying extra water is beneficial. And this is where mulches come in.

Most mulches are applied as a 2"–3" (5.1–7.6cm) layer on the surface of the soil. This creates an almost impenetrable barrier for most weeds. As well as preventing water loss from weeds, it also helps to prevent water loss from the soil. Quite a high proportion of water is lost in evaporation from the soil surface on hot and breezy days. The mulch acts as a blanket over the soil, keeping the ground beneath it nice and moist, while almost entirely eliminating any water evaporation. Not only does mulch conserve water, but it also provides an excellent home for a wide variety of beneficial predatory insects that need a cool place to hide during the hot, sunny summer days. The downside of this is that it also provides a home for slugs and snails, but this should not be a problem if enough predators have been encouraged in the garden.

can be seeded among standing crops in late summer; or they can be planted in strips between food crops in large gardens.

Fall-seeded green manure crops serve a dual purpose: they decrease wintertime soil erosion and leaching of nutrients, and when chopped and turned under the following spring, they nourish soil organisms. Annual ryegrass is a popular green manure crop and can be sown in the spring or fall. Buckwheat is usually sown in early to midsummer. In the South, annual crimson clover is favored for late summer or fall seeding.

Allow about a month between turning under green manure crops and planting vegetables. This will give the green matter time to be greatly reduced by decomposition.

Straw is an inexpensive option if you have to buy mulch. Placed around sweet corn as shown here, it will suppress weeds, keep in moisture, and eventually break down into the soil.

The act of applying a layer of mulch to the soil around plants is one of the most useful and simple strategies for saving time in your vegetable garden. Beyond the annual mulching of the garden with nutrient-rich compost and farmyard manure, using all kinds of mulches in different situations is immensely useful throughout the growing season. If at any time an area is empty, a covering of sheet mulch will keep it pristine and weed free until you are ready to use it.

Many of the materials already discussed in this chapter can be used as mulches, including garden compost, manures, leaf mold, and grass clippings. There are some special concerns when using these items as mulches (they all have jobs for which they work best). There is also a wide range of other materials that can be used as mulches on both long-term and short-term crops.

## Leaf Mold

Leaf mold is a great soil conditioner; it does not add nutrients to the soil but adds organic bulk, opening its structure and increasing its ability to hold water. A blanket of leaf mold between rows of vegetables at least 7" (17.8cm) thick is excellent for suppressing weeds and preventing the evaporation of valuable moisture from the soil. As with garden compost, it is one of the incredibly useful ways of recycling free garden waste into something valuable. In fact, making leaf mold is even simpler than making compost.

## Shreddings

This option is free since it involves using the shreddings generated from tree and shrub prunings, as well as herbaceous stems removed from the garden. If your garden is not large enough to generate enough shreddings, you can also request prunings from your friends and neighbors. All that is required is a good-quality shredder that will chop the materials into usable pieces. You also need to compost them down in a heap for three to six months to prevent them from removing vital nitrogen from the soil surrounding a crop.

Due to the timing of pruning and cutting back of herbaceous perennials, the majority of shredding needs to be carried out in the winter, when it is not possible to get it onto the garden. You'll shred it into a heap and, during the winter, cover it with a piece of plastic just to keep off the worst of the rain—then uncover the heap during the drier summer months. The shredded material can be used as a pathway material or as a weed suppressant around long-term crops, such as soft fruits, fruit trees, artichokes, or rhubarb.

## Farmyard Manure and Garden Compost

As well as being an excellent organic matter for incorporating into the soil, well-rotted farmyard manure can be used as a thick layer around crops. It has excellent weed-suppressing and moisture-retaining qualities but is not suitable for walking on, as it can be very slippery. The same principle that applies when using manure as a soil conditioner also applies to sourcing farmyard manure for mulching: the farm should be "clean" to prevent importing unwanted weeds.

Farmyard manure can be used for all crops except for roots, because even with the shorter-term crops, it can be dug in once the crop has been harvested. It is not a good idea to apply a mulch of farmyard manure to any root crop, because they will not like the extra nutrients available and will be inclined to produce forked roots. Ensure that the manure is well rotted and not fresh; fresh manure is too potent and will damage crops. Manure and garden compost should only be used in the general mulching of beds for fertility, not where the aim is to suppress weeds only.

## Mushroom Compost

This is a by-product of the mushroom-growing industry that is available to buy in bulk. A generous layer will suppress weeds, keep the moisture in, and add organic bulk to the soil, but its nutrient content is minimal.

## Straw

If you are short of compost, have no leaf mold, and are faced with the prospect of having to buy some mulch material, then straw is a good option. It is inexpensive,

Straw mulch protects young grapevines from cooler temperatures.

**TIP**
You can also use a mulching mower with a sharp blade to return grass clippings to your lawn in a super-pulverized form, providing half the food your lawn needs in a season. It's always better to let mulched clippings lie.

very quick to get onto beds, is usually heavy enough to stay in place, and reflects light onto ripening fruit. A reasonable layer will keep weeds at bay, warm the soil, and help to preserve moisture.

Put onto the ground as a thick layer, straw will suppress weeds very well, although it is not a good material for use on windy sites. It can be walked on easily to reach a crop and will rot down slowly. It can be used on long-term crops, especially strawberries, or on shorter-term vegetables. Once you've harvested the crop, remove the straw and put it onto the compost heap.

## Grass Clippings

Research has shown that the dried clippings from an herbicide-free lawn are a well-balanced and good source of nutrients. Dried clippings from an herbicide-free lawn are one of the absolute best mulches for keeping down weeds, as well. Spreading cut grass straight onto the vegetable garden is just as easy as tipping it into the compost heap. Grass clippings will benefit the soil and save the gardener time. As with leaf mold, a layer

2"–3" (5.1–7.6cm) thick will prevent some evaporation from the soil and help to stop weeds from growing, while also adding valuable nutrients to the soil.

**The clippings must come from a lawn that has not been treated with herbicides.** Clippings from herbicide-treated lawns can kill garden plants if used as mulch. Compost made from treated clippings has also been shown to kill plants. So, if you're not certain of your clippings' provenance, don't take the risk. Also, they must be dried. Green clippings are too "hot" (nitrogen-rich) and can burn plants. Green clippings mat down into a wet, green, slimy mess.

Don't be tempted to pile on the grass cuttings too thickly, as the grass at the bottom may be deprived of oxygen and rot anaerobically, forming an unpleasant slime. You can use grass cuttings to cut down the weeding around beans, brassicas, rhubarb, cucurbits, and artichokes. They quickly fade to brown and eventually disappear into the

These still-slightly-green, herbicide-free grass clippings are almost ready to use as food and mulch.

Do NOT use lawn clippings for mulch or compost if you have an herbicide-treated lawn.

soil. In summer, grass cuttings are likely to be in good supply, but only use them once or twice on the same bed as they may add too much nitrogen to the soil.

## Newspaper, Cardboard, and Purpose-Made Paper Mulch

Newspaper and cardboard are laid on the soil to prevent weed growth. The newspaper needs to be several sheets thick, anchored in place with stones or by burying the edges in the soil, and watered thoroughly as soon as it is put down. This takes a while to put down, but it lasts a season and can then be left to rot into the soil. A thin layer of hay, straw, or compost can also be added, but that is more work, basically double the mulching. Deliberately made rolls of paper are also available for organic gardeners.

## Black Plastic

Available cut from a large roll at most garden centers, hardware stores, or DIY shops, heavyweight black plastic is a versatile, reusable mulch, effective in preventing weed growth. It can be spread over the soil, anchored securely by burying the edges in the soil or holding it down with stones. Young plants can be planted into the soil beneath by cutting holes in the plastic. In very warm areas, this can have the unwanted side effect of baking the soil, but it can be used to great advantage in colder areas at the end of the winter to warm the soil for early planting. The plastic is expensive, but it can be reused.

## Seaweed

Gathered from the seashore, seaweed is full of all kinds of nutrients that will be valuable in promoting fine growth in your vegetable garden. Few people are likely to have a vast supply, so adding a thick layer to thwart weeds is likely not an option. Seaweed dries out quickly and shrinks, leaving gaps, but a thin layer works well to give soil an extra boost. It should be washed thoroughly first to remove some of the salt.

## Wood Ash

As long as no plastics have gone onto the firewood, ash is a useful mulch high in potash, and is good for fruiting plants.

Seaweed mulch dries out quickly, but provides an abundance of nutrients to your soil.

# CHAPTER 4
# Planning and Design

Having a large, beautiful, and bountiful kitchen garden is a wonderful dream, but it pays to not get too adventurous too soon, especially if you are a first-time gardener. Getting behind with the work on the vegetable plot or having too many problems with pests and diseases to deal with can soon lead to poor yields and, worse, disillusionment. It is much better to start with a patch that is a half or quarter of the size of your dream garden, so you can learn and enjoy the time you spend in the garden and gather a healthy harvest. Your garden can be a pleasure and a triumph rather than a burden, and you can always expand your plot as your knowledge and confidence grows.

> **THE BASICS**
> Start small, gain confidence and skills, then expand your plot.

If you have a community garden plot, and the space is too daunting to begin with, try sharing with friends or offering a section to a fellow community gardener whose plot is bursting at the seams. It is also perfectly acceptable to allow half to lie fallow for a while under a mulch of heavy black plastic or green manure until you are ready to expand.

## Planning for Crop Rotation

Using a crop rotation is a very traditional way of managing a vegetable plot or allotment. Basically, similar vegetable types are grouped together in order to give them the conditions they like for growth and to avoid a build-up of pests and diseases. The three main groups are brassicas, including cabbages, cauliflowers, and Brussels sprouts; root crops, including carrots, parsnips, beetroot, and potatoes; and legumes, the whole range of peas and beans. You can make a fourth group with miscellaneous and tender vegetables, such as zucchinis, sweet corn, celery, and tomatoes.

You'll divide your plot into three or four areas, and the crop groups are moved around in these areas over a three- or four-year period. Using this process hopefully avoids the build-up of pests and diseases that can occur when the same crops are always grown on the same land. You should also try to treat the soil in the ideal way for each crop. Peas and beans are rich feeders so try to add manure or organic matter before planting these crops. Brassicas need a high pH so aim to add lime before planting them. Root crops do not grow well with lumpy organic matter in the soil, as it causes the roots to be misshapen, so aim to grow these one or two years after manuring, so that the manure will be well absorbed into the soil. Salads are not particularly fussy, and can be squeezed in wherever there is a gap. Onions can be grown with root vegetables. See page 284 for more on the practical application of crop rotation during the growing season.

## Companion Planting

Growing a combination of plants together for the benefits they bestow upon each other is known as companion planting. Harnessing these qualities keeps the garden healthy and productive. There are a number of specific ways that growing different plants in combination can make your vegetable gardening easier. In general, growing a range of plants of different types, such as flowering plants and herbs, among the vegetables around the edges and between the rows will improve the biodiversity of the garden, keep pests from easily locating the productive plants, and also attract beneficial insects. Adding flowering plants and herbs also contributes a burst of welcome color and scent to the garden.

One plant making the soil more fertile for another is an alternative meaning of companion planting. Peas and beans fix nitrogen in the soil, a characteristic used in traditional crop rotation schemes, but the crops can be combined from the outset, growing brassicas, sweet corn, sweet peas, or cucumbers in the same area.

Attracting beneficial insects into the vegetable patch, those that will feast on the pests that inhabit the vegetable garden, is another very worthwhile method to keep potential problems with pests under control. Lacewings, hoverflies, and ladybugs will consume vast numbers of aphids and caterpillars, while parasitic wasps will lay their eggs into the pests, their larvae eating the host once it hatches. Plants such as Tagetes, nasturtiums, Limnanthes, and many others are very effective in attracting the adults of a wide range of beneficial insects into the productive garden and will also add color and interest. The poached eggplant, calendula, and California poppy will all attract beneficial insects, as well, and punchy, orange calendula petals are great sprinkled over a crisp green salad.

Other flowers have the ability to repel pests: pungent marigolds will repel whitefly, nasturtiums will mask the smell of brassicas, and chives will repel aphids. Tagetes planted in a greenhouse will dissuade whitefly from attacking tomatoes. Garlic is also said to deter many pests.

Nasturtiums can also be used as a "fall guy" to take the hit of blackfly that might otherwise blight fava beans (broad beans), although this does of course make them much less appetizing. Growing spring onions with carrots to mask the scent of the carrots from the carrot root fly is another example of companion planting, a simple strategy that really works (although some research has shown that you need to grow at least ten rows of onions or garlic for each row of carrots).

Alternatively, a plant can be used that will attract a predator, which will naturally control the pest. French Marigolds attract beneficial hoverflies, which feed on aphids, so these are useful next to crops, such as beans, which are liable to be attacked by aphids.

Some of these companion plants can be productive, useful parts of the garden, as well. Garlic, of course, is a flavorful addition to any dish. The leaves of fresh chives can be snipped up and used to give an onion kick to plenty of dishes. While pretty, purple chive flowers and peppery nasturtium flowers are also another fantastic way

Poppies are among the plants that attract beneficial insects to the garden.

the soil. If they grow too strongly, they might even crowd out the crops you are trying to protect.

# Raised Bed Gardening

Growing in beds, raised or otherwise, is an alternative to the open or community garden. It is very efficient and offers plenty of benefits for those trying to cut down on the time spent maintaining their vegetable garden. It reduces an overwhelming expanse of land into easily tackled chunks, saving time and effort.

A raised bed is a planting area with a soil level significantly above the natural soil level, normally contained within a frame and surrounded by permanent paths. Although often constructed from wood, raised beds can be made from just about anything durable that will form a frame to hold soil. Brick, stone, or low fences all work well, although fencing is usually not particularly robust or long-lived. The simplest raised bed

to give a salad a touch of pizzazz, and the leaves have a taste that is similar to cress.

Having a diversity of nectar-rich flowers also has the advantage of encouraging pollinating insects into the plot, ensuring that vegetables, such as peas and beans, are well pollinated. A word of caution, these companion plants are performing a valuable service, but they are also occupying space and taking up nutrients and water from

Chic metal raised beds give the vegetable plot a contemporary feel.

## RAISED BED KITS

Most garden equipment suppliers sell raised bed kits, basically shallow wooden or plastic squares that you fill with potting mix or topsoil. They work like giant containers and using them means you don't have to be as vigilant about your garden soil. Just break up the earth at soil level before you put the raised bed on top, so you don't compromise drainage. Raised bed kits are popular because they look very neat and tidy. You do have to construct them, so factor in some time and effort.

These chunky lumber beds look fantastic, are incredibly practical, and will last for years.

## THE BASICS

Raised above the normal soil level and constructed of wood, brick, or other durable materials, raised beds allow you to create excellent, fertile soil and escape problems with bad drainage or thin soil. Crops can be grown more intensively in raised beds, giving you a better harvest for less effort.

## Advantages of Raised Beds

**Perhaps the most important advantage of raised bed gardening is that it allows you to escape unfavorable soil.** This enables you to ensure the best growing conditions possible by filling your beds with a 50-50 mix of good-quality topsoil and well-rotted organic matter to produce great soil and, in turn, vigorous, productive plants. Where the underlying soil is very wet, you'll need to till the ground below and work in some gravel or sand before the new soil is added to ensure good drainage. In most circumstances, the beds only need to be about 12" (30.5cm) deep, though in very damp areas you may want a depth of up to 24" (61cm) or more to ensure good drainage. Higher beds are also an excellent option for gardeners with back problems.

is constructed of lumber—reclaimed wooden boards are perfect—that is nailed or screwed to stakes hammered into the ground. They are effectively freestanding "flat pack" beds that can be taken apart and rearranged or reused elsewhere.

Garlic and strawberries love a raised-bed system.

When growing in raised beds, you only need to maintain, water, weed, and cultivate the core growing area. The beds can be planted more intensively by arranging the plants with less space between them than in the traditional open vegetable garden or community garden plot, so you get more tasty produce for the area maintained. Closer spacing also cuts down on weeding, too, since more of the soil is covered with plants, and the weeds are deprived of light.

The soil in raised beds warms up more quickly in the spring than soil in an open vegetable garden or community garden plot. This allows plants and seeds to get a faster start.

Having neat islands of raised garden surrounded by paths makes working in the garden convenient and allows you to harvest crops in all kinds of weather since there is no need to walk on the soil. This is very handy when you are short of time and can't be picky about when you venture outdoors. Growing in beds also works very well with the timesaving "no-dig" method.

Plants are more easily protected from frost or pests in a neat, regular, confined area. You can use wire or plastic pipe hoops that neatly span the bed to hold row covers, chicken wire, or insect-proof mesh.

A crisp pattern of well-constructed beds will give you a head start in keeping the garden looking neat and well-tended. A pretty arrangement of beds instantly makes the garden look more appealing and decorative, adding value and elevating the humble vegetable patch to "truly beautiful kitchen garden." Taking the time to give your plot what is often termed "good bones"—a strong, structured design—will go a long way toward giving the illusion of tidiness even through those inevitable times of slight neglect.

If you are lucky enough to have great soil, raised beds may seem unnecessary. In this case, laying out a series of low beds at the existing soil level bounded by permanent paths will give many of the same advantages and can be managed in the same "no-dig" way.

## Layout

The way you choose to lay out your beds will have a big impact on how simple they are to tend and how the garden looks. The neatness and beauty of your plot may not trouble you (perhaps you're only interested in

## THE BASICS

Beds should be narrow enough to be tended without stepping on the soil, ideally between 3' (91cm) and 4' (1.2m) wide, and as long as is practical. Complex-shaped beds will likely be less convenient.

the delicious food), but for most gardeners, creating a wonderful space and an area to be proud of helps make tending the garden more of a pleasure and less of a chore.

The growing area you choose to fill will be governed by how much space you have available, what kind of crops you hope to grow, and how much you want to take on in the first year. If you aim to concentrate on salad greens, tomatoes, and cucumbers, you will only need a few small beds, perhaps measuring 3' x 4' (91cm x 1.2m). If you want to grow bulk crops like onions and potatoes, then more cultivated space and larger beds will be more practical, perhaps 10'–16' x 4' (3–4.9 x 1.2 m). A combination of large and small beds will suit most people and will make for interesting design possibilities.

The basic rule regarding shape and size is that a bed can be as long as you like but only ever less than twice your arm's length wide, meaning that you can tend the bed, weed, harvest, and mulch without ever having to walk on the soil. In reality, very long beds can become a nuisance as you move around the garden. Square and rectangular beds are easiest to cultivate. Intricate shapes, triangles, and circles may look fantastic, but they are hard to construct and tend. It is well worth carefully measuring your area and drawing out your proposed pattern to scale, leaving space for decorative elements like benches, trees,

## HOME-BUILT HOSE GUARDS

You may need to pull water hoses through your vegetable garden, and hoses tend to knock over plants, especially those at the corners of beds. Hammer 30" (76.2cm) pine contractors' stakes into the corners of your beds. About 2" (5.1cm) of each stake will stick up above the ground, enough to shunt hoses to the side to prevent them from ruining your plants. You can also buy plastic hose guards that rotate as the hoses rub against them.

or whatever else you may want. There is nothing wrong with taking the easy option either; if you plan to use scaffolding boards, making beds the length of each board or half a board cuts down the work and is economical. If you have old paving stones to use for paths, make the length of your beds fit neatly with these to avoid cutting stones or having oddly constructed paths and corners.

## Designing the Beds

It's best to be practical when designing your beds, but practical and delightful can go hand in hand. If you are concerned only with the practical, you have less to think about in laying out your garden, but also much less to look forward to!

A simple geometric pattern of beds works well in both respects. This approach naturally creates vistas and spaces for focal points—for example, a simple bench, a rustic scarecrow, or even a piece of sculpture. It is your

The best temporary garden seating is the traditional deck chair—perfect to relax in after a burst of gardening.

garden—you can make it as decorative as you want, using your own style to create a space you'll enjoy. Ballerina fruit trees, teepees, standard bay trees, and trellises can all be used to add some height. As you draw out the pattern of your beds, don't forget to leave space for some decorative and fun elements if the idea appeals to you.

One word of caution—the kitchen garden tradition, seen perhaps at its most grand in the chateaux of France, often employs a multitude of small box-edged beds, or beds edged with lavender. This looks fantastic but really cuts down on the growing space in each bed, and larger beds are required for bulk crops, such as potatoes. It can be frustrating to see a large part of the growing area you have worked hard to create supporting an unproductive plant and suffer the inconvenience of working over the low hedge.

If you start small, your successes will undoubtedly inspire you to extend your vegetable patch. It is worth considering how you might do this when planning phase one, leaving options for the further seamless development of the plot. After a couple of seasons of growing, you will have a better idea of what works for you and your family.

## The Productive Patio or Deck

Patios and decks may not seem like encouraging places to grow vegetables. However, paved surfaces absorb and radiate warmth from the sun, so a patio can be the perfect spot for plants. Containers will give you the opportunity to grow delicious crops on both patios and decks.

**Raised beds can be built directly on top of a paved area.** Filled with good-quality soil, they will provide enough depth for growing a number of plants. You can even grow root vegetables, such as carrots—if you choose short-root types— as well as climbers growing up supports. Provide plenty of drainage holes at the bottom of the raised bed walls—and a place for the water to drain to.

**Small areas of raised beds are quick and easy to maintain and are attractive.** Raised beds can be decorative landscape features as well as places to grow crops. The patio is the ideal place to relax after a day's work,

Neat, weed-free rows of vegetable plants look great on a patio or deck.

A waist-high raised garden bed is the best option for people looking to protect their back and joints.

A raised bed situated on a paved walkway is convenient and attractive.

and a little gentle weed pulling while admiring your crops in the evening warmth is a great way to round off the day.

**Beds raised to waist height are ideal for gardeners who are not especially agile, since they cut out the need for bending.** This "tabletop" type of bed is also a suitable design for wheelchair users, enabling them to get up close to the plants. Metal hoops allow for the bed to be covered with insect-proof netting to protect against pests or with a floating row cover as protection from excessive cold or heat.

## Wooden Raised Beds

If using wood to construct your raised bed, the dimensions should not be any less than 5" x 1" (12.7 x 2.5cm). The length is totally up to the person using it and how far they are prepared to walk in order to get around to the other side. Bear in mind that the farthest distance will be from the center of the bed on one side to the center of the bed on the other.

When considering wood for building an organic garden bed, remember that you cannot use chemically treated wood because it has been impregnated with chemicals in order to lengthen the wood's life. You can use wood in its natural, raw state, or treat it with an

You must not use chemically treated wood for organic raised beds.

# NOT GOING ORGANIC—SHOULD YOU STILL AVOID TREATED LUMBER?

One frequently asked question that comes up regarding raised beds is whether or not you should use pressure-treated lumber. Most outdoor projects like decks, stairs, and patios make use of pressure-treated lumber since it is resistant to rot and decay. But the pressure-treating process of lumber uses chemicals that can gradually leach into the soil. In a garden, these chemicals might be taken up by food you grow.

Much of the attention has been focused on arsenic, used in the chromated copper arsenate (CCA) treatment. CCA-treated lumber is no longer available for purchase by general consumers, but other types of copper-treated lumber are still in widespread use.

Some research suggests that health hazards from treated wood are minimal, but there are instances in which excessive levels of arsenic, copper, and other metals can build up in soils and be taken up by plants, especially if the soil is low in phosphorus or is acidic. Especially vulnerable are root vegetables like potatoes or carrots, since the roots are more likely to absorb and contain metals. Other plants—such as lettuce or spinach—can have higher concentrations of metals in their edible leaves, so the treated lumber problem doesn't apply just to root vegetables.

One simple solution is to just avoid treated lumber in the construction of garden beds. Instead, you might opt for wood that is naturally rot-resistant—cedar or locust are good choices. Your raised beds made from untreated lumber might not last as long as beds made from treated lumber, but the peace of mind that untreated lumber provides can be a worthwhile tradeoff for its shorter lifespan.

Treated lumber often includes materials you don't want leaching into your garden soil.

approved organic wood preservative. If you only have chemically treated wood, be sure to line your beds so the chemicals do not enter the soil. Unless you are concerned about the finished look, use sawn lumber rather than the planed alternative, as this will be considerably cheaper.

You'll keep the wood upright by nailing or screwing it to stakes that are knocked into the ground on the inside of the bed. Having the stakes on the inside keeps them hidden by the soil, making the beds more aesthetically pleasing to the eye and preventing any tripping hazards. If attaching the wood to the stakes with nails, it is better to use annular ring nails as these will not pull out under the weight of the soil.

The ideal pathway between the beds is one just wide enough to be able to work from and walk down while pushing a wheelbarrow. Remember, however, that the wider the path, the lower the potential crop for the whole area (since much of the essential raised bed space is being taken up by path space).

Once your bed is constructed, double dig the soil. This initial digging should be the last time anybody's foot is allowed to stand on the soil bed. It is important that the soil structure is maintained, and that no compaction of any sort occurs, so all future work should be carried out from the pathways on either side of the bed. This is why it is important to be able to easily reach the center of the bed. Because most plants will be grown in staggered rows across the bed, and the plants should all be reachable from the pathways, there is no need to have room between each row in the bed. This means that crops will be grown with a closer spacing, producing a bigger harvest for the area used.

## Other Types of Raised Beds

There are other materials besides wood that can be used very effectively as edging for raised beds. Everybody will have something that they prefer, so there are far too many to mention them all.

**Railroad ties** tend to be treated with either tar or creosote and cannot be bought for use in the garden. It is possible to buy new landscape timbers made to the same dimensions from new wood, however. These new timbers

Placing bricks horizontally in rows is just one way to use bricks for a raised bed.

are often treated wood, so inquire before purchasing. They make excellent raised beds, usually having dimensions of 6" x 9" (15.2 x 22.9cm), and can stand directly on the soil surface or be stacked to a higher. If stacking timbers, you will need to attach wood between them to secure them.

When using a very deep bed, it is always worth ensuring there is a means for the excess water to pass out of the bed. Do this either by cultivating the soil at the original ground level so that excess water can filter away in this direction, or by making sure that the bed's edging is not too tightly sealed, allowing excess water to pass out gradually through the joints in the timbers.

**Round fence posts**, 2" to 3" (5.1 to 7.6cm) in diameter, can be cut into the lengths required. Bury about 18" (45.7cm) in the ground to ensure that the bed's edging is secure and won't move under the weight of the soil. Beds deeper than 24" (61cm) will need to have the posts buried deeper into the ground. You are most likely to find untreated posts at a lumberyard.

**Synthetic wood** is becoming more and more available. It is made from recycled plastic and is very effective. It can be nailed, cut, and even planed like real wood but obviously lasts much longer. Synthetic wood beds are constructed in the same way as with sawn lumber.

**Bricks** can be used in several ways, although their use tends to mean permanent beds rather than ones that can easily be changed at a later date. If the bricks are going to be laid flat and mortared into layers, the final height of the bed has few limits, as long as you've put a proper footing in place. It is very effective to lay the bricks at a 45-degree angle, and this arrangement can be held in place just with the soil. Bricks held in place in this way will move fractionally over time. To keep bricks totally in place, they need to be set in mortar. A variation on this theme is to lay the bricks vertically, which creates a slightly taller bed than if set at an angle.

**Tiles** that are specially made for edging raised beds tend to be either Victorian in style or very modern. As with bricks, they can be set in the soil or in mortar, and they do not create a great depth of soil above the original soil surface. This edging style should be seen primarily as a decorative feature—to obtain a decent depth of soil above the original level the tiles would really need to be three times the size.

**Bamboo rolls or larger bamboo poles** cut into length can be used and set in the ground using the same principles as for fence posts. It suits a definite style, which may or may not work with your garden design.

**Woven willow or hazel** gives a lovely old-fashioned look to beds but does not last very long—maybe only two or three seasons—when used to contain soil. It would be far better, if you want to achieve this look, to make the beds out of a longer-lasting material and surround them with the willow or hazel.

**Concrete blocks, slabs, and paving stones** make excellent raised beds and will last a lifetime. They are all very heavy, and thus require setting into the soil or in mortar in an adequate way to avoid any risk of them falling over and causing injury.

**Overturned wine bottles** make a very decorative edging for raised beds. They are quite tough and will take knocks and bumps to a point, but once they are broken, they are obviously very dangerous and need to be replaced immediately.

# Project: Making Raised Beds

**Difficulty Level:** Easy | **Time Required:** 2–3 Hours

As enjoyable as gardening is, there's no question that it can also be a lot of work at times. From hauling soil or compost, to building fences and weeding, gardening is bound to keep you busy. With that in mind, building a raised garden bed is an easy—and quick—project that you can wrap up in just a couple of hours. You can always make your raised beds more elaborate and decorative if you'd like, but the construction of a simple raised bed doesn't have to be complicated— it can even be fun!

The instructions included here are for a 4' to 8' (121.9 to 243.8cm) raised bed, with the sides being made of 2x12s, giving the bed a final height of 11¼" (28.6cm). This is a handy height for a raised bed. You can also build a cover for the raised bed out of hardware cloth stretched across a frame. This feature can help reduce trouble with small critters or birds while still allowing the plants access to sun and water. The cover won't work with tall plants; however, it will help protect shorter plants (lettuce, strawberries, etc.) and seedlings.

| PARTS LIST | TOOLS NEEDED |
|---|---|
| • 3" (76mm) screws | • Electric drill |
| • 4' × 8' (121.9 × 243.8cm) section of ¼" or ½" (6 or 13mm) hardware cloth | • Circular saw |
| | • Tape measure |
| • ½" (13mm) staples | • Framing square |
| • Three hinges (optional) | • Staple gun |
| • Hook-and-eye latch (optional) | • Safety glasses |
| | • Gloves |
| | • Pencil (optional) |
| | • Wire cutters |

**CUT LIST**

| Number of Pieces | Dimensions | Type |
|---|---|---|
| 3 | 8' (243.8cm) | 2x12s |
| 3 | 8' (243.8cm) | 2x2s |

## INSTRUCTIONS

**1. Make the cuts.** Even if you've purchased 8' (243.8cm) lumber, you'll find that the pieces are slightly longer. So, to prepare the long sides of the bed, trim any additional lengths off the 2x12s so that they are exactly 8' (243.8cm) long. For the short sides of the bed, trim a third 8' (243.8cm) 2x12 to 90" (228.6cm), and then cut this piece in half to create a pair of 45" (114.3cm) 2x12s. Next, prepare the 2x2s for the hardware cloth frame in exactly the same way, ending with two 8' (243.8cm) 2x2s, and two 45" (114.3cm) 2x2s.

**2. Lay out the bed.** With your lumber prepared and all your cuts made, begin construction on the raised bed. Lay out the bed with the two 8' (243.8cm) 2x12s running parallel to each other and the two 45" (114.3cm) 2x12s on the ends, placed "inside" the 8' (243.8cm) 2x12s.

**3. Fasten the corners.** Use a framing square to help make sure that each corner of the 8' (243.8cm) and the 45" (114.3cm) 2x12s are square. Use 3" (76mm) screws to secure the lumber at each corner.

**5. Begin installing the hardware cloth.** Carefully roll out the 4' x 8' (121.9 x 243.8cm) hardware cloth and lay it across the top of the 2x2 frame. Use staples to fasten one end (the short end might be easiest) securely in place.

**4. Assemble the cover frame.** With the raised bed completed, you can construct the frame for the hardware cloth. Repeat Steps 2 and 3 using the 2x2s instead of the 2x12s. Put your hardware cloth frame on top of the garden bed frame.

**6. Continue installing the hardware cloth.** Next, stretch the cloth tightly across the frame and staple all the sides down. Wearing gloves and safety glasses, trim away any sharp points or excess hardware cloth. If you built your raised bed in a different space, get some help to carry it as needed. Fill it with quality soil.

**7. Add hinges (optional).** If critters are a problem in your garden and you'd like to give your bed some extra security, you can use two or three hinges to attach the hardware cloth frame to the bed so that it can't get knocked out of alignment by curious critters. You can also add a hook-and-eye latch to pin down the other side.

# Project: Above-the-Ground Raised Bed

**Difficulty Level:** Easy | **Time Required:** 3 Hours

Now that you know how to build a simple raised bed, another type of raised bed you can make is an elevated "above-the-ground" raised bed that is kind of like a tabletop garden. The advantage here is that you can garden while standing up, with no bending over whatsoever—plus the bed may be less susceptible to small critters like mice or squirrels.

The design here is fairly simple, and the dimensions are easy enough to adjust to your own preferences. For example, you might want to keep the bed 3' (91.4cm) wide but might prefer to extend the length to 5' or 6' (152.4 or 182.9cm). This sort of change would only require adjustments to a few measurements.

### PARTS LIST

- 3" (76mm) exterior screws
- Piece of 36" × 36" (91.4 × 91.4cm) weed mat/landscape fabric
- Paint

### TOOLS NEEDED

- Circular saw
- Miter saw (optional, useful for cutting the 45-degree angles)
- Electric drill
- Square
- Pencil
- Tape measure
- Paintbrush
- Framing square
- Staple gun and staples

### CUT LIST

| Number of Pieces | Dimensions | Type |
| --- | --- | --- |
| 2 | 36" (91.4cm) | 2x12s |
| 2 | 33" (83.8cm) | 2x12s |
| 4 | 36" (91.4cm) | 4x4s |
| 4 | 38" (96.5cm) | 2x4s |
| 3 | 33" (83.8cm) | 2x4s |
| 2 | 26" (66cm) | 2x4s |

## INSTRUCTIONS

**1. Create the square frame.** The raised bed is based around a 36" x 36" (91.4 x 91.4cm) square constructed out of 2x12s. To create an exact square, the two "inside" 2x12s should be 33" (83.8cm), and the two "outside" 2x12s should be 36" (91.4cm), as shown in the photos. Use a framing square to help ensure that the corners are square. Fasten with 3" (76mm) screws.

**2. Add the legs.** Install the four 36" (91.4cm) 4×4s to each corner to make legs and elevate the raised bed (note that we're building the bed upside down at this point for ease of construction). Take care to place the 4×4s tight against both sides, and make sure they're flush with the top (remember, if you're building upside down, the top is on the ground). Use a good number of 3" (76mm) screws to ensure a solid hold. Once all four legs are attached, you can flip the raised bed over and stand it upright.

**3. Prepare the trim.** You'll use four 38" (96.5cm) 2x4s as trim for the top of the raised bed. To make a good fit that looks nice, cut a 45-degree angle at each end of the 2x4s as shown. Use 3" (76mm) screws to fasten the corners together.

**4. Attach the trim.** Add the completed 38" x 38" (96.5 x 96.5cm) trim to the top of the raised bed, and secure it down with 3" (76mm) screws.

**5. Add the floorboards.** Use five evenly spaced 2x4s to create the floor of the raised bed and support the landscape fabric. The three 33" (83.8cm) 2x4s are used as the three middle supports, while the two shorter 26" (66cm) 2x4s are used on the ends (they're shorter so that they can fit in between the 4x4 legs). To create even spacing, leave 3⅞" (9.8cm) gaps between each 2x4. Use 3" (76mm) screws to attach them. For the 33" (83.8cm) 2x4s, you can screw into the ends through the 2x12 boards, but for the 26" (66cm) 2x4s, you have to screw into their sides.

**6. Add the landscape fabric.** Place a 36" x 36" (91.4 x 91.4cm) section of landscape fabric on the floor of the raised bed to keep the soil in but still let water escape. The landscape fabric will be a bit larger than the floor of the raised bed. Use a staple gun to quickly and easily attach it as shown.

**7. Paint the wood.** Adding a couple coats of exterior paint will help protect the wood and help make it look nice. We used white paint, but you can use a color that best fits the theme of your garden.

**8. Add a garden design (optional).** To upgrade the style of your raised bed, consider painting a design on the front. You can do something similar to the design shown in the photos—a garden quote and flowers—or try something different. Use this step to have some fun.

**9. Set up and use.** Fill the bed with quality soil.

# Container Gardening

Most fruits and vegetables can be grown in pots—in fact, some, like figs and blueberries, prefer it. You can fit masses of container-kept plants on a small terrace, from herbs to fruit trees. In fact, pretty much any crop can be grown in a pot, if the pot is big enough. If you treat them as mini beds, cramming in different plants—salad leaves, zucchini, and nasturtiums, or purple French green beans and California poppies at the base of a fig tree—pots can look surprisingly lush. Most plants love the sheltered atmosphere of a sunny deck—and most gardeners appreciate it, too, finding it an ideal place to take a breather on a summer's day. A mixture of flowers and edible crops makes a pleasant view and large terra-cotta pots, weathered with lichen, can be objects of beauty on their own.

Where size is concerned, generally it's a case of the bigger, the better (within reason), although the size will

Vegetables and herbs, like this upright pepper plant and trailing thyme, can be partnered in container planters.

Fruit trees and other crops can grow out of containers and create a beautiful, productive space.

## "CROCKS" IN FIRST

You may have heard about adding "crocks" in the bottoms of your pots or window boxes. Crocks are bits of broken terra-cotta pot that stop the drainage holes from getting clogged up with soil and roots and waterlogging the plants. Years ago, large gardens would have had a constant supply of smashed terra-cotta but these days, with a small garden, you probably don't have any. Stones or broken-up pieces of polystyrene will do the job just as well. They're light, and you can use them again and again.

## POTATO POTS

A small crop of potatoes can be grown in a large pot, a tub, or a special potato bag. Start with about 8" (20.3cm) of good potting compost in the bottom. Plant the potatoes and keep them well-watered. As they grow, top up the compost in stages, no more than 3" (7.6cm) at a time. At harvest time, just tip out the whole pot and separate the potatoes from the compost. Remember that potato roots must grow in the dark or they become green, so don't try using clear plastic drums.

vary according to the plant and variety. You can grow small plants, such as annual herbs and cherry tomatoes, for example, in a 1 gallon (4L) pot, but 3–4 gallons (12–15L) is a better minimum size for most vegetables. Remember that large pots need a lot of potting mix to fill them—and they will be heavy to move once filled and planted.

Use your imagination—in this case, a kitchen colander has been converted into a "hanging basket" of sorts for delicious, sweet strawberries.

The best thing about growing in containers is that you don't have to worry about the type of soil you have because you're not using it. Just buy some organic all-purpose potting mix to fill your pots with, and you're good to go. If you don't have time to sow crops, you can buy them as seedlings and plant them directly. It's pretty much instant gardening. Any container can be used to grow plants as long as it has holes in the base to allow water to drain away. The following are just a few popular options.

**Hanging baskets.** These are less commonly used for vegetables because they contain such a small volume of potting mix, but they are great for trailing herbs, such as thyme and cherry tomatoes.

**Window boxes.** They don't offer much growing space, but compact varieties of carrots, bush beans, tomatoes, herbs, and leafy salad greens will all do well in window boxes. However, you need to make sure you feed and water them frequently.

**Terra-cotta pots.** Old terra-cotta pots—with their faded charm and patina of lichen and calcification—are so much more appealing than the brand-new, orange, machine-made plastic pots you find at big-box stores. For starters, they make it look like you've been gardening for ages and actually know what you're doing. Round pots are the most common shape of all. However, you can get a range of different shapes, such as the square Versailles planter. Many planters have a slightly tapered shape so that you can stack them inside each other when not in

**Terra-cotta pots**

**Glazed pots**

## GALLON POTS

Pots come in many shapes and sizes, so it's often more useful to give their volume. As a guide, a round pot that is 13" (33cm) across and 7½" (19.1cm) tall holds 4 gallons (15L); a pot that is 9" (22.9cm) across and 10" (25.4cm) tall holds 2½ gallons (10L).

use—this is a useful feature in a small garden where storage space is in short supply.

To make terra-cotta look older, mix some baking powder with a few drops of water to make a paste, and brush it onto the outside of the pot with a soft brush. Leave it to dry, and then brush off any excess powder to leave a whiteish patina. To keep rain from washing away the powder, finish with hairspray or fixative.

**Glazed pots.** These pots are common in the Mediterranean and have become popular among home gardeners. They usually come in deep vivid blues, turquoises, and greens.

**Old wooden wine crates.** These are perfect for salad crops. Ask for them at your nearest wine store, as they often have some they're throwing out. They're somehow the perfect size to grow a decent patch of greens or even tomatoes, and their imprinted logos give them a certain élan.

**Fiber cement pots.** Fiber cement (fiberclay) pots are also available. Light, large, and deep enough for fruit trees, they look just like the heavy lead planters you see in the gardens of stately homes without the high price or weight.

**Metal containers.** Metal containers—for those aiming for a clean, modern look—work really well, whether made of

Old wooden wine crates

## ODD LOOKS BEST

For some reason, odd numbers of containers always look better than even ones—the same rule applies when planting seedlings out in the garden. Three or five plants make a nice cluster—a group of two or four looks unnatural.

Fiber cement pots

Metal containers

galvanized tin, copper, zinc, aluminum, or brushed steel. Even regular tin cans can be co-opted for growing herbs, salads, and even hot peppers. Paint them with exterior masonry paint for a subtler effect, or leave them to rust naturally. If you can find large, attractive, colorful cans—such as those used for olive oil or tomatoes in delis—they look great planted up.

**Plastic**

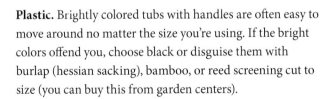

**Improvised**

A wine bottle cooler has found new life as a container for a chili plant.

**Plastic.** Brightly colored tubs with handles are often easy to move around no matter the size you're using. If the bright colors offend you, choose black or disguise them with burlap (hessian sacking), bamboo, or reed screening cut to size (you can buy this from garden centers).

**Improvise.** If you're feeling creative you can use anything—colanders, hats, teapots, or even old boots—as growing containers. Vegetables will grow in all sorts of containers as long as they are deep enough and have drainage holes in the bottom. Disused builders' bags make excellent small beds, and plastic compost sacks make useful large pots, excellent for growing potatoes.

Old farm sinks are popular, but beware, they are incredibly heavy and require plenty of crocks and gravel (grit) at the bottom since the drain may not allow for the best drainage. Some people seem to like the challenge of turning any incongruous old thing into a container, such as tires, buckets, old bathtubs, etc.

# MAKE YOUR OWN CONTAINERS

These containers are easy to make because they are molded around an existing pot (or a cardboard box, if making a trough). Due to its makeup, the hypertufa requires some strengthening. Use pieces of chicken wire sandwiched in the center to provide extra support. The principles for making both pots and troughs are the same.

### COIR HYPERTUFA MIX INGREDIENTS

- Two parts coir
- One part coarse sand
- One part fresh cement
- Yellow cement dye

### OTHER MATERIALS AND TOOLS NEEDED

- Two strong cardboard boxes or containers
- Chicken wire
- Bamboo canes
- Wire cutters
- Pliers
- Wire brush

DIY hypertufa containers are great because you can create your own custom shapes and sizes.

**1.** Find two boxes or containers that fit into each other so that there is about a 2" (5.1cm) gap between the two around the edges. The inner container needs to match the internal dimensions you want for your container. Place the outer container on the floor in an area that is out of the way and free of frost (if you're working in the winter).

**2.** Mix the hypertufa and put a 1" (2.5cm) layer in the bottom of the outer container. Form your strengthening wire into the required shape (the same shape as the containers), and place it inside the outer container. This shape should be 1" (2.5 cm) smaller than the outer container and 1" (2.5 cm) larger than the inner one so it will be spaced evenly between the two containers. The top edges of the wire need to be 1" (2.5cm) lower than the top of the finished container.

**3.** Cut six 2" (5.1cm) pieces of bamboo cane taken from the thick ends. Push them into the hypertufa mix so that they are evenly spaced, until they hit the bottom of the container. This should leave about 1" (2.5cm) of each cane sticking up. These holes will help with drainage.

**4.** Pour the next 1" (2.5cm) layer of mix onto the wire base, and level it with the top of the bamboo canes. It is important to firm the mix well to eliminate any air pockets that could weaken the container once it is dry.

**5.** Place the inner container in the center of the outer container so that the gap around it is even.

**6.** Force the hypertufa mix in between the two containers, ensuring that the wire support is sandwiched evenly in between. Make sure to firm the mix well to eliminate air pockets, but be careful not to deform the outer or inner containers. Placing bricks inside the inner container will help ensure that the internal dimensions remain as required.

**7.** Leave everything for at least 48 hours to dry fully before removing the internal and external containers. Push out the bamboo canes to leave drainage holes.

**8.** Remove any glossy areas where the hypertufa mix was in contact with the outer or inner containers by giving the outside of the trough or pot a light brushing with a wire brush. Do not get too carried away, otherwise the supporting wire may become visible. Also, rounding the edges slightly will give the finished product a nicer appearance.

## Tips for Growing in Containers

Just about anything will grow in a container if it is lavished with enough care and attention. A range of attractive containers can transform even a small balcony, terrace, or courtyard into a pretty and productive garden. Vegetables in pots are far more reliant on the gardener for all their needs as the soil in containers can dry out quickly and the nutrients in the soil soon deplete. So, feeding and watering are very important—most containers will need watering twice a day in the hottest part of the year to ensure a good crop.

If it is not possible to check containers for water regularly, a watering system is the answer. This can range from a timer-controlled system that operates from an electrical supply through various degrees of complexity right down to ones that are just a water-filled bag with a tube that goes from the bag down into the container. A drip feed irrigation system is a simple solution that will ensure an adequate supply of water even if you are away for a few days, and an occasional liquid feed from a watering can should keep nutrient levels high.

Mulching the tops of the pots with garden compost, pebbles, or a landscape fabric can help reduce moisture

Recycled kitchen equipment—in this case, an old enamel bucket and flour container—add a retro-style touch. Just be sure to add drainage holes.

loss. Once the plants are in the pots and the watering and feeding is taken care of, there isn't a great deal more to do except keep watch for pests and diseases. It pays to have a few companion plants in pots, such as nasturtiums, marigolds, or calendula, to keep aphids away and encourage pollinators.

Compact varieties are best suited to growing in containers and most seed catalogs have a number of miniature cultivars developed for growing in pots and window boxes. There is no reason, however, why you shouldn't grow runner beans or raspberries up cane obelisks, or a crop of early potatoes, ruby chard, zucchinis, ballerina fruit trees, or dwarf fava beans (broad beans) alongside the more obvious tomatoes, strawberries, and salad leaves. Growing in pots can even make life easier if you are trying to grow something like blueberries, which need an acidic soil, and your soil doesn't suit. They will thrive in a container filled with good-quality acidic compost.

You can grow annual crops in multipurpose compost. They require feeding about a month to six weeks after planting. All soil bought from a garden center or DIY store will have a proportion of fertilizer in it, but not a great deal, so this supplementary feeding will be required

When arranging your planters, put smaller ones in front to make sure the plants get enough sun.

## BIG POTS

If you use a large container, make sure you place it in its final position **before** you start filling it with potting mix. A large pot filled with soil will be heavy and difficult to move. Special pot caddies with wheels are designed to help make heavy plant containers more portable.

## THE BASICS

- Vegetables and fruits grown in containers are more dependent on the gardener.
- Regular feeding and watering are essential.
- Almost anything can be grown in a pot if the pot is large enough.

to maximize crop production and ultimate harvest. The organic feed you use will depend on the vegetable or fruit grown, although the simple rule is to apply a fertilizer higher in nitrogen to stimulate the plant's leaf growth, whereas a fertilizer higher in potash is used to maximize the production of flowers and subsequent fruits. These are easily applied when watering, as most come in the more quickly absorbed liquid form or are water-soluble. Different fertilizer brands are applied at different rates and varying intervals, so follow the package directions.

For very hungry vegetables, such as runner beans and zucchinis, you can beef up the multipurpose compost with some garden compost or well-rotted manure if you have it. At the end of the season, the compost will be spent and can be tossed onto your compost heap or used as a mulch. If you are growing plants that mature quickly, you can also replant the pots with a different crop in that season.

Anything that will be in its pot for a long period, such as fruit trees, needs a different treatment; use the largest pot reasonable for the plant, and start by putting something weighty, such as a few bricks, in the base of the pot to make it less likely to blow over in the wind. Use a loam-based compost mixed with multipurpose compost and a few handfuls of grit—this mix holds onto nutrients and water well and won't become compacted. If you live in a cold area, it may be necessary to wrap permanent pots in layers of bubble wrap, or bring the pots inside in the winter to prevent the compost and roots from freezing.

Some plants, such as tomatoes or beans, will need some type of support as they mature. Put these in place early, before the plant has time to grow too much, to avoid root damage and to give the plants support as soon as they need it.

## Vegetables and Containers

It's surprising how many vegetables you can grow successfully in containers. You might not get as high a yield from some plants as you would if they were planted in the open ground, but that's a small price to pay for being able to grow your own food where open-ground planting is not an option. Container-grown vegetables often are ready for harvesting more quickly, too, making them a great choice for time-conscious growers.

Vegetables with large frames are not suitable for container growing. Even the compact varieties of summer squash will flop over the rims and demand frequent watering. Bush beans, peas, and corn are impractical because you can't harvest enough from a single container to make a meal. Pole beans attached to tall stakes and lashed together at the top with twine might give you enough pods for a meal for two from a single picking.

Herbs, strawberries, and small, quick-growing vegetables, such as leaf lettuce, onions from sets, and

The flowers on a zucchini make it an attractive vegetable choice for a container—as pretty as any ornamental flower in bloom.

Swiss chard's colorful stems make a spectacular display in containers.

## VEGETABLES SUITABLE FOR CONTAINER GARDENING

- Baby beets
- Blueberries
- Carrots (short-root varieties)
- Bush and pole beans
- Herbs
- Kohlrabi
- Lettuce
- Peppers and chilies
- Potatoes
- Radishes
- Salad greens
- Strawberries
- Tomatoes

spinach, all grow well in containers. Swiss chard puts on a spectacular show all summer with its multicolored appearance. In the South and warm West, give chard afternoon shade to maintain the moisture.

Vegetables growing in containers are often exposed to both drought and waterlogging because there is a limited amount of potting soil around the roots, which can cause problems. Roots need air as well as water, so while there should always be enough water in the soil for a plant's needs, excess water must also be able to drain away freely. The smaller the container, the more difficult it is to get this juggling act just right.

When you choose a container, make sure that it has enough drainage holes. If you decide to transform another object into a container, you may need to make drainage holes—make sure you select a container in a material into which you will be able to make holes. (This could involve drilling, so choose wisely.) You may also want to raise the container off the ground on pot feet, blocks of wood, or bricks so that water can more easily drain.

## WATERING HANGING BASKETS

Hanging baskets are so packed with plants and roots that water tends to run straight off the surface of the potting mix, making the watering process messy and time-consuming. When planting a hanging basket, sink a small plastic flowerpot into the soil mix so that its top is level with the surface. Pour into this pot when watering—it will act as a reservoir and make watering the basket much easier.

## Choosing Container Soil

When you are selecting potting mix, choose bags that are not faded or worn—the older the bag, the longer the potting mix will have sat around releasing its nutrients. In this case, the mix will come with no available fertilizer, and that's a big part of what you're paying for. What you also need to consider, however, is that this fertilizer may be put into the soil at too high of a rate, which will mean that plants sown or potted into it may be scorched off. Always buy potting mix that looks as if it has just been delivered.

It's important to choose a soil mix that will not dry out too quickly. You can use regular soil from your yard, but you may transfer diseases along with it. Instead, use a good-quality potting mix, which will be free of pests and diseases. Soil-based potting mixes have long-lasting supplies of nutrients and retain water best, but they are heavy, making the bags and filled pots awkward to move. Soilless growing media are based on peat or a peat alternative, such as coir (coconut husk) or bark. They are lightweight and clean to handle, but they dry out quickly and need frequent watering and feeding. They can be difficult to rewet if they dry out, but good brands have a wetting agent to help them reabsorb water more quickly. You can mix water-retaining granules with the potting mix as you fill the container. These granules soak up water like a sponge and hold it for plants to use without the soil mix becoming waterlogged. The downside is that they can be damaging to soil life.

For shorter- and medium-term vegetables, such as lettuce, radishes, scallions, carrots, multisown beets (beetroot), tomatoes, melons, or new potatoes, you can simply use a mix straight out of the bag. If growing longer-term vegetables, such as brassicas, it is beneficial to add a proportion of soil to the mix because they like a firm and "meaty" soil in which to grow. A mixture of equal parts soil, proprietary potting mix, and compost is ideal, although this may make moving the container difficult, due to the weight of the soil. Still, once the containers are in position, you shouldn't need to move them.

Keep a careful eye on the moisture level of the potting mix, especially on hot or windy days. Most containers need daily watering, and hanging baskets may even need watering twice a day. Aim to always keep the potting mix slightly moist. After you plant the vegetables, you can cover the surface of the soil mix with a mulch—a layer of gravel, pebbles, or shredded bark, for example. Not only will it help prevent water from evaporating, thereby cutting down on the amount of water needed, but it will also look more attractive.

### SPRINKLE WITH PEA GRAVEL

Make your vegetables in pots look tidy by covering the top of the potting mix with a layer of pebbles, shingle, or gravel. It not only looks smart and reflects light, hiding all that dark earth, but also keeps moisture in the mix and reduces the amount of watering you need to do. A medium-sized bag of pea gravel is easy to find in garden centers and goes a very long way.

Soilless growing substrates, like coir, are lightweight and easy to use, but they need to be watered more frequently.

# Project: Planting in Containers

**1. Fill the container halfway to two-thirds with potting mix.** Carefully support the plant's stem as you remove the plant from the plastic pot by giving the rim of the pot a firm tap; gently loosen the roots a bit if necessary.

**2. Pull back the potting mix to make room for the plant's roots and gently break up the roots so they are not tightly bound.** It's important to loosen the root ball before replanting. If the container will hold only one plant, put it in the center; otherwise, check the position of all the plants before you plant the first one.

**3. Once all the plants are in position, fill in around them with more potting mix; then press them in gently but thoroughly.** Finally, water them thoroughly to help them get settled.

Container gardening can be useful in any garden, not just those with limited space.

## Container Gardening with Limited Space

Not having any outdoor space does not mean all is lost. You can position a hanging basket indoors near a sunny window using a ceiling hook or wall bracket. Planters filled with herbs and compact, short-rooted vegetables are also an option for a sunny window with a wide ledge or on a table nearby. Outdoor window boxes are a third option. If you live above the first floor, make sure any window boxes are securely attached to the wall.

Balconies provide outdoor growing space even in a high-rise apartment building. Planters, window boxes, and hanging baskets are all good choices. Consider using hanging baskets with a pulley system to raise and lower the planters for watering and harvesting.

The weight of soil-filled containers may limit the size and number of containers you can use. If you're not sure of the safety of your balcony, have a structural engineer survey it. Always make sure outdoor containers on a balcony are safe, and there's no risk of them being knocked to the ground.

## Container Gardening in Larger Spaces

It always seems to be assumed that growing fruits, vegetables, and herbs in containers is limited to gardeners who have no garden or larger space in which to grow vegetables in the ground. This should not be the case. Fruits, vegetables, and herbs can be grown in containers for a variety of reasons, with some being driven by necessity, while others are aesthetic, and some purely for greater control. It is a method that is available to every gardener.

Most fruits, vegetables, and herbs can be quite beautiful, and there is no reason why they cannot be used as decorative container plants that have the added bonus of producing a food crop. Containers can also control and limit the growth of aggressive plants. Jerusalem artichoke, for example, is a rampant spreader in the soil. If grown in a container, it can be contained and controlled.

### SMALLER SCALE: GROWING IN A BAG OF POTTING MIX

Turn a bag of potting mix into a planter. Tomatoes and peppers are good choices for bags. Lay the unopened bag flat on the ground where the plants will grow, and use a sharp knife to make three planting holes (cut a cross in the plastic and tuck the flaps in). You can also remove the plastic over the top surface of the bag, leaving a few inches around the edge, and sow salad greens or lettuce directly in the soil.

You can also repurpose odd containers (like old copper hot-water tanks) for climbing vegetables, such as French beans, runner beans, outdoor cucumbers, or summer squash (marrows). The plants climb up the supports, and when the copper has aged, the whole thing looks very attractive. The arrangement has the added benefit of preventing any slug or snail damage to the plants (these pests will not travel over copper).

## Reusing Containers

At the end of each growing season, you need to empty the container and either spread its contents on the garden or put it on the compost heap. Unless the contents of the container are primarily soil-based, it is best to replace it each year. Soil-based potting mixes can be used again, but not for the same crop because there may be a risk of pest or disease buildup like there would be for crops grown in the ground. If you replace the contents of containers annually, you won't need to worry about crop rotation (see page 284) and what crops to grow in each container because there will be fresh potting mix each year and, thus, no chance of pests and diseases building up.

## Using Grow Bags

Plants in commercial grow bags always seem to thrive, even if plants in the soil or other pots struggle. You can make shallow wooden boxes to fit the bags in, then cover the bags with pea pebbles. You can buy ready-made burlap covers that will neatly slip over the grow bags, too, giving them a more natural look.

Commercial growbags can be used for quick-growing vegetables, but are too shallow for deep-rooted vegetables or long-term crops. They can be used for salads, dwarf French beans, stump-rooted carrots, beetroot, and tomatoes.

# Vertical Options and Support Pieces

All vegetable gardens need some vertical structures, if only to support beans, sweet peas, and cucumbers. These offer the chance to add a new dimension to the design of the garden and are a space-saving way to grow. Simple cane tunnels work, but there are plenty of other options—climbers can be grown over arches or tunnels spanning

Standard bays and formal teepees give this pretty garden height and structure.

Trailing plants are particularly appropriate for hanging baskets; there are a lot of tomato types specially bred for basket growing.

## CROPS THAT COMMONLY NEED SUPPORT

Check the descriptions of the cultivars and varieties in your seed catalog. Many are bred to be especially compact, so some varieties are much less likely to need staking than others.

- Climbing beans (depending on the variety)
- Bush beans (depending on the variety)
- Chilies
- Peas
- Tomatoes

paths or gateways, or up obelisks in formal gardens. You can buy ready-made vertical structures or try something more homespun: old tools or painted wooden posts tied together at the top and pushed into the ground add height and interest. These are temporary, low-cost features, so you can use your imagination and have a bit of fun. Providing supports will let the plants grow by extending upward instead of rambling over the ground, which is especially important in small gardens. In addition, keeping the vegetables off the soil will help keep them protected from attack by pests, such as slugs, and diseases that thrive in damp conditions. Always get supports in early, before they are needed, which will help to prevent root damage.

The recent houseplant revival has breathed new life into the humble hanging basket. Clay, plastic, and even concrete planters suspended from the ceiling are adorning interiors, and, inside or outside, they make ideal homes for tumbling tomatoes, strawberries, herbs, and baby salad

Multitier hanging baskets are a great way to use vertical space. Be careful to position them where watering overspill will not cause a problem and firmly secure them to their supports.

Vertical structures help you make the most of container gardening.

from growing your own food. You can use every inch of space, including the vertical surfaces, to grow a range of delicious and beautiful vegetables and fruits. Raised beds and containers can provide perfect growing conditions, but climbing pole beans on vertical structures are also perfect for the courtyard; if they are well fed and watered, they will continue to provide regular batches of beans all summer long.

## Walls and Fences

Probably the easiest and most obvious structure on which to grow the productive crops mentioned is a wall or fence. In order for this to be suitable, it must be south- or west-facing, so that the vegetables will gain enough sunlight to be as productive as possible. These vegetables are annuals and do not hold themselves to walls or fences, so they would need supports on which to cling. Use a strong galvanized wire running horizontally across

leaves. Just make sure you don't hang them with string that will rot and break when it gets wet; metal chains and nylon or plastic string are best. Hanging baskets dry out quickly in hot weather. Regular watering is essential, but you can make life a bit easier by mixing a handful of water-retaining gel into the potting mix when planting.

Half-standard bay or gooseberries or ballerina fruit trees all make striking vertical punctuations. Bays instantly evoke traditional formality, while gooseberries are a little more wayward. Ballerina fruit trees grow a single stem straight up to about 6½' (2m) and require no pruning. They are productive, pretty space-savers with both blossom and fruit, and the space beneath them can be planted.

Your courtyard garden may be completely paved over and surrounded by walls, but don't let that deter you

Bamboo canes are often used to support climbing beans.

Wooden trellises are quick to construct and are perfect for creating accessible gardens with easy-to-pick produce.

all your fences; if growing beans on a fence, add much thinner vertical wires to these horizontal wires. The main horizontal wires should be spaced 12" (30.5cm) apart, and the thinner vertical wire should use the same spacing so that squares are formed.

If preferred, garden twine can be used instead of the vertical wire. At each point of contact, the vertical wire is wrapped around the stronger horizontal wire so that it is the stronger wires that take the strain from the weight of crop. The vertical wires are in place for the beans to twine around as they climb upward (the horizontal wires are too far apart for this purpose). The bean shoots may need gentle persuasion to direct them in the desired direction to prevent clogging of shoots on one or two of the vertical wires. If training zucchini, spaghetti squash, gherkins, or other squashes, tie them onto the horizontal wires as soon as they are long enough. As these are not twining vegetables, they do not necessarily require the vertical wires for growing upward. The wires must be firmly attached so that they can cope with the weight of the crop. In years when climbing vegetables are not grown against these wall or fences, rotate in annual flowering plants instead.

## Trellises

A nice trellis is perfect to for your plants to grab on to. In addition to maximizing your potential garden space, a trellis can help your climbing plants receive ample sunlight and proper airflow around the leaves, which keeps them healthy and helps them avoid disease or wet conditions. Plus, it's easier to find, select, and harvest vegetables like cucumbers when they are hanging vertically.

A wooden trellis secured to a wall or fence is useful for climbing beans to scramble through. You can use a freestanding trellis to support spreading zucchini and squash plants, making them an attractive feature. (Check whether your particular squash is a sprawling vine variety or a more compact bush type.) Your trellis needs to be permanently attached with strong screws or nails to prevent the weight of the crop from pulling it off. Bean shoots may need to be gently directed to ensure a good, even coverage of the trellis, while non-twining plants can be tied regularly. When using garden twine to tie in these very delicate shoots, ensure that it is soft in nature and not coarse. If the string rubs on the shoot, coarse twine may cause irreversible damage.

# Project: Make a Decorative Trellis

**Skill Level:** Intermediate | **Time Needed:** 2 Hours

A trellis can be as elaborate or simple as you wish, and some designs are easier to build than the one demonstrated here, but this trellis provides a nice compromise between form and function—simple enough to build and sturdy enough for the plants, yet decorative enough to add an ornamental touch to your garden space.

| PARTS LIST | TOOLS NEEDED |
|---|---|
| • ½" x ⅞" (1.3 x 2.2cm) wooden strips from wider lumber (see Cut List and Step 1) | • Table saw |
| | • Circular saw or miter saw |
| | • Pneumatic pin nailer |
| | • Tape measure |
| • 1¼" (32mm) finishing nails or staples | • Pencil (optional) |
| | • Jigsaw (optional) |
| • Paint (optional) | • Paintbrush (optional) |
| | • Ruler (optional) |

**CUT LIST**

| Number of Pieces | Dimensions | Type |
|---|---|---|
| 2 | 28" (71.1 cm) | ½" x ⅞" (1.3 x 2.2cm) pine strips |
| 2 | 31" (78.7 cm) | ½" x ⅞" (1.3 x 2.2cm) pine strips |
| 4 | 40" (101.6 cm) | ½" x ⅞" (1.3 x 2.2cm) pine strips |
| 2 | 35¼" (89.5 cm) | ½" x ⅞" (1.3 x 2.2cm) pine strips |

## INSTRUCTIONS

**1. Make the cuts.** This trellis design is built entirely out of ½" x ⅞" (1.3 x 2.2cm) wooden strips in varying lengths. You won't find these dimensions just off the shelf from your lumber provider, as they are a unique thickness and width. You'll need to use a table saw to modify ("rip") a wider piece of lumber into these thinner strips. You can also modify the dimensions slightly to make them work more easily with whatever lumber you have on hand. For example, using 1-by material—with an actual thickness of ¾" (1.9cm)—can work well, too, and be easily modified into strips that are ½" x ¾" (1.3 x 1.9cm). However, for a slightly sturdier build, you can rip ⅞" (2.2cm) or even 1" (2.5cm) strips out of wider lumber. The instructions here assume you're working with ⅞" (2.2cm) strips. Be sure to take extra care when ripping narrow pieces on the table saw. Use a circular saw or miter saw to create the various lengths required.

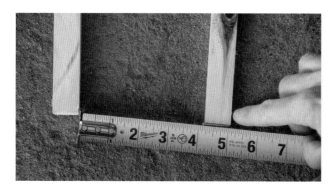

**2. Begin laying out the design.** Achieving the precise spacing between the slats requires a bit of careful measuring and placement, so it's a good idea to have an extra person or two around to help you get the layout correct and hold it in place while adjustments are made. If you have a table or workbench that is large enough, you can assemble the trellis there; another good option is to lay out the trellis on a concrete floor in a garage or shop. In any event, a large level surface is essential.

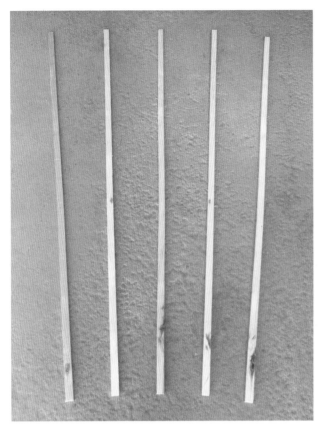

**3. Take your time and have patience as you work on the layout.** At the bottom of the trellis, the spacing between each vertical pole should be as close to 4¼" (10.8cm) as you can get. At the top, the spacing between each vertical pole is wider, creating a fan shape. The spacing here should be 8¾" (22.2cm). One way to achieve the proper spacing is to work from the middle pole outward; first get the correct spacing between the middle pole and its immediate neighbors, then work on the spacing from those neighbors to the outermost poles. As long as you keep spacings of 4¼" (10.8cm) at the bottom and 8¾" (22.2cm) at the top, you should arrive at the fan shape shown in the photos. (When finished, the overall span at the top of the trellis will be about 39½" [100.3cm], and 21¼" [54cm] at the bottom.)

**4. Continue laying out the design.** Add the horizontal struts to the trellis. One easy way to achieve the proper spacing is to place a tape measure alongside the entire length of the center vertical pole (make sure that the 5' [152.4cm] mark on the tape measure is at the top of the center pole). Now place your horizontal struts at 11" (27.9cm) intervals. Start from the bottom and place struts at 11", 22", 33", 44", and 55" (27.9, 55.9, 83.8, 111.8, and 139.7cm). The shortest strut—the 28" (71.1cm) one— should go at a height of 11" (27.9cm), the next longest of 31" (78.7cm) at a height of 22" (55.9cm), and so on up the trellis, with the 40" (101.6cm) (longest) strut placed at a height of 55" (139.7cm). Each strut should be perpendicular to the center vertical pole.

**5. Fasten the pieces.** The easiest and fastest way to assemble the trellis is with a pneumatic pin nailer; this greatly speeds up the process and helps limit the wood cracking or splitting that might otherwise occur. You can make the entire layout first and then nail, or you can do as shown in the photos and nail each horizontal strut in place as you work; this method can help maintain the shape as you go.

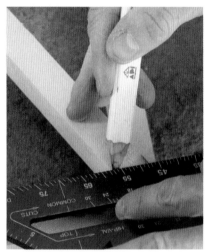

**6. Add the diagonals.** To provide additional places for plants to grip and add a bit of decorative flair, attach two diagonal struts. These are each 35¼" (89.5cm) long and form an *A* shape across the front face of the trellis. The top point of the *A* meets at the center of the top-most horizontal strut, and the feet of the *A* each land on the second strut from the bottom, as shown in the photos. For an optional, more precise look, you can make marks with a pencil and ruler on the bottom ends of these diagonals and cut off the angles with a jigsaw; these will make the diagonals flush with the horizontal struts for a cleaner look.

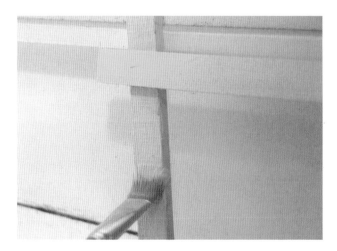

**7. Paint the trellis.** Painting is a final option that will help protect and extend the life of the trellis, as well as add a dash of color to the garden landscape. We used a bright yellow, but you can use any color you like.

# Project: Make an A-Frame Trellis

**Skill Level:** Intermediate | **Time Required:** 3 Hours

If you'd like to have multiple trellises around for form and function, it's fun to shake up the design and vary the style somewhat. One simple design is a "teepee" trellis, which uses three or more wooden poles tied together near the top to make a simple vertical structure. Gardeners will often add twine, as well, to give the climbing plants something else to grab onto and hold the teepee together.

This is a fairly quick and easy project, but the stronger design means that you'll likely be able to get more than one season out of it. As long as it's stored indoors during the winter (and perhaps painted), you and your plants should enjoy several seasons of use with this trellis. Plus, you can always make multiple versions for larger gardens.

### PARTS LIST
- ½" x ⅞" (1.3 x 2.2 cm) wooden strips from wider lumber (see Cut List and Step 1)
- 1¼" (32mm) finishing nails or staples
- Paint (optional)

### TOOLS NEEDED
- Circular saw or miter saw
- Table saw
- Jigsaw (optional)
- Pneumatic pin nailer
- Tape measure
- Pencil (optional)
- Paintbrush (optional)
- Gloves (optional)

### CUT LIST

| Number of Pieces | Dimensions | Type |
|---|---|---|
| 6 | 48" (121.9cm) | ½" x ⅞" (1.3 x 2.2cm) pine strips |
| 9 | 16" (40.6cm) | ½" x ⅞" (1.3 x 2.2cm) pine strips |
| 1 | 22" (55.9cm) | ½" x ⅞" (1.3 x 2.2cm) pine strip |
| 2 | 10" (25.4cm) | ½" x ⅞" (1.3 x 2.2cm) pine strip |

## INSTRUCTIONS

**1. Make the cuts.** This design is built entirely out of ½" x ⅞" (1.3 x 2.2cm) pine of different lengths. These unique dimensions mean that you'll need to have access to a table saw so that you can easily and safely rip (cut lengthwise) wider lumber into these thinner strips. This task doesn't take very long with a table saw; you can simply set your saw's guide to the width desired, and then repeatedly make the long rip cuts without having to remeasure your wood over and over. You can also modify the dimensions to make them work more easily with whatever lumber you have on hand. For example, using 1-by material—with an actual thickness of ¾" (1.9cm)—will work well, too, and can be easily modified into strips that are ½" x ¾" (1.3 x 1.9cm). But for a slightly sturdier build, you can rip ⅞" (2.2cm) or even 1" (2.5cm) strips out of wider lumber. The instructions here assume you're working with ⅞" (2.2cm) strips. Be sure to take extra care when ripping narrow pieces on the table saw. Use a circular saw or miter saw to create the various lengths required.

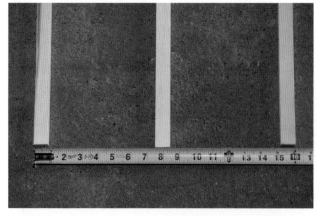

**2. Begin laying out the design.** Begin by laying out three of your ⅞" x 54" (2.2 x 137.2cm) pine poles on a flat surface (a concrete garage or shop floor works nicely), and make them all parallel to each other. The entire span should measure 16" (40.6cm), with the middle pole centered on 8" (20.3cm), as shown in the photo.

**3. Continue laying out the design.** Add the horizontal struts to the trellis. Take four of the ⅞" x 16" (2.2 x 40.6cm) pine pieces, and lay them out across the three vertical poles at 90-degree angles. The first horizontal strut should be placed at 11" (27.9cm), the second at 22" (55.9cm), the third at 33" (83.8cm), and the fourth at 44" (111.8cm). Use your pin nailer and finishing nails to carefully secure everything together at this point (if possible, have another person help hold the pieces in place while you fasten them).

**4. Repeat Steps 2 and 3 to create the second side of the trellis.** You can speed up this process by building your new layout right on top of the first one. This saves you the time of having to remeasure everything.

**5. Add the top strut.** Stand up the two halves of the A-frame, and lean them against each other (you might want to have someone help you hold them). The spread on the ground between them should be about 26" (66cm). Now take the final 16" (40.6cm) piece of ½" × ⅞" (1.3 × 2.2cm) pine, and nail it to the top of the A-frame.

**6. Add the side braces.** Take the two ⅞" x 22½" (2.2 x 57.2cm) pieces, and nail them to the sides of the A-frame at a height of 11" (27.9cm) to match the other horizontal struts. The two ⅞" x 10½" (2.2 x 26.7cm) pieces should likewise be placed at 33" (83.8cm). You'll notice that the corners of the side braces will extend a little and won't match the angle of the A-frame. You can stick with this "rougher" look, or, for a more precise fit, you can use a pencil to mark the angle of the cut needed (as shown in the photos), and then remove the excess with a jigsaw.

**7. Finish and set up the trellis.** Add a coat of paint or leave it natural. Your A-frame trellis is now complete and ready for its job in the garden.

## Tepees and Obelisks

Tepees or obelisks can be used to great effect in the productive garden. Green and climbing French beans are traditionally grown up long bamboo canes pushed into the ground to create an upturned *V* and connected together by a cane ridge. Although very effective, this method does require a reasonably large area, whereas individual tepees or obelisks do not.

Both types of climbing bean are very ornamental when in flower, and you can use them in flower borders to give color most of the summer, up to a height of 6' (1.8m). To get the shoots long enough to carry a big enough crop of beans, 8' (2.4m) bamboo canes must be used to make your tepee. Push these about 12" (30.5cm) into the ground, at about a 75-degree angle, with 12"–18" (30.5–45.7cm) of space between each of the canes. About 12" (30.5cm) from the top of the canes, bunch them together and tie them using garden twine. Rather than growing the beans straight up the canes, you can train them so that they wrap around the outside, potentially giving a greater

length of shoot and therefore a heavier crop. Homemade or bought obelisks are very ornamental and can be used in the same way.

## Pergolas

You can use pergolas as supports for growing climbing vegetables. One option is to push long bamboo canes into the ground, and then tie them to the top of the pergola at 24" (61cm) intervals, but this can be somewhat obtrusive. The other option is to use soft but strong string that can be tied to the top of the pergola, then held in the ground with a homemade wire stake. In the case of non-twining plants, wrap the string around the growing tips of the plants to hold them in position.

## "Pea Sticks"

The majority of peas are not self-supporting, and even with those that are, you'd still invariably have to use supports in windy sites. The use of twiggy "pea sticks" is a practice that has been carried out very successfully over

Tepees not only provide support, but also help to save space in a small garden.

# BEAN TRENCH

The only real problem with runner beans is that they can become stringy and inedible. There are two reasons for this: either they are too old (green beans are always better when picked young and fresh) or the plants have been allowed to become too dry. Both problems are easily avoided by picking regularly and ensuring that there is always moisture at the roots of the plants.

The best way to keep runner beans moist throughout the summer is to grow them over a bean trench. It is a simple method that involves digging a 36" (91.4cm) wide trench where the crop will be grown. The length of the trench depends on what is required to accommodate the runner beans. The depth of the trench only needs to be about 9" (22.9cm), with the soil piled along one edge. The bottom of the trench is then filled with organic matter that would usually be destined for the compost bin, such as Brussels-sprout leaves and shredded newspaper, as well as other moisture-retaining materials, such as well-rotted horse manure. The idea is to half-fill the trench, if possible, with all this type of material. As it rots down to good organic matter, it will help to conserve moisture in the bottom half of the trench and in the area feeding the green bean roots.

It is prudent to have a contingency plan in place in case of a very long and hot summer, so that water can be applied to the plants if the bean trench cannot cope. If you've erected tepee supports over the trench to be used for the beans, you can run a length of soaker hose along the inside edge of each row of canes. It needs to be buried just under the soil surface so that water evaporation is kept to a minimum. Each end of the soaker hose is connected to a *T* piece, then one pipe runs to a water source (ideally a rain barrel). It can run from very low pressure because the water leaks out of the pipes, which can be made from recycled rubber car tires, as small droplets. When using this system, it is very easy to forget what stringy runner beans are like.

You'll fill in the bottom half of your bean trench with organic materials that will break down and conserve moisture.

many years. There is usually no need to buy pea sticks; you can use long, twiggy branches—24" to 36" (61 to 91.4cm) long—from any tree.

Sweet peas are delicious, and they make beautiful additions to your garden as they twine up trellises or other vertical structures.

Due to the tendrils pea plants have in each leaf joint, which will twine around and grip onto almost anything, fancy supports are not required. Once the peas have been planted outside and any cloche covering has been removed, the sticks can be inserted into the ground on either side of the row of peas. They are pushed into the ground at a slight angle, so that the twiggy tops meet over the row of peas, giving the plants ample support. As the peas grow, they will grip onto the twigs for support with no assistance needed.

## Tree Trunks

You can support climbing vegetables by making use tree trunks that may have lost their top halves in very windy weather. You can attach a thin wire vertically to the tree so the vegetable plants are able to hold themselves up.

## Cages

Good for tomatoes and peppers, plant cages are three-dimensional supports in which the plant is set in the center and grows up through the structure. They save time because plants growing in them need less tying than when grown with other types of supports.

Cages come in all kinds of three-dimensional forms, including square, triangular, circular, and tapering spiral shapes.

## Individual or Grouped Stakes

Vegetables, such as tomatoes and chilies, are reasonably stocky. However, as they grow and, hopefully, carry a heavy crop, they tend to lean, sometimes down to the ground. At planting time, provide each plant with a sturdy stake set about 12" (30.5cm) deep; then tie the main stem to it at intervals as the plant grows taller. Make sure the tie isn't so tight that it will cut into the stem as the plant grows.

In small gardens, support climbing beans on less formal versions of tepees made from tall stakes or poles arranged in a circle and tied or clipped together at the top. This method saves space and looks attractive, too. You can also arrange the stakes in a double row in an A-frame shape, with pairs of stakes tied together and more stakes laid horizontally and tied firmly into place to keep the structure secure. You can attach horizontal string or wires to the end stakes to provide supports for the plants.

## Netting

Wide mesh netting, supported on sturdy stakes, will soon be covered by the scrambling growth of peas or beans. However, be careful: unless it is firmly secured, the weight of the plant can pull it down or cause it to fall as the season progresses. Disentangling dead plant growth at the end of the season can be a frustrating job. This often means that the netting gets only one season of use before being disposed of, making it an expensive option.

## Branched Brush

Supports made of winter prunings taken from live hardwood shrubs are perfect for plants that have twining tendrils, such as peas. They will also help to hold up bushy plants, such as bush beans. Use branches with plenty of twigs about 3' (91.4cm) tall. Push them into the soil about 12" (30.5cm) apart along the row as soon as you see seedlings emerging.

Use garden string, plastic plant ties, or strips of cloth to gently tie a plant to a supporting stake.

Branched brush will keep plants upright and the crop off the ground.

# RAISED BED ROPE SUPPORTS

Vegetable gardens can be a bit flat, so to give them some permanent height, build some triangular rope supports in L-shaped beds at the corners. They'll prove to be very practical, with hairy, synthetic hemp-like rope giving good grip to beans and sweet peas, and they'll look good even when not being used. Synthetic rope looks natural but also provides years of service in the garden.

## MATERIALS AND TOOLS NEEDED

- Raised bed with precut half joints (see Step 1)
- Sturdy posts with precut half joint (see Step 1)
- Power drill
- Screws
- Screwdriver
- Synthetic hemp-like rope

**1.** Sturdy posts are slotted into the corners of the beds using a half joint precut by a carpenter. Drill holes at regular intervals on the edge of the frame and the vertical posts.

**2.** Screw into the half joint to add stability and secure the posts into the frame. Predrill the holes to make this easier.

**3.** Pass ropes through drilled holes. They should run from one side of the frame through the post to the other, keeping the rope taut.

# CHAPTER 5
# Preventing Pests, Diseases, and Weeds

The traditional method of controlling any pest or disease is to spray a chemical pesticide onto the plants to kill the pest. The side effects are possible contamination of the crop and the environment, and also potential destruction of beneficial creatures, such as ladybugs. The use of pesticides on fruits and vegetables always raises the question of residues left at harvest. For these reasons, the range of pesticides available for dealing with plant pests is severely restricted. This is a good thing for both safety and environmental reasons and indeed many gardeners may wish to choose alternative, nonchemical treatments for pests and diseases.

You should try to use a minimum of pesticides and, wherever possible, look for alternative ways of controlling pests. The effects of pests and diseases can be reduced by growing and feeding plants well enough to make them healthy and able to withstand those pests and diseases. A weak, poorly fed plant is much more likely to succumb to attack. There are also varieties of fruits and vegetables that are resistant to diseases and sometimes pests. These are well worth growing. Other garden techniques, like crop rotation and companion planting, are also effective methods for controlling pests and preventing diseases.

Exactly what problem strikes your plants will depend on where you live and what kind of season it is. Some years can be almost trouble-free, while in others, a gardener can face an onslaught of problems, one right after another. Just to complicate matters, there are a host of other problems that can adversely affect plants that cannot be blamed on pests or diseases. When the situations in which plants grow are less than ideal, plants will start to suffer and show various symptoms. High temperatures will cause scorch, as will frost, high winds, or a shortage of water. Excess water causes roots to die, resulting in wilting. Low light will cause plants to be thin, spindly, and pale. It can be difficult to pin down whether the issue is pests, diseases, or environment, so it's best to prevent pests and diseases from the start.

## Preparing Your Crops

The first step to giving your plants a fighting chance is to grow them in the best possible conditions so that they are strong and vigorous. It won't make them any less attractive to pests and diseases, but it will give them the best opportunity to fight off the effects. Avoid putting the plants under any form of stress because this will make them less able to withstand pest and disease attacks.

Choose vegetables that suit your soil and climate, and provide them with a reasonably sheltered, warm position in fertile, fine-textured soil. When you plant them, space them correctly so that there's plenty of air for ventilation. Keep weeds under control so there is no unnecessary competition. Fertilize the vegetables as needed; however, don't overfeed—soft, lush growth is more vulnerable to pest and disease attack. Keep plants watered during dry spells to avoid moisture stress, but don't water foliage excessively, especially in the evening. Damp, cool conditions increase the spread of fungal diseases. Water the plants overhead in the mornings so that excess moisture has time to evaporate during the sunny part of the day.

> ### TIME-SAVER
> Breeders have developed cultivars that are resistant to, or tolerant of, various pests and diseases. For example, tomato 'Legend' has excellent blight tolerance; spinach 'El Grinta' has high resistance to downy mildew; and carrot 'Flyaway' is resistant to carrot-root maggots. Growing resistant cultivars will cut down time spent on checking for and treating problems.

# Use Perfect Timing

Some vegetable plants have a peak season in which they are attacked by pests. By sowing them early or late, you can avoid their maturing just at the time they are most likely to be attacked. For example, turnips are often attacked by flea beetles, a pest that creates tiny holes in the leaves. If you live in Zones 3–7, try sowing seeds in midsummer instead of spring to early summer, so the plants miss the worst season for attacks. Similarly, if Colorado potato beetles are a problem, plant potato tubers in early summer instead of spring. When the adult beetles emerge from the soil and find no potatoes on your land, they will go elsewhere.

This can be easily demonstrated with carrots, which are particularly susceptible to the carrot fly when the roots are young and tender. The carrot fly lays its eggs in the soil next to the developing roots, with the emerging larvae burrowing into the roots before emerging as adults. There can be up to three life cycles per year, but it is the first, at the end of May or early June, that seems to cause the worst damage. The carrot flies are attracted by the smell of the young carrots, with the larvae finding it easier to burrow into the softer, tender flesh than that of more mature roots. You should therefore time the sowing of carrots so that they are more mature by the period that the carrot flies are active, or so that they germinate and grow after the life cycle has been completed. As

This map is based on the hardiness zone maps developed by the US Department of Agriculture and divides the United States into hardiness zones based on average minimum winter temperatures. Some plants do well in certain zones and struggle in others, so you need to know which zone you are planting in when choosing vegetables and cultivars to plant. Other elements may also affect how a plant grows in your specific area, so along with checking which zone you live in, you should also discuss your plant choices with your local nursery, water department, or cooperative extension service.

This is not an official USDA Plant Hardiness Zone Map.

the flies are attracted by smell, it is also prudent not to thin carrots at this time of year. The process of thinning releases a strong odor that will only attract the carrot fly to your vegetable garden.

# Create Barricades

Many pests can be kept at bay by using physical barriers, and this is particularly appropriate in small gardens. It's much more practical to erect an insect-proof screen over a raised bed than to try to protect an entire large vegetable patch. Fast-growing vegetables will also need protecting for a relatively short time; a protective structure does not have to be as sturdy and solidly built as if it had to stay in place for a long season.

Glass or plastic cloches or tunnels are handy because they are easy to move from one row of plants to another. Floating row covers and fine-mesh netting are ideal for keeping out insects.

To keep out large pests, such as birds and four-legged furry mammals, consider a "cage" made of stakes forming a boxlike frame with a covering of small-mesh

Lightweight floating row covers are ideal for keeping flying pests away from carrots. They are so light that you won't need a frame to support them.

Tunnels supporting a netting material will keep birds and smaller pests at bay. Make sure the ends are firmly secured to keep out these critters.

## IT'S A CUTTHROAT WORLD

The nasty larval form of a useless but otherwise harmless moth, cutworms are the worst kind of garden pests. These larvae live about 1" (2.5cm) deep in the soil and can demolish seedlings as you sleep at night. Cutworms kill only young plants, severing transplants at the soil line so the young plants will topple over. They later consume them without much effort. It's really easy to thwart cutworms. Just make a circle of relatively hard material, and shove it into the dirt around the young transplant (these are known as cutworm collars). Sink the collar around the plant at planting time so that it's at least 2" (5.1cm) into the ground.

Homemade collars of cardboard, tin, or plastic will provide barriers against cutworms:

- **For small plants, make a tubelike collar using a toilet paper or paper towel roll or tin cans without a lid or bottom.** Remove both ends of a soup (or similarly sized) can, and insert the metal cylinder over the transplant, sinking it 1" or 2" (2.5 or 5.1cm) into the soil.
- **Use a plastic soda bottle.** Cut the top and bottom off of large soda bottle, and use it as you'd use the tin cans.
- **Try magazine "blow in" direct response cards.** Open up any new copy of any magazine, and select the biggest card inserts. Fold them over into circles to surround your plants.

The cutworm is shown here in its egg, larva, and pupa stages. PHOTO BY DOWNTOWNGAL.

netting. To deter rabbits, bury the bottom edges at least 1' (30.5cm) underground, forming the edge into an outward-facing *U* shape.

See Using Covers on page 188 for more information on structures and materials to protect soil and plants from weather, pests, diseases, and other concerns.

# Fighting off the Enemy

Once pests or diseases attack a plant, it's important to treat the problem promptly before they do too much damage. This means you need to check your plants frequently—and be ready to go on the offensive quickly.

Get into the practice of inspecting your vegetables regularly. Look at the undersides of leaves—where trouble often starts—as well as the tops. It can rapidly build up to damaging levels if undetected. You will soon develop an eye for singling out a plant that does not seem quite right and needs additional investigation.

Most gardeners prefer to enjoy produce that they know is chemical free. Manufacturers of pesticides have increasingly concentrated on producing short-lived safe products, often made from naturally occurring ingredients. All garden chemicals are thoroughly tested to ensure they are perfectly safe to use as directed. However, there are other methods you can use on your plants before reaching for a chemical application.

## Handpicking

For larger insect pests, such as caterpillars and beetles, you can pick them off plants and drop them into a bowl of soapy water. (If you are squeamish about handling insects, wear gloves.) Where individual picking is not practical, spread a cloth on the ground and shake pest-infested stems over it to dislodge unwelcome visitors. You can use a strong jet of water to dislodge smaller, more tenacious pests, such as clustering aphids—a much quicker option than handpicking.

## Trapping

**Slug and snail traps.** Sink a trap in the ground to capture slugs and snails. Bury an old margarine container with

You can use a store-bought trap filled with beer to entice slugs and snails to enter. Alternatively, recycle any plastic container or even a tin can (just be careful of sharp edges).

the rim just above soil level (to make it less likely to catch ground beetles, which are garden helpers). Fill the container with diluted beer to attract the slimy critters. They will crawl in—and drown. See Dealing with Garden Critters on page 182 for more information on trapping rodents.

**Flypaper.** Flypaper controls flying pests in the greenhouse using a strip of plastic that is coated with a very sticky glue. Some flypaper also has a sweet substance to attract the bugs, and some even contain an insecticide. You hang the strips up in the greenhouse, and the pest flies into it, sticks to the glue, and is unable to fly away. Flypaper can also trap some beneficial insects—although it usually catches far more pests. The traps can also be considered excellent pest detectors because regular monitoring of the glue will indicate a pest problem.

**Cardboard grease traps.** The combination of cardboard, grease, and a small wooden stick (like a tongue depressor) makes another sticky trap that is very effective in trapping flea beetles. The sure signs of attack

from this pest on crops, such as turnips and radishes, are tiny holes in the leaves. These holes cause a reduction in the size of the roots harvested because they reduce the amount of leaf area able to photosynthesize, slowing the plant's growth.

This very simple method involves cutting a rectangular piece of cardboard 4" (10.2cm) wide and about 6" (15.2cm) long and coating one side of it with grease. Any grease will do as long as it has a similar consistency to petroleum jelly. When small insects come into contact with the trap, they stick to the grease.

To use this type of trap, you hold the stick in one hand and the cardboard in the other. Turn the cardboard so that the grease side is facing down, about 2" (5.1cm) above the leaves of the crop. Run the stick along the row of plants so that it hits the tops of the leaves and move the cardboard along with it. Flea beetles jump when disturbed— hence their name—so they will jump straight onto the grease, where they become stuck. Discard the cardboard once you reach the end of the row. All of the flea beetles should be stuck to it and none left on the leaves of the crop.

**Pheromone traps.** A pheromone trap is a triangular box that has a sticky card placed on the bottom, and is laced with the pheromone of the female codling moth. Gardeners hang these traps among apple and pear trees during mid-May at a ratio of one trap per five trees. This type of trap works because the female pheromone attracts the male codling moth into the triangular trap, where it then gets stuck on the sticky pad and dies, meaning that it is unable to fertilize the female's eggs, preventing new larvae that would have burrowed into and damaged the fruit crop.

**Grease bands.** Adult female winter moths are wingless, and because they overwinter in the soil at the base of apple and pear trees, the most effective method of control is to stop them from climbing these trees to lay their eggs. Because they begin to emerge starting in mid-November, you should tie a grease band around each stem and supporting stake of all susceptible trees by the end of October.

You can buy grease bands from garden centers and home stores, but they are very easy to make. Each trap is a 4" (10.2cm) strip of plastic that circles the tree trunk about 18" (45.7cm) from the ground and is tied in place with soft string. You coat the plastic with some thick grease so that when the female winter moths try to climb the tree to deposit their eggs, they become stuck in the grease and cannot progress any farther. You will need to use new bands each October.

## Biological Controls

Naturally occurring organisms are the biological controls that prey on pest species. Companion plants will attract a range of naturally occurring predators, most of which are common to gardens, and it is the larvae of some and the adults of others that will eat the pests. For example, lacewings, hoverflies, and ladybug larvae, as well as wasps and earwigs, eat aphids. Ground beetles, centipedes, frogs, and toads consume slugs and snails.

Ladybugs require something in which to crawl, and a bundle of canes tied together and hung up is ideal. The canes need to be only 3"–4" (7.6–10.2cm) in length and the holes in the center of the canes wide enough for the adult beetles to crawl into. Lacewing adults easy to

overwinter. A soda bottle cut in half, filled with rolled-up corrugated cardboard, and then hung up, is ideal. Ground beetles and centipedes require a leaf, soil, or mulch cover under which to hide.

Birds and bats should also be encouraged into the garden. Place birdhouses in trees because many bird species feed on pests—many small nesting birds are voracious. While raising their brood of chicks, a pair of adult birds can collect between 7,000 and 14,000 caterpillars to feed themselves and their chicks. Not all of these caterpillars will be pests, but the majority of them will be. Also, place bat boxes in trees; an average bat can consume up to 3,500 insects per night. Again, not all of these insects are bad, but it's likely that the majority of them will be. Frogs and toads require a water source, which may be something as simple as something that will enable the animals to get in and out of a bucket.

There is no doubt that attracting wildlife into the garden not only increases the diversity and pleasure of one's productive areas, but also makes the job of pest control much, much easier. Having a population already there at the start of each year will only make growing much more pleasurable.

A homemade bat box is a great way to attract bats that will eat many harmful insects.

# BENEFICIAL CREATURES AND INSECTS TO PROTECT

Many of the insects and other creatures that live on plants and in your garden are not pests but are beneficial in the garden. Be sure to differentiate between the friends and foes. Ladybugs, lacewings, spiders, and centipedes are all garden friends that act as natural predators feeding on the pests. The ladybug is probably the most common example and eats many aphids each day to stay alive. Bees are, of course, pollinating insects and essential for many fruit crops. Larger creatures, such as frogs and toads, are valuable, too, in controlling slugs. By minimizing the number of pesticides we use, we can encourage these beneficial creatures and move toward holding pests in check with natural means.

Ladybugs eat aphids and scale insects.

Praying mantises are useful for biological pest control.

Lacewing larvae feed on many pests that affect fields and greenhouses.

Bees are integral pollinators for your vegetable garden.

Several different types of biological controls are available from specialty suppliers online or by mail order. Many of these come from much warmer climates, and thus need to be bred in a controlled environment and introduced into the crop on a regular basis. Many biological controls are specific and target just one pest: ladybugs and lacewings will attack aphids and other insect pests; nematodes attack slugs and snails; and bacteria attack caterpillars. Some newer mixes of nematodes are available to control a whole range of pests: carrot root flies, cabbage root flies, leatherjackets, cutworms, onion flies, sciarid, caterpillars, gooseberry sawflies, thrips, and codling moths. Depending on the pest you're combating, you apply the product to the soil or the crop. These products are totally safe for use on edible crops and provide no risk to children, pets, or wildlife.

It should be noted however, that biological controls keep infestations down to acceptable levels rather than wiping them out completely. The purpose is to keep the pest under control so that it does not cause too much damage. The reason the predator will never completely eradicate the pest is that, if it did, it would have nothing to feed on. The following are just a few of the types of purchasable biological controls on the market.

- *Aphidius* is a tiny black insect that lays its eggs into aphids. When the eggs hatch, the resulting larvae feed on the aphid, killing it. These predators need a regular temperature of 64°F (18°C) to survive and work efficiently.
- *Encarsia formosa* is a small parasitic wasp that looks very much like a miniature hoverfly. It controls whitefly by laying its eggs in the whitefly scales (eggs), which then turn black. The resulting larvae eat the contents of the scales before they develop. *Encarsia formosa* requires a temperature of 61°F–68°F (16°–20°C).
- *Phytoseiulus persimilis*, just like its prey, is a small mite. It devours red spider mites by crawling from leaf to leaf. Because it can only crawl, the leaves of the crop must be touching for it to cover a wide enough range. To work properly, *Phytoseiulus persimilis* also requires a temperature of 61°F–68°F (16°–20°C).
- *Cryptolaemus* beetles are relatives of the ladybug, with both the adults and larvae feeding on mealybug eggs and nymphs. The adults lay their eggs directly into the eggs of the mealybugs. They require an average temperature of 68°F (20°C) to work well.
- Nemasys is a microscopic nematode that comes dehydrated in a packet and is brought back to life by adding water. There are three types of nematodes that each work on either vine weevil, daddy longlegs larvae, or chafer grubs. They require a constant soil temperature of no lower than about 41°F (5°C) to work.
- Nemaslug is also a microscopic nematode that kills slugs and snails. It requires the same minimum temperature as Nemasys to work, which means that it is usually effective from April to September.

As you can see by the required temperatures, only the latter two predators can be used outside. All of these predators need to be reintroduced on a regular basis in order to keep any pests under control.

# Organic Products for Fighting Pests and Diseases

There are only a small number of pesticides that an organic gardener is permitted to use to control pests and diseases. It is therefore vital not to let problems get out of control and to spray at the first sign of a problem; if you are vigilant enough, you can keep any problem to a minimum. Remember, though, that you should use spraying as a last resort in your productive organic garden because some pesticides will also kill beneficial insects.

*Chrysanthemum cinerariaefolium* are the natural producers of pyrethrum.

**Pyrethrum**—Pyrethrum is an insecticide made from parts of plants, in this case, the flowers of *Chrysanthemum cinerariaefolium*. It kills pests only if it comes into contact with them. The insecticides that contain pyrethrum do not have as long of a toxic period as some other insecticides, but they will kill aphids, small caterpillars, ants, and flea beetles. Vegetables and fruits can be harvested a day after spraying with pyrethrum because of its rapid rate of breakdown. This insecticide is also poisonous to fish and kills a wide variety of beneficial insects, including ladybugs. Bees are surprisingly unaffected, however.

**Organic slug pellets**—These are formed of ferric phosphate and are only harmful to mollusks; therefore, they will not harm wildlife, pets, or children unless eaten in very large quantities. The pellets are blue, which is generally a warning color to wildlife, and will break down into iron and phosphates as they pass into the soil, adding goodness to your plants.

**Insecticidal soap**—This insecticide is made from the potassium salts of fatty acids and kills pests on contact. It breaks down very quickly after application, so can be used up to the day of harvest. The product works by breaking down the pests' protective coating and works well on soft-bodied pests, such as aphids, red spider mites,

caterpillars, thrips, whitefly, and mealybugs. It does not seem to affect most beneficial predatory insects except for the introduced greenhouse predators, such as *Aphidius* and *Encarsia formosa*.

**Horticultural soap ("soft soap")**—Although made from vegetable constituents, soft soap has very similar attributes to insecticidal soap and can also be used up to the day of harvest. It will kill aphids, scale insects, red spider mites, mealybugs, and whitefly it comes into contact with.

**Diatomaceous earth**—Apart from boiling water and pyrethrum, this is the only effective way of dealing with ants. This insecticide comes in powder form and absorbs the protective coating of the ants, causing them to die.

**Canola oil**—Colza (rapeseed) is becoming a common agricultural crop, and oil extracted from the seed makes an insecticide that will kill aphids, thrips, scale insects, red spider mites, and whitefly.

**Sulfur**—Sulfur is used to control powdery mildew on fruit flowers and vegetables both outside and in the greenhouse. Note, however, that certain fruits are susceptible to sulfur.

**Skim milk**—This works very well against rose black spot because it coats the leaf and prevents the spores from attaching themselves to the surface. It is a preventative method, not a cure. Therefore, you should begin application as soon as you notice the first signs of the disease. It will stay active for a few weeks but should be reapplied after rain. It is important to use only skim milk because the more fat in the milk, the less effective this method will be. You can use a mixture of equal parts milk and water.

**Potassium bicarbonate**—When used as a control, not as a preventative, potassium bicarbonate works well against rose black spot as well as both powdery and downy mildew on cucurbits, roses, and fruits.

# The Future of Organic Options

Scientists are making huge strides in understanding life processes in the soil, the organisms that inhabit it, and what causes the outbreaks of pathogens that trigger plant diseases. Some of their discoveries are astonishing in their potential. Unfortunately, new organic products developed as a result of these discoveries are often slow to reach the home gardener, mostly because of the expense involved in funding their research, development, and marketing. Here are some of the things in the pipeline.

With the aid of electron microscopes, scientists are identifying and naming even more of the thousands of species of microorganisms in soil. They are gaining a better understanding of their functions, how they interact with other micro and macroorganisms, and how to propagate beneficial species and apply them to garden soils. A few universities are evaluating simple, "bland" compounds, such as diluted bleach, for controlling foliar diseases. But don't try using bleach in your garden without following qualified instructions for dilution and safe application.

**Disease-fighting organisms**. BioWorks, Inc., is one of the companies that is developing and marketing biological fungicides. Their products, which include Rootshield and Plantshield HC, contain beneficial fungi and bacteria that control plant diseases by "eating" harmful pythium, rhizoctonia, and fusarium pathogens. Because they are living organisms, these products are perishable and should be used soon after purchase.

The squash vine borers that killed this plant, as well as squash bugs, can be controlled by organic materials.

A praying mantis egg case will soon hatch beneficial garden insects.

**Simple, relatively safe fungicides**. Bioworks, Inc., also markets Milstop, which is an organic fungicide made from potassium bicarbonate, a benign compound. It kills the spores of powdery mildew, black spot of roses, and numerous other pathogens on contact by pulling water out of them. Early tests indicate that Milstop is harmless to many beneficial insects.

**Fatty acid herbicides.** Monterey Lawn and Garden Products, Inc., makes an herbicidal soap concentrate. Diluted as directed and sprayed on weeds, it kills all but the toughest kinds within four hours. It is made from a naturally occurring organic material. This and other organic items are available through large, independent garden centers.

## ATTRACTING BIRDS AND GOOD BUGS

Birds devour the bugs that picking and squashing miss. To attract them to the garden, provide them with plenty of water for drinking and bathing. A row of conifers gives them a place to nest, roost, and hide from neighborhood cats. As an added incentive, you can scatter birdseed on the ground and keep hanging feeders full.

You can also get a big assist in bug control from praying mantises. To ensure their protection during the growing season, collect their egg cases from the shrubs and trees in winter and early spring, and then place them throughout the garden. When the eggs hatch, hundreds of tiny mantises will patrol your garden, eating aphids and flea beetles off the vegetables.

Another helpful insect in the garden is the braconid wasp, which lays its eggs inside the tomato hornworm. So, when you spy a fat, green worm covered with hundreds of tiny white cocoons, let it be. The cocoons are feeding off the worm, which eventually dies. These cocoons hatch and become wasps. As the wasps multiply, you'll see fewer and fewer hornworms in your garden.

Green cabbageworms feed voraciously on the leaves of vegetables in the Brassica family, which includes cabbage, broccoli, Brussels sprouts, cauliflower, kale, and collards. One of the best ways to prevent them from devouring your crops is to cover the young plants with Agronet, a floating row cover made from porous plastic. This prevents the white cabbage butterfly from laying its eggs. If you don't want to use this covering, check your plants daily, and handpick the worms.

—Walter Chandoha

This potato beetle is about to be plucked and dispatched in kerosene.

Braconid wasps lay their eggs inside tomato hornworms, protecting your plants and lowering the hornworm population.

The West Coast is a bit further along than the rest of the country in the availability of organically approved pest controls, especially beneficial insects and predatory microorganisms. Thankfully, most producers and distributors of these products invest a lot of money in research and development and are sure of the safety and efficacy of their products before they put them on the market.

**Simple, relatively safe snail and slug bait.** Monterey Lawn and Garden Products, Inc., manufactures Sluggo, which combines iron phosphate with a bait that attracts slugs and snails. It is safe to use around pets and wildlife and is replacing metaldehyde-based slug and snail baits, which can be harmful to pets.

**Fermentation products.** Monterey Garden Insect Spray can replace synthetic sprays that can be toxic to humans and pets. Its active ingredient is Spinosad, a broad-spectrum insecticide made by fermenting certain soil microbes. Trials have proved that Spinosad can control caterpillars, leaf miners, thrips, borers, and more.

**Botanical and biological insecticides.** Neem oil, which is pressed from the seeds of a tree that is indigenous to India, has been used to repel insects in North America for several years. It has been proved effective against numerous species of insects and mites, as well as certain foliar diseases. According to the Environmental Protection Agency, neem oil works by deterring the normal life cycle of certain insects, including feeding, molting, mating, and egg laying.

**Beneficial insects for controlling aphids.** We are now seeing beneficial insects, such as ladybugs and praying mantises, offered for home garden use. Several species are already being multiplied and sold to commercial vegetable growers and greenhouse operators. However, the greatest promise may be with predatory nematodes, which are microscopic, worm-like organisms that have an insatiable appetite for targeted pathogens. Several companies operate insectaries for producing beneficial insects and nematodes. Most of these specialists market primarily to organic farmers and fruit-tree orchards and secondarily to organic home gardeners.

# Guidelines for Spraying

It is very important, whether spraying more potent products or fairly nontoxic products, to always follow the same procedure. Never use the product for any plant other than those specified on the label because some crops may be damaged by some of the products. If in doubt, contact the manufacturer or the store or site through which it was purchased.

When mixing and applying the product, it is worth being as protected as possible. Gloves are crucial, as your hands are most likely to become contaminated, and it's very easy to unconsciously rub your lips, face, or other parts of your body. Not only do gloves protect your hands, but they also make your hands more noticeable, so you are less likely to touch your face, rub your eyes, etc., with them on. Another very important part of the body that needs protecting is the eyes. Goggles are the easiest protective eyewear to obtain, and they are fairly inexpensive.

It is always very difficult to imagine what damage is being done when the perpetrator is not usually visible, with fine sprays being no exception. If you wear nothing else, at least use a dust mask. Dust masks are easily

No matter what type of sprayer you use, be careful to protect yourself from inhaling any fine particles.

purchased from home-improvement and DIY stores at a low cost, and they help prevent you from inhaling a lot of the spray. The best piece of equipment to wear to prevent all spray from being inhaled is a respirator mask, which is also available at DIY stores for reasonable costs. If possible, wear waterproof jackets and trousers to protect your clothing, preventing it from getting contaminated. If these aren't available, change immediately after spraying, and put your clothing straight into the washing machine.

Keep in mind that spraying is much better for the plants themselves if it's carried out early or late in the day. At each end of the day, there is little strength in the sun's rays, whereas spraying in the part of the day when the sun is at its strongest will invariably cause vegetable leaves to be scorched, potentially reducing the amount of crop harvested. Also, beneficial insects are generally at their most active during the warmer parts of the day. Spraying with chemicals that kill any insect they come into contact with is best carried out when minimal damage will be done to the insects you want to encourage.

The actual spraying equipment available varies enormously, from small handheld products to much larger motorized sprayers. Never spray with any equipment that is not in perfect working order because it may be detrimental both to you and to the crop being sprayed. For obvious reasons, never spray when it is windy because the spray will be blown onto areas where it is not required and where it may cause damage, and always try to allow at least an hour for the spray to dry before applying water. Most insecticides and fungicides deteriorate once mixed and will become ineffective if left to stand for weeks, so try to mix only what is required; any leftover spray will be wasted and can harm the environment if poured away. Keep sprays only in the containers they came in, and keep these in a locked container or at least on a high shelf out of reach of people who may be unaware of their danger.

When spraying, the most important factor to remember is that organic pesticides work on contact. Therefore, ensuring a good covering of the affected vegetables, fruits, or herbs, by spraying to give a total coverage of the upper surface of the leaves as well as the undersides of the leaves, is the only way to eradicate the pest. But remember, there is no point spraying beyond the point of "run-off," when the spray begins dripping off the end of the leaves.

# Common Pests and Controls

Pests are small creatures that live in or on plants, eating them for food. Some may be very obvious, such as slugs and snails. Other pests include greenfly and, smaller still, there are microscopic pests, such as eelworm, which live within the plants but still have devastating effects. Some pests carry other diseases, for example greenfly on their own are a relatively harmless pest, but the viruses they spread can be extremely serious.

## Slugs and Snails

Probably the most hated of all pests because of the devastating damage they do, slugs and snails are most active in wet weather and feed at night.

**Control**—Do NOT use blue slug pellets containing metaldehyde. This material is highly toxic to children, pets, and wildlife, and has been banned in many places. Instead, use ferric phosphate pellets. These include iron, which kills slugs and snails, and they break down into basic soil nutrients. Scatter the pellets sparingly.

Slugs can eat a lot very quickly.

Aphids are tiny but can do a ton of damage and spread viruses.

Red spider mites are so small they often go unnoticed until you have an infestation, like this one on a tomato plant.

Alternatively, spread sharp sand or crushed eggshells around plants, set up beer traps to drown slugs, or collect them at night by torchlight. Biological control in the form of nematode worms or encouraging frogs and toads to move into your garden can also be used.

## Aphids

These include greenfly, blackfly, and also woolly aphid. Aphids are small, often winged insects up to about ¼" (6mm) in size that are usually found on the undersides of leaves and around young growths. They suck the sap out of a plant, which weakens it and can turn the leaves yellow. They leave a sticky excrement that turns black and is called sooty mold. Aphids spread viruses.

**Control**—Contact insecticides, such as soft soap products, will have an immediate effect. Winter washes can be used to control the eggs of overwintering aphids on fruit trees. Various biological controls are available.

## Red Spider Mite

This is a pest that is often not noticed until there is a massive infestation. Red spider mites can affect garden plants, such as fruit trees, but they are more commonly seen on greenhouse plants, such as cucumbers, melons, or peppers. These are tiny creatures and so visible only as a fine, dust-like coating underneath leaves. For this reason, they are often missed until the attack is well established and the leaves show a dull yellow mottling, become brown and brittle, and drop. With a bad attack, a fine mesh like a spider's web is formed around plant tips.

**Control**—Under glass, the pest can be deterred by maintaining a damp atmosphere, but this will not control an established infestation. Most readily available pesticides will not control red spider mite and a specific acaricide must be obtained. Alternatively, biological control by means of the predator Phytoseiulus is very successful.

## Whitefly

Whitefly is commonly found on glasshouse plants, such as tomatoes and cucumbers, but also outside on crops, such as brassicas. The creature itself is like a tiny white moth, and they fly off in large numbers when disturbed. They feed by sucking the sap from plants, living on the undersides of the leaf. They also leave behind sticky honeydew and sooty mold. They breed rapidly, so numbers and damage can escalate fast.

Whiteflies live on the undersides of plant leaves.

**Control**—Contact insecticides, such as soft soap, are reasonably effective, as are some of the synthetic pyrethroids. The trick with whitefly is to spray frequently at about four-day intervals, rotating the chemical used. Under glass, the parasite Encarsia is very effective, particularly on individual vegetables, such as tomatoes or cucumbers. It may have to be reintroduced several times in a season.

## Flea Beetles

These are tiny jumping creatures that eat holes in vegetables, particularly in seedlings of members of the Brassica family, including radishes and turnips.

Flea beetles can do a lot of damage to cabbage leaves.

**Control**—One of the easiest control measures is to drag a yellow sticky trap through the rows. The flea beetles jump and get trapped.

## Leaf Miner

This is a pest that lives inside the leaf and creates a distinct pattern, leaving twisting, whitish tunnels as it moves through the leaf, feeding. With a bad attack, the tunnels will end up linked together into large, blister-like patches that turn yellow and brown. In the vegetable garden, they can be found on celery, tomatoes, and mint.

**Control**—This is difficult, as the pest is inside the leaf and many pesticides will not control it. When there is relatively little damage, either destroy the individual creatures with your thumbnail or pick off the infected leaves. Removing too many leaves, however, will slow down the plant's growth.

## Vine Weevil

This pest can be found on a wide range of plants and can sometimes be brought in with new plants from a garden center. The adult vine weevil is a grayish beetle that eats notches out of leaves. It disfigures plants but rarely causes major damage. The larva, which is the juvenile stage, is a small white grub, up to ½" (1.3cm) long with a brown head. This causes major damage, as it lives on the roots of plants,

Leaf miners are small, but the damage they cause is easy to spot.

The caterpillars of the cabbage white butterfly are some of the more troublesome caterpillars you'll encounter in the garden.

The most dangerous vine weevil stage is the larva. This grub can destroy plant roots.

which wilt and eventually die. Outside, it particularly attacks strawberries, raspberries, and black currants.

**Control**—If vine weevil is suspected in potted plants, the simplest treatment is to tip it out and examine the roots. If infected, wash the roots thoroughly, removing the infected compost and grubs. Repot in fresh compost and keep in a damp atmosphere until re-established. Surprisingly, plants will often recover from such drastic treatment. With a more widespread problem outdoors, it is possible to use a chemical root drench of Armillatox. Biological controls are not so effective against this pest outdoors.

## Caterpillars

These come in a whole host of sizes and colors, often camouflaged to hide in the plants they are feeding on. Cabbage white caterpillars are common on brassica crops. Tortrix and winter moth are pests of fruit trees. The damage occurs in the summer. Many others may be a problem.

**Control**—On a small scale, hand picking is both effective and very safe. Contact insecticides can be used. A biological control based on the bacteria Bacillus is also available for use on brassicas. Winter washes are valuable for controlling the overwintering eggs on fruit trees. Winter moth caterpillars can be controlled with grease bands applied to the trunk in mid-autumn. These trap the wingless female moth as she climbs from the ground into the tree to lay eggs, which will ultimately become caterpillars.

# Common Diseases and Controls

These are distinct from pests in that they are caused by another organism, such as a fungus, bacteria, or virus. Diseases may attack any part of the plant, including the root system. Sometimes the effects may be clearly visible as a mold on the leaf surface or a distortion of the overall plant, whereas other diseases may be inside the plant and only show as the plant's health declines.

The control of diseases is slightly different from the control of pests in that many diseases, such as mildew or botrytis, are very difficult to eradicate once they are established on a plant. The emphasis is therefore on prevention. Initially, it is good practice to modify the conditions where your plants are growing to deter diseases. However, with some plants and situations where diseases are particularly likely to occur, some gardeners will choose to use a preventative spray of a fungicide to protect the plant. For example, this is often done with seedlings in a greenhouse to protect them from damping-off disease. The spray or drench will need to be repeated at intervals to maintain the protection.

## Powdery Mildew

Many plants suffer from this, particularly apples and peas. It is immediately visible as a white mealy deposit over leaves and sometimes flowers or fruits. Strangely, while it is most prevalent on plants in dry conditions, it spreads from plant to plant in damp weather and by means of water splashes. So, a rainy spell followed by dry weather is an ideal set of conditions for a mildew outbreak.

**Control**—Do not let susceptible plants go short of water. With important crops, use a protective fungicide spray as a routine precaution. Vary the fungicides to avoid any resistance developing.

## Rusts

There are many different types of rust that affect different plants. Rust usually appears as bright orange or brown patches on the undersides of leaves, with a yellow spot showing on the upper surface. Rusts are not particularly common on vegetables but may appear on asparagus, tomatoes, and beans. A particular type of rust may infect apples.

**Control**—Affected leaves can be removed and burned, or a protective fungicide spray used if susceptible plants are being grown.

Powdery mildew spreads as a white mealy layer usually over a plant's leaves.

Rusts aren't common on vegetables, but fava beans are among the crops that might be affected.

## Botrytis (Gray Mold)

This fungal infection can attack almost any plant, although soft, young plants are most likely to succumb. It is also most prevalent under poor conditions, such as a cool greenhouse early in the year when the light is poor, and growth is weak. It shows as a gray, fuzzy mold on leaves, shoots, or in the growing points of plants. The tissues underneath the mold rapidly go mushy and rot.

**Control**—Avoidance is, as always, best, which in this instance means trying to grow strong, healthy plants. In greenhouses, good ventilation and air circulation helps. There are some products that can be used to protect in advance of an attack. Apply them to susceptible seedlings and crops, such as glasshouse lettuce, in winter.

## Armillaria

Also known as honey fungus due to the honey-colored toadstools that are eventually produced, this devastating disease attacks fruit trees and woody plants, such as soft fruit bushes. Initially it will show as a general yellowness of the leaves, followed by wilting. Quite quickly the plant will start to die, and large trees can go from appearing healthy to being dead within a single season.

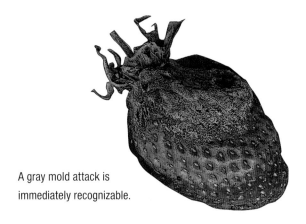

A gray mold attack is immediately recognizable.

The presence of this disease can be confirmed in two ways. Scrape the bark near ground level and check for the presence of a white mold that smells of mushrooms. Alternatively, dig down to the root system and look to see if there are any black, thread-like growths. These give the disease the alternative name "boot-lace fungus." It easily spreads from plant to plant through the soil, so on privet hedges, for example, which are particularly susceptible, you can see the disease working its way down the row.

**Control**—Initially, infected plants should be dug up and burned. You can use a soil drench of Armillatox to prevent further spread, especially if there are other

Armillaria affects fruit trees and woody plants via the roots.

valuable trees or bushes nearby. Soil infected with armillaria can only be used for nonwoody plants—vegetables are not susceptible. Replacement of the soil is possible, but large quantities will usually have to be dug out, and it is difficult to be certain that all the fungus has been removed.

## Viruses

A wide variety of plants are attacked by viral diseases, although they are less likely on annual plants, such as fast-growing vegetables, as viruses are less commonly seed transmitted. Both tomatoes and cucumbers, however, can suffer from viruses. They cause a wide variety of symptoms, which include distortion of leaves or flowers, spotting, mosaic patterns or streaking, and reduction in vigor or cropping potential. Viruses rarely kill plants completely, but they can so distort or weaken a plant that it is no longer productive. Viruses in fruit plantations, such as the reversion virus of black currants, are more serious because the only real treatment is to destroy the crop and start again.

**Control**—Viruses are almost impossible to control. In general garden terms, if a plant has acquired a virus, it is infected for life. This is not entirely true since there are sophisticated techniques by which specialist nurseries can produce virus-free stock under laboratory conditions. So, for example, you may see virus-free stock of old favorites, such as the 'Royal Sovereign' strawberry, offered for sale. This is a rare exception, however.

In general, virus-infected plants should be dug up and destroyed. Viruses are usually spread by sap-sucking insects, such as aphids, so these should be controlled to avoid the spread of the virus. Viruses can also be passed from plant to plant on a propagating knife. So, where plants are propagated by cuttings, the knife or secateurs should ideally be sterilized between cuts, by passing through a flame or with a horticultural disinfectant.

One pest that produces similar symptoms to virus is eelworm. These are tiny, microscopic worms that live inside the leaves and cause distortion. They may appear on onions, peas, beans, cucumber, tomato, salad crops, and soft fruits—especially strawberries. They are a particular problem for potatoes, where the swollen bodies of the egg-laden females can be seen as cysts on the roots.

# Dealing with Garden Critters

For any gardener who has experienced the devastating effects of a rabbit in their garden, chicken wire (also known as poultry netting) is an absolute must. Rabbits will not only devastate vegetables and herbs, but they also will strip the bark from fruit trees. It is important to use netting with 1" (2.5cm) holes and a width of 48" (121.9cm). Stretch strong galvanized wire between round fence posts at a height of 36" (91.4cm). Dig a trench 4" (10.2cm) deep and 8" (20.3cm) wide on the outside of the posts to carry the underground part of the netting, placing the soil on the nonproductive side of the trench. Attach the netting to the posts using construction staples, and attach the top of the fence to some of the supporting wire using thin galvanized wire. Lay the wire netting across the bottom of the trench and cover with 4" (10.2cm) of the soil that you removed.

If you follow these instructions to install chicken wire around the entire area to be protected, the crops will be completely safe from attacks by rabbits. When rabbits approach the fence, because it is a barrier, their instinct will be to dig straight down. When they do this, the wire that extends 8" (20.3cm) will stop them again, and they will hop away. Rabbits will jump over a 36" (91.4cm) fence if they are being chased, but they will not do so when approaching a fence in a normal, stress-free situation.

In a productive garden, deer can be just as devastating as rabbits. Deer are not a problem in some suburban developments, but in other neighborhoods, they can wreak havoc on the landscape. Wild animals tend to follow parkland, creeks, and ravines into housing areas. They tend

## SMART GARDENER

Nonvenomous snakes can keep rodents under control in your vegetable garden. The larger nonvenomous snakes help keep voles, moles, and field mice under control, and they also eat insects. To avoid being bitten, use a hoe handle to guide any snakes out of high-traffic areas in your garden or out of it completely.

## HAIRY DEER DETERRENT

Unless you erect an 8-foot-tall (2.4m) fence, it can be difficult to keep deer away from tempting vegetables. One solution worth trying is hanging balls made of human hair wrapped in cheesecloth around the plot to scare them away.

to avoid yards where they have to cross streets or highways to gain access. Dogs can also be a deterrent, but not always. Many gardeners who are troubled by deer live in rural areas or areas that border countryside, which means that they also have the potential for rabbit damage. It is therefore necessary to consider deer protection only above the height of the rabbit fencing that is already in place.

Where deer are a problem, the right type of fence is the realistic solution. Unlike rabbits, deer can jump up to 6' (1.8m) high in their normal activity, particularly if there is a juicy crop to be nibbled. A determined buck can clear a 6' (1.8m) fence easily, and with a running start, an 8' (2.4m) fence. To protect against deer, erect 8' (2.4m) posts to which you can attach the rabbit fencing, as well as the galvanized wire used to fend off deer. Knock the posts about 24" (61cm) into the ground, leaving at least 6' (1.8m) sticking out of the ground. Stretch three strands of strong galvanized wire above the

rabbit fencing, and attach it using construction nails at 12" (30.5cm) intervals up the posts. It will be possible for some larger deer to leap this height, but only when being chased. You can also plant shrubs around the outside of your fences, so deer will not be able to get close enough to see what is inside and, since they're cautious by nature, will not risk jumping over.

Another effective barrier is a picket fence topped by tall pieces of electrical conduit strapped to posts, with taut wire running at 6' and 8' (1.8 and 2.4m) levels. Some gardeners prefer shorter posts with electrified wires at 6", 12", and 48" (15.2, 30.5, and 121.9cm) levels. Farm supply stores are among the best sources of information on electrified fences to keep out deer, but you should also check the internet and your State Extension Service.

Eight-foot-high, plastic-net deer fences are cosmetically acceptable and do a good job of keeping deer out. Even when deer are not a problem, gardeners may still deal with rabbits, groundhogs, squirrels, and, in the South, armadillos. As mentioned, rabbits can be kept out of the garden with chicken-wire barriers, but groundhogs and squirrels can climb and are best controlled by electrified fencing. Groundhogs are vigorous diggers, as are armadillos. You'll need to sink chicken-wire barriers at least 1' (30.5cm) into the ground to discourage them. As a last resort, use a humane trap, and ask your wildlife agent where to relocate the animals.

## Mole Traps

The only way to deal successfully with a mole problem is to trap the moles. When used correctly, mole traps will execute a quick kill, preventing the moles from suffering. You set the traps so that they are part of an active tunnel that runs between two molehills. Because moles have a very sensitive sense of smell, you must wear gloves when setting the traps; otherwise, they will detect a foreign smell and not use that particular tunnel.

## Mouse and Rat Traps

There are two types of traps for catching these rodent pests. The humane traps are wire cages that have bait inside. The rodent enters to eat the bait and cannot exit. It can then be released into an area where it will do no harm to the crops. The other type of trap is one that works on a highly tensioned spring that kills the rodent as it attempts to eat the bait. Neither of these rodents is of any benefit in the productive garden, and they can cause a lot of damage to seeds, growing vegetables, and stored produce.

## Scarecrows

People have long used scarecrows to scare birds away from freshly sown seed and growing vegetables. Stationary scarecrows are of no real use because birds quickly realize that they are not angry gardeners ready to kill them and will happily roost on the outstretched arms. Scarecrows that swivel in the wind seem to be much more effective.

## Shiny Discs

Old CDs, DVDs, and other shiny discs make excellent deterrents to birds. You can hang them on strings from branches in fruit orchards, and you can place them on a stick stuck in the ground at an angle near vegetables. It is important that the discs be able to spin because it is the changing reflection of light that scares away the birds.

# Combating Weeds

Weeds are bad news. They make your garden look untidy, and more importantly, they compete with your plants for light, space, food, and water. They can also harbor pests and diseases that will attack your vegetables.

Weeds are everywhere. Hundreds of weed seeds already lie dormant deep in the soil, gradually working their way up near the soil's surface where they can germinate. Seeds float in on the breeze from adjoining yards, or they hitch a ride on the dirt that clings to the soles of your shoes. Fresh weed seeds and seedlings arrive with every new plant you bring into your vegetable garden. You can't avoid them—but you can keep them under control.

Dealing with weeds should not be backbreaking or time-consuming work. It's only when you let them get out of control that they become a real problem. Do what you

Scarecrows are most effective if you build them to swivel in the wind.

The reflection of light from a shiny disc scares birds away from crops.

> ### TIME-SAVER
> While hot, dry weather is the best time for hoeing since severed weed tops will shrivel and die quickly, hand weeding is quicker and easier when the soil is moist.

can to prevent weeds from occurring in the first place, then take a few moments each day to deal with the stragglers. Little and often is the key to keeping weeds at bay.

## Prevention Is Best

Keep down the number of weeds by following a few basic rules from the very beginning.

**Start with clear soil.** When preparing the ground for a new vegetable garden, try to remove all the roots and stems of perennial weeds that you come across. Let freshly dug soil lie empty for a couple of weeks. A flush of weeds will crop up from seeds that have been brought near the surface with the digging. Use a hoe to remove them before you start sowing and planting.

**Don't let weeds flower.** "One year's seeding, seven years' weeding," as the saying goes. Remove weeds before they have a chance to flower, and you will prevent hundreds more weed seeds from being sprinkled over your soil to plague you in the years to come.

**Cover bare soil.** Bare soil is an open invitation to weeds. Use a mulch to cover the soil surface. There are plenty of packaged products available based on materials, such as shredded bark and cocoa hulls, or you can use well-rotted compost from your compost pile, if you have one.

**Try black plastic.** Spread sheets of black plastic over a whole area before planting. Although not

Use a sharp knife to cut X-shaped slits through black plastic to create planting holes.

## CLEANING WEEDY GROUND WITH POTATOES

If you have moved onto a property where the garden has been neglected, the best way to get this type of ground under control and clean for growing vegetables, herbs, and fruits is to grow vegetables—more precisely, potatoes. This crop is an excellent ground "cleaner" due to the amount of soil cultivation the crop requires before planting and while the time the crop is in the ground and the soil coverage of the potato tops (stems).

You will need to clear the ground of weeds by digging out the perennial weeds and hoeing off the annual ones. Once the weed tops have been cleared, the soil can be prepared by digging and adding organic matter. The potatoes are then planted into furrows or planted using a trowel. Once they are planted, it is a good idea to grow a quick catch vegetable between the rows, such as radishes, scallions, or lettuce transplanted from seed trays (flats) with individual cells. Once these vegetables have been harvested, the potato tops will require earthing up. This is the process of drawing up soil from between the rows of potatoes so that the new tops are almost completely covered with soil. This will keep the developing potatoes covered with soil and not exposed to any light. If the potatoes do push out of the ground into the light, they will turn green and become inedible.

It may be necessary to earth up, or hill, the potato tops three times. As the tops fill out, they cover the ground, excluding light, making the conditions beneath this foliage unattractive to growing weeds. It is also wise to sheet-mulch between the rows, which will not only conserve vital moisture for the crop but also prevent weed growth. At the end of the growing season, the soil is again cultivated to harvest the main-crop potatoes, clearing any weeds that may have grown. It is then too late for weeds to germinate and grow successfully before the winter sets in. This is a great organic method for clearing ground, with the added bonus of food at the end of it.

When weeds appear too close to plants for hoeing, hand weeding is the best method for removing them.

particularly attractive, the plastic is perfect for preventing weed growth.

**Target food and water application.** Apply water and fertilizers directly to the plants for which they are intended, instead of spreading them over a larger area where weeds can benefit from them, too. A soaker hose is ideal for precision watering of rows of vegetables. Apply plant foods in a narrow band alongside the plant row instead of spreading them over the whole bed.

## Dealing with the Enemy

All weeds in the productive area are a problem. Not only do they use vital water required by the crops, but they remove essential nutrients from the soil as well. If left unchecked, weeds will cause a reduced harvest for these reasons. In addition, with vegetables and herbs, they may smother crops, at best preventing them from growing, or at worst, killing them completely.

One of the best ways of eliminating weeds from a productive area before crops are grown is to use the stale seedbed method described on page 262. The easiest way to control weeds in orchards of apples, pears, cherries,

The long handle on a hoe lets you remove the weeds without having to bend down, taking the strain off your back.

Hoeing between rows is hard, but effective, work.

or plums is to cover the bare soil with grass. This may prevent a small amount of water and nutrients from being available to the trees, but for the amateur gardener it has a minimal effect on the subsequent crops and makes controlling weeds much easier. The reason it is excellent as weed control is because the grass will need to be regularly mowed, which not only cuts the tops of the grass blades but also cuts down any weeds. The competition from the grass also makes it harder for weeds to get a firm hold.

This method is not really feasible in vegetable, herb, and soft fruit areas because the crops will not remain in exactly the same places each year. There are four basic methods of weed control in this situation: mulching, hoeing, closer plant spacing, and green manures. Mulching in the vegetable areas has to be short term because even the longest crops will generally not be in the ground for more than eight to nine months. You should therefore look to use materials that can be dug into the soil as a soil improver once the crop has been harvested, like compost, green compost, well-rotted horse or cow manure, grass clippings, and cardboard. Permanent or longer-term herb and soft fruit crops can be mulched with the full range of mulches.

If mulching is not an option, hoeing between the crops works well. Keep a well-sharpened hoe on hand near your vegetables, and deal with weed seedlings as soon as they appear. Don't try to dig them up—slide the hoe along the ground to slice off the top growth. Where weeds are growing right up against plants, carefully weed by hand to avoid accidents with the hoe. Draw hoes, Dutch hoes, onion hoes, or wheeled hoes can be used, with the latter only suitable for vegetables grown in rows. Once the weeds have been hoed off, they are left on the soil surface to dry out before being taken to the compost bin. Remember to hoe walking backward, so that you do not replant the hoed weeds by pushing them back into the soil with your feet.

When using the bed system, weeds are kept at bay by planting the vegetables closer together so that they cover the ground better. This inhibits water and vital light getting to the weed seed, preventing them from germinating and growing. The closer spacing also helps to minimize water evaporation from the soil surface.

Hand weeding is not an arduous job if it is done often, while the weeds are tiny. In a small garden, it should only take a few minutes each day. While a few weeds will pop up in mulching material, such as compost or bark, the loose nature of the material makes it easy to pull them.

Chemical weed killers are rarely necessary in a small garden, but products such as glyphosate can be useful in clearing a truly weed-infested plot when starting from scratch. There are several weed-killing products based on natural ingredients, such as citrus oils and fatty acids. However, if it kills weeds, it will kill your vegetable plants, too, so you need to be careful when applying herbicide sprays.

# Using Covers

A little extra protection for the soil and your plants can help your crops reach harvest time more quickly and securely. There are several easy ways to protect vegetables from the extremes of Mother Nature.

## Protecting the Soil

In early spring, sowing and planting can be held up because the soil conditions are not right, even if the weather itself is fine. While a light, crumbly soil warms up early, enabling you to get going as soon as the weather allows, heavy clay soil takes a long time to warm up and dry out. The first step is to improve drainage and soil texture by working in organic matter.

However, placing a cover over your sowing and planting area will also help the soil to warm quickly. You can use glass cloches, which act like mini greenhouses to trap the sun's heat, but their main warming effect comes from keeping the cooling rain off the soil. Using a sheet of black plastic will also absorb the sun's heat, warming the soil and keeping it dry.

## Protecting the Plants

Once you sow your seeds or plant young plants in the ground, you can encourage them to grow more quickly by giving them protection from the weather. You will need to take your garden conditions into account when deciding whether it's worth giving plants extra protection. In a sheltered, warm, and sunny yard, they will grow well without additional help. However, if they are in an open spot exposed to cold winds in a chilly spring, it's a different matter.

Protection is often necessary only when the plants are getting established early in the season, but a physical barrier is also sometimes the only way to keep your vegetables completely pest- and disease-free. At the other end of the year, it will also help to keep tender plants, such as tomatoes, producing a crop longer into the cooler fall days. There are several different ways of providing that little extra help for your plants. Some of the techniques used involve everyday materials, while others require a special purchase, but all the methods are cheap and easy to employ.

---

### RAISED BED PROTECTION

You can buy raised bed kits complete with covers, providing you with a metal frame that fits neatly over the bed and a fine mesh cover to slip over the frame. The sides of the mesh cover can be opened for access, and there is plenty of headroom for the vegetables, which will be protected from both adverse weather and pests.

---

**Cloches and tunnels:** Cloches, which are also sometimes called "hot caps," are plant covers originally made from glass (like bell jars), but today plastic is more popular. While plastic is not as efficient at trapping heat, it is lighter and easier to move than glass, and much less fragile. Larger cloches may be semicircular or an A-frame or barn shape. They are usually about 2' (61cm) long so that they can be moved from plant to plant or placed end to end to form a continuous row.

Tunnels consist of wire hoops set over the row of plants to be protected, covered with a thin polyethylene plastic sheet. Sometimes sheets of other materials are used. The material used often depends on their desired function. Gardeners often use plastic-covered cloches over early crops that require protection from the weather. If the plastic is held down in a way that prevents pests from getting underneath it, it will both provide a barrier that flying pests cannot penetrate and protect the vegetable from the cold weather.

If you are erecting a cloche over a crop strictly for the purpose of protecting that vegetable from pests, plastic may not be the best covering material, particularly as the season extends and the weather warms. With the buildup of potentially damaging heat under the cloche, the answer is either to ventilate—which creates an obvious entry point for flying pests—or to cover the cloche with a breathable barrier. Either garden fabric or enviromesh will prevent flying pests from attacking the crop while allowing water and air to pass through freely so that the plants will not overheat in hot weather.

**Floating row covers:** This material, also called garden fabric, comes in different types. It's used primarily to protect vegetables against frost, but it also creates an excellent barrier against flying pests. Some are so light that you can lay them directly over the plants without

Plastic cloches come in many shapes and forms, such as this semicircular example with ventilation openings. You can remove them during the daytime to let plenty of fresh air reach young plants, replacing them at night to provide protection from the cold.

Individual plastic coverings are similar to the soda-bottle cloche concept in the box on page 190.

## QUICK CLOCHE

Make a quick and easy temporary cloche to cover a young plant by cutting off the bottom of a large, plastic beverage bottle. Place the top of the bottle directly over the plant, and remove the screw cap for ventilation during the day. This is a great method for protecting tender plants, such as tomatoes and chilies, when they are first planted outdoors.

Recycled soda-bottle cloches can also be very handy tools to protect plants from flying insects, birds, slugs, and snails. If using the bottle for protection against small flying pests, it is advisable to put a piece of netting, old stocking, or something similar over the hole left by the cap and hold it in place with a rubber band. Be sure to use a breathable material to cover the hole so that the plant inside does not overheat.

Once the plant has grown enough to touch the sides of the bottle, remove the bottle and use it elsewhere. It's important to note that, if you are gardening on a windy site, soda-bottle cloches are probably not the best option for protection because the bottles are lightweight and will blow away in a medium-strength wind.

damaging them. These are made of a lightweight material of woven plastic fabric. Although this looks insubstantial, it can make a surprising difference to plant growth.

Weigh down the corners and edges with stones, or dig them into the soil, to keep the cover from blowing away. Alternatively, stretch them over hoops to form tunnels, or make frames to support them over beds. You can also use a floating row cover over soil in early spring to help it warm up more quickly. However, because it lets rain through, it is not as effective as a solid barrier, such as black plastic sheets.

If you plan to use the fabric to protect a vegetable against subzero temperatures, it needs to lie directly on the crop because the air trapped between the fibers is what provides insulation. If you plan to use the fabric for vegetable protection against flying pests, however, the fabric needs to be above the crop but not necessarily directly on top of the plants.

This material is ideal for protection against the carrot root fly. You can place it over the vegetables when sowing or planting, and leave it in place until either the flies have completed their first life cycle or the vegetable becomes large enough not to be troubled by the carrot fly. The material is also light-, water-, and air-permeable, so you can leave it on or over a vegetable (the only problem is the chance of slight leaf scorch on sunny days where the fabric touches the plant). Although garden fabric is permeable to all of the important elements that a vegetable requires to grow successfully and without hindrance, it provides a completely impenetrable barrier to all flying pests if attached to the ground correctly.

Enviromesh is a type of row cover material that lies over the vegetable to keep all flying pests from getting to and damaging the produce beneath. It is made from plastic and contains thousands of tiny square holes that are small enough to allow the easy passage of water and air but not pests. The material is light and easy to move, and it can lie on any structure placed over the vegetable. Enviromesh is pliable and long-lasting; it will continue to protect against pests for many growing seasons as long as the edges are sealed to the ground.

Even when vegetables and fruits are almost ready for harvesting, a floating row cover will be beneficial because it acts as a barrier to pests.

When held in place properly, plastic covering over a tunnel creates an impenetrable barrier to flying pests.

Carrot plants are protected from carrot flies under an enviromesh cover.

Spots where the leaves touch the netting are vulnerable to cabbage white butterflies.

**Plastic netting:** Green or black plastic netting is less obtrusive, and therefore, more pleasing to the eye than other colors. Netting with ½" (1.3cm) square holes is not penetrable by cabbage white butterflies or birds, particularly pigeons, and thus is ideal for covering and protecting brassica crops. Position the netting above the vegetable so that it is not touching any of the plants. If the netting is allowed to lie on the vegetable, cabbage white butterflies will be able to lay their eggs through it and onto the brassicas. Knock four fence posts into the ground, and support the netting with strong twine stretched around all four posts and across diagonally from corner to corner. There is no harm in leaving the netting on for the life of the crop because the large holes will not allow too much shade to be cast over the plants.

**Cotton string/twine:** If crops such as brassicas or cherries are plagued by birds, you can stretch cotton string or twine between supporting posts or sticks so that the birds cannot fly through the strings and onto the crop. The problem with this method, though, is that birds can easily become trapped in the string, which can badly injure or even eventually kill them.

**Cabbage root fly squares:** The material you use to create this barrier can vary depending on what is available at the time. You can make your own squares because they are very easy to construct, and you can usually use free carpet-padding scraps from local carpeting stores. Cut the padding into 4" (10.2cm) squares. With each square, make a cut from one edge into the center, and then make two smaller cuts at the top of your first cut (to resemble a *Y*). Then place the cut squares over the plants at ground level to prevent attacks.

If your young brassica plants are unprotected, cabbage root fly adults land next to them and lay their eggs where the stems meet the soil. After hatching, the larvae burrow down into the soil and feed on the roots of the brassicas, stunting the plants and badly affecting the crop yield. The carpet-padding squares prevent the adults from laying their eggs next to the plant stems, providing an extremely simple barrier against cabbage root fly attack. Once the plants are more mature, you can remove the squares and use them on the next crop of young brassica plants; the carpet-padding squares will last for at least three years. You can use cardboard instead, but it will deteriorate over the season to a point where it disintegrates and thus cannot be reused.

**Hedges:** Hedges are very useful against the carrot fly, because this pest flies very close to the ground and will not usually fly any higher than 6" (15.2cm). A dense evergreen hedge that is more than 6" (15.2cm) tall will prevent carrot flies from reaching the young and tasty carrots beyond. An excellent hedge for this purpose is box (*Buxus*), which is also very easy to maintain and looks very formal.

**Peach umbrella:** Many peaches and nectarines suffer from peach leaf curl. Although it is unsightly, it rarely causes the trees too much harm. In a severe attack, however, the tree will drop leaves, which affects the final yield of the tree. The spores of this disease are spread by rain, so the best way of controlling it is to keep the rain away from the tree leaves. This is easier on fan-trained specimens than freestanding trees, but you can adapt an umbrella for any type of tree.

An easy but time-consuming method is to attach a sheet of plastic above the fan-trained tree and, every time rain is in the forecast, roll the plastic down to keep the leaves dry; you then roll it up again once the rain has passed. A less labor-intensive method is to construct a semicircular plastic-covered frame above the tree that will act as an umbrella, keeping the majority, if not all, of the rain off the leaves.

Those with expert woodworking skills, however, can construct a frame from ¾" x 1" (1.9 x 2.5cm) lumber as the outer frame and use strong wire for the supporting ribs. Attach the plastic with roof battens and nails. This structure will last many seasons and is not as obtrusive as a plastic sheet.

Carefully planning what to grow and where to grow it is just as important for making your vegetable patch efficient as planning your garden layout and structure. This kind of planning is invaluable for beginners and experienced vegetable growers alike.

The ideal time to plan what to grow is in late winter. Make a realistic list of what you would like to grow. Use a photocopy of your garden layout plan to mark what you plan to grow where—this will help to curb over-ordering and ensures you have space for everything. If it is your first year, leave space in your plan for the permanent plants that will produce year after year. Choose their location carefully and consider the shade that tall plants, such as raspberries, might cast over neighboring beds.

The most efficient way to obtain plants and seeds is by mail order. Seed catalogs and the internet have a wealth of varieties available and solid information on each variety. You can place your order early in the year, and the plants and seeds should arrive at your door in good time to get them in the ground.

### THE BASICS
Make a well-thought-out "what to grow" list early in the year and stick to it. Place orders with online or mail-order nurseries in time for delivery to your door at the right time for planting.

A sturdy box with index cards and a lid is a practical way to keep seed packets tidy.

A vegetable garden notebook and a basic plan of what is going to grow where help the vegetable plot to run efficiently.

## THE BASICS

Keep a simple notebook with lists of plants ordered. Use it to plan your time and keep track of repeat sowing.

If you plan and place a mail order early in the year, young plants, like these leeks, arrive at your door carefully packaged, ready to plant out at just the right time of year.

If you are a busy person, crops that need repeat sowing are easily forgotten, so a simple list of what to sow when is invaluable. This second batch of peas is being sown just a few weeks after the first; as the first batch finishes producing, the second should begin.

Keep records in a vegetable garden notebook. Other than the plants you're ordering, another important list to make is a more-detailed inventory of every variety of any crop you have grown with comments. It is a handy reminder of what has done well, what has tasted particularly good, and, most importantly, what has failed to thrive. While it is always fun to try new varieties, it is good to have the guaranteed bumper plants in your garden that have been successful in the past. You can also use this notebook to record a timetable for repeat sowing of crops to ensure an extended harvest. Also, use it to note any other tasks to be done.

If you choose the right plants for your garden, ordering is a once-a-year task. The varieties recommended here, which are all grouped by type, are tried-and-true vegetables that have had abundant growth for vegetable gardeners with a range of experience levels. Each plant profile includes all the information you need to get growing.

# Salads and Greens

Salad greens are one of the best vegetables to begin your vegetable-growing experience. They're usually fairly forgiving and highly productive and they're easy to work into regular rotation in your kitchen. The types listed here are the best of the best.

## Perpetual Spinach (Spinach Beet)

These young plants have already provided several harvests and will go on to produce tasty leaves for months to come.

Delivering exceptional value for its space in the garden, spinach beet will provide a succulent crop of leaves for salads or cooking, from not long after planting through the following spring, with only the minimum needed care. It is an obliging plant used in place of spinach; a few leaves are harvested from several plants each time. In fact, it is one of those plants that reward regular harvesting with yet more tender leaves. Spinach beet is a tidy grower, especially when picked regularly, and can be used to edge beds. Spinach beet tastes good, cooks well, keeps growing in more temperate areas even through winter when spinach won't grow, and will deliver a great crop in dry soils. This is a perfect beginner's vegetable crop that will also grow well in a container.

## HOW TO HARVEST LETTUCE

### Cut-and-come-again lettuce

Sow about 1" (2.5cm) apart, and when the plant is about 4" (10.2cm) high, harvest the top, cutting just above the smallest new pair of leaves. The plant will then resprout from here and can be harvested once or even twice more. This will give you small, fresh leaves ideal for adding to salads, garnishes, and sandwiches. Best for small spaces.

### Harvesting "around" the lettuce

Sow lettuce 8" (20.3cm) apart and let them grow to maturity. Once they have bulked up nicely, you can start taking the outside leaves, tearing, or cutting them gently away at the base and leaving the rest of the lettuce intact. You can continue to take two or three leaves this way every few days while the lettuce continues to grow. Once the middle of the lettuce starts to shoot upward, though, stop harvesting, since it is now bolting and the leaves will start to taste bitter.

### Harvesting the whole lettuce

Sow lettuce 8" (20.3cm) apart and let them grow to maturity. Then cut the whole lettuce off at ground level with pruners (secateurs) or a sharp kitchen knife, or simply pull up the whole plant.

### VARIETIES TO TRY
Named varieties are rarely available.

### PLANT OR SEED?
Plants.

### SPACING AND PLANTING
6" (15.2cm) between plants, 12" (30.5cm) between rows. Stagger plants. Grows well in blocks.

### WHEN TO PLANT
Mid-spring.

### WHEN TO HARVEST
Early summer, just a few weeks after planting depending on weather conditions.

## HOW MANY?
Twenty plants should give a good harvest.

## REPEAT SOWING
No.

## IDEAL CONDITIONS
Very unfussy.

## MAINTENANCE
Pick a few leaves from each plant regularly, but start by picking lightly so plants get well established. In temperate areas, they will grow through the winter without protection, but in some areas, the ferocity of the weather may damage the leaves, so to avoid this, they can be protected by floating row covers (fleece).

## WHEN TO WATER
Will withstand dry soil but rewards watering in very dry spells.

## COMMON PROBLEMS AND SOLUTIONS
None of note.

# Swiss Chard

With large, crinkled leaves and thick, colorful stems, midribs, and veins, Swiss chard may be unfamiliar since it is one of those vegetables that can only really be enjoyed at its best if you grow your own. It soon wilts once harvested and isn't often available to buy. Picked young, the leaves can be cooked whole, but larger leaves need the tough stems removed before cooking. These can either be composted or cooked separately. Young leaves with their bright stems liven up a green salad.

## VARIETIES TO TRY
- **Swiss chard**, sometimes known as silver chard, has deep green leaves and thick white stems. It reaches about 20" (50.8cm) high and is the most productive and robust of the chards.
- **'Northern Lights'** has a mixture of brightly colored, shining stems. This chard will certainly add a burst of color to the garden, though it is not such a strong grower as the less flashy Swiss chard. For color, go for

A few of these succulent young leaves can be taken from each plant and used in salads.

'Bright Lights' or Rainbow chard. Gourmets prefer the classic Swiss chard with thick, white stems. Sown again in late summer or early autumn, a few plants dotted throughout the border are a very welcome sight in the lean times of winter.
- **Ruby chard**, as its name suggests, has glowing, ruby-red stems, and its leaf is a very dark green, making it a real eye-catcher. Like 'Northern Lights', it is easy to grow, but won't deliver as much leafy greens as Swiss chard. Very ornamental and will grow well in containers.

## PLANT OR SEED?
Transplants or small plants.

## SPACING AND PLANTING
8" (20.3cm) between plants, 16" (40.6cm) between rows. Stagger plants.

## WHEN TO PLANT
Late spring.

## WHEN TO HARVEST
Start cutting the leaves, a few from each plant, as soon as they are large enough to use. As the stems are quite thick, you will need to cut them with a knife rather than picking

or pulling them. They can be harvested until cut down by the frost, but even then, if left in the ground, they may regrow a little in the spring. At any time, they can be cut to the ground and will sprout a crop of succulent baby leaves.

## HOW MANY?
Twenty plants.

## REPEAT SOWING
No.

## IDEAL CONDITIONS
Very unfussy.

## MAINTENANCE
Pick regularly to ensure plenty of new leaves. Large, coarse, or battered leaves aren't worth eating—instead, put them on the compost pile.

## WHEN TO WATER
In dry spells.

## COMMON PROBLEMS AND SOLUTIONS
Protect small plants from slugs and snails if they are a problem in your garden.

# Lettuce

There is an astounding range of lettuces available to grow in your vegetable garden with an amazing range of leaf shapes and colors, from frilly red to crisp green and undulating bronze. They are the backbone of summer salads, looking equally attractive in the garden as on the plate. There are cultivars recommended for growing over the winter months, although since these aren't easy to manage, it is better to choose one of the hosts of other salad greens, such as spinach beet or Swiss chard, that are more reliable. Summer lettuces take up little time and thrive if the soil and watering are right. Choosing varieties that work well as a cut-and-come-again crop suits the low-maintenance gardener because it means you can have a constant supply of small leaves for salads and sandwiches from just one planting.

Eaten just moments after it is picked, homegrown lettuce retains all of its crisp juiciness and bite.

## VARIETIES TO TRY
- **'Can Can'** is a green non-hearting lettuce with sweet, crisp, frilly leaves suitable as a cut-and-come-again crop. It also has good disease resistance.
- **'Salad Bowl'** is a large, fast-growing cut-and-come-again lettuce that should produce leaves for a whole season. Slow to bolt.
- **'Pinokkio'** is a short romaine-type lettuce that produces a good heart and is resistant to downy mildew.
- **'Sentry'** has very decorative, wavy-edged, reddish leaves and can be used as a single head or as cut-and-come-again. It has a good resistance to mildew.
- **'Fristina'** is a reliable oak-leaved variety with a good flavor.
- **'Little Gem'** is a small hearting lettuce that produces crisp, pale hearts. It is fast-growing and compact, so even though you do have to wait for the heart to form, you don't have to wait long. Don't be tempted to grow too many hearting lettuces because they will all be ready at about the same time.
- **'Lollo Rossa'** is a lavishly frilly, Italian non-hearting lettuce that can be harvested as a

Picking a few leaves from a number of plants makes for an interesting salad and means that one plant will produce for weeks.

cut-and-come-again crop. It is a wonderfully attractive plant with a great taste.

## PLANT OR SEED?
Plants and later sowing of seed.

## SPACING AND PLANTING
Plants can be set as close as 4" (10.2cm) for small varieties or 10" (25.4cm) for larger.

## WHEN TO PLANT
Late spring.

## WHEN TO HARVEST
Start picking a few leaves as soon as the plants are large enough. Always pick just one or two leaves from each plant, leaving at least four or five at the center. In the summer, each plant will rapidly regenerate, slightly more slowly in the spring and autumn. Eventually, the lettuce will bolt, and the plant can be removed.

## HOW MANY?
Twenty plants.

## REPEAT SOWING
Start the season with a selection of cut-and-come-again plants, and once these have been producing for a while, direct sow a selection of lettuces to take their place. This way the whole season is covered.

## IDEAL CONDITIONS
Lettuces enjoy a rich soil that is not compacted.

## MAINTENANCE
Young plants can be affected by competition from weeds, but if they are planted close together, they will soon cover the ground.

## WHEN TO WATER
Lettuces need regular watering to thrive, but it is important to water the soil and not the leaves as they can be damaged and rot.

## COMMON PROBLEMS AND SOLUTIONS
Slugs and snails love tender lettuce leaves and are a particular threat to seedlings and young plants. Larger plants can withstand a little damage. Use the methods outlined in Chapter 5, starting on page 164, to protect your crop.

Aphids (greenfly) are particularly unpleasant if they are plentiful. This problem can be avoided by growing lettuces under a floating row cover (fleece) or fine insect-proof mesh from the outset.

Bolting can be a problem in hot weather or if watering is inconsistent. Generally, the leaves of plants that bolt are bitter and inedible and should be composted.

> When you've spent years buying ready-prepared salad in bags, it can be easy to forget that you actually might have to wash the stuff before eating. You don't need to eat waterlogged salad. A simple, plastic salad spinner gives you crisp, dry leaves in a few seconds.

## Salad Leaves

This mix of leaves, including mizuna, mustard leaves, and arugula (rocket), will deliver a good mix of tastes, textures, and colors.

Salad leaves are close to effortless to grow; just sprinkle the seed, water, and wait. Sometimes they can be picked after only three or four weeks, because the plants start producing long before they are mature. There is a plethora of plants that can be grown, and you can very easily produce an enormous variety of salad leaves with a whole range of exciting tastes, colors, and textures. Many of the leaves are from immature plants, such as kale or beets (beetroot), or a mix of oriental greens, such as komatsuna, mizuna, Chinese cabbage, and mustard greens. The simplest way to go about growing an interesting mix of salad leaves, especially for beginner gardeners, is to try some of the mixed packets of seed on the market. Many are ready for eating in just a few weeks and will contain a vast array of different and interesting plants. Some are themed, promising spicy leaves, fast-growing varieties, or a winter mix, and most can be treated as a cut-and-come-again crop, so you can pick from each plant several times. Add a few snippets of fresh herbs and some colorful edible flowers, and you have something infinitely superior to the salads sold in sealed bags. They also grow well in containers.

## VARIETIES TO TRY

Any salad leaf mix. Or create your own by mixing packets of seeds of your favorite leaf lettuces.

## PLANT OR SEED?

Seed.

## SPACING AND PLANTING

Sow thinly in shallow, wide furrows about ⅜" (1cm) deep. Thinning out is not necessary. Mixed salad leaves can be broadcast (sprinkled over the soil in a wide area rather than in straight rows). This is an efficient use of space, and pretty, too. When the plants initially come up, they are indistinguishable from weeds, especially if they are new to you, so neat lines make it easier to see what needs to be weeded out.

## WHEN TO SOW

Depending on the varieties chosen, from early spring through to early autumn.

## WHEN TO HARVEST

As soon as the leaves look large enough to enjoy, you can start harvesting, probably when they are about 4" (10.2cm) high. Use scissors to snip the leaves or pinch them from the plants. Alternatively, when the plants are

It is tough to distinguish weed from plant at this stage, so it pays to sow seeds in neat bands or rows.

about 4"–6" (10.2–15.2cm) tall the whole plant can be cut to about 2" (5.1cm) above ground level as needed. Within three to four weeks there should be another harvest ready and another about four weeks after that.

## HOW MANY?

Probably a quarter to half a packet of seed at one time.

## REPEAT SOWING

Yes, plant a new batch of seeds just before you start harvesting the first and so on.

## IDEAL CONDITIONS

Moist, rich soil.

## MAINTENANCE

Keep weeds down, especially when plants are young.

## WHEN TO WATER

Salad leaves are one crop where you really cannot hold back on the watering as they need a constantly moist soil to grow well. Water the soil, not the plants—a soaker hose works well.

## COMMON PROBLEMS AND SOLUTIONS

Insect pests including aphids (greenfly) and flea beetle are likely to be the most significant problems depending on the mix of leaves you are growing. Both can be kept from the plants by growing them under a floating row cover or the finest insect-proof mesh in the summer months.

Slugs and snails will also enjoy the lush leaves. Use the methods outlined in Chapter 5, starting on page 164, to protect your crop.

Harvest salad leaves once they reach about 4" (10.2cm) by snipping them with scissors or pinching them away from the plant.

# Podded Vegetables

Podded vegetables come in a variety of flavors and textures. From crisp snap peas to tender green beans, the plants listed here are prolific growers that work well cooked, added to salads, or just as a crunchy snack.

Harvest podded vegetables once the pods are well filled out.

Most podded vegetables benefit from having ropes or other supports to twine around.

## Peas and Snow Peas (Mangetout)

Peas fresh from the garden are nothing like those in the stores—as soon as peas are picked, the sugars that make them so delicious start becoming starches, and while frozen peas may be okay, they are nowhere near as good. Peas grow well but keeping up a constant supply requires planning and space—it is perhaps better to make two or three sowings and have the harvest in bursts of a few weeks at a time. The most labor-intensive part of growing peas is the shelling. Growing snow peas (mangetout) cuts out the work of shelling as the pods are tender and eaten in their entirety, although they can get stringy if left on the plant too long. Shelling peas are either wrinkle- or round-seeded—the round varieties are generally hardier, and the wrinkled varieties are generally thought to be sweeter.

### VARIETIES TO TRY

- **'Kelvedon Wonder'** can be planted from early spring through early summer, so there is no need to buy more than one variety of pea. It is a shelling variety that produces a bumper crop of pods crammed with good-sized and sweet-tasting peas that are quick to mature. It also has the advantage of being mildew resistant, growing to about 20" (50.8cm) tall.
- **'Hurst Green Shaft'** is worth trying; it also produces a heavy crop of sweetly flavored peas and promises good disease resistance. This is a taller variety, growing to about 30" (76.2cm) and is a main crop cultivar.
- **'Onward'** is another main crop variety, and also offers some disease resistance and a good flavor. Grows to about 1 yd. (1m) in height.
- **'Little Marvel'** is a very sweet dwarf pea, only reaching about 17¾" (45.1cm) tall, but it produces a wonderful harvest very early in the year.
- **'Oregon Sugar Pod'** is a great, fast-maturing variety of snow peas. When gathered young, the pods are crisp and fleshy and great in salads, stir-fries, or steamed.

The young tips of the pea plant can be added to salads. Harvest just a few at a time so as not to ruin your crop of peas.

## PLANT OR SEED?
Seed.

## SPACING AND PLANTING
Direct sow early varieties from mid-spring in wide furrows about 8" (20.3cm) wide with two or three rows of peas so that the peas are about 2" (5.1cm) away from each other. Leave about 18"–24" (45.7–61cm) between rows for the shorter varieties. Alternatively, if you are working in small beds, sow a block of peas aiming at about 8–10 seeds per 1' (30.5cm) square, although remember you will need to be able to reach into the center of the block to harvest the peas.

## WHEN TO SOW
Early varieties can be sown from early spring, while main crops can be sown from mid- to late spring. Some varieties are very hardy and can be sown in the autumn to produce a crop very early the following year. The ground is likely cold and damp, and the seed is liable to rot, plus mice and birds are hungry, so are likely to eat the seed, and some protection may well be needed. Better to wait a little longer and not waste time or seed.

## WHEN TO HARVEST
The first peas of cultivars sown in the early spring should be ready in early summer, about 10–12 weeks after sowing. Pick snow peas as soon as pods are about 1½" (3.8cm) long, because old snow peas are tough and stringy.

## HOW MANY?
One 6½'–10' (2–3m) row each at sowing.

## REPEAT SOWING
Sow two or three batches about three weeks apart, or when your previous sowing reaches 3"–4" (7.6–10.2cm) tall. Sow one batch of an early variety and one or two of a main crop or make more sowings of 'Kelvedon Wonder'.

## IDEAL CONDITIONS
Peas appreciate a soil with plenty of organic matter. In cold, wet soil pea seeds tend to rot, so well-drained soil is necessary, especially for early sowings. Other than that, peas are very unfussy and will even survive a little shade.

## MAINTENANCE
All peas benefit from some support framework to grow through, even short varieties. The easiest support frameworks are ranks of twiggy hazel or birch sticks pushed in along the rows of peas. These can be cut from woodlots or garden hedgerows or should be available from good garden centers. Plastic pea netting can also be bought at garden centers. This can be strung along the rows, but requires stout supports to keep it from drooping under the weight of the peas. Twigs are much easier and probably free. Once the plants are growing strongly, they will tolerate a few weeds.

## WHEN TO WATER
When in flower and when pods are forming. Peas are one of the crops where knowing just when to water can save you time and water while maximizing your crop. Watering during flowering and while the pods are forming really boosts yields, but you can happily not water once the seedlings have emerged until flowering begins unless they wilt. Too much water before flowering encourages too much leafy growth.

## COMMON PROBLEMS AND SOLUTIONS
Generally, peas are trouble-free, but there are just a couple of problems that can easily be avoided. Birds and mice

# OVERVIEW: GROWING PEAS FROM START TO FINISH

**1.** Pea seeds are a tasty treat for rodents. Dipping them in seaweed fertilizer before planting should help to protect the seeds from attack.

**2.** Sow peas in a flat-bottomed furrow about 8" (20.3cm) wide in staggered rows so that the peas are about 2" (5.1cm) apart, or grow them in a block with 8–10 seeds per 12" (30.5cm) square.

**3.** When the pea plants begin to show, add hazel or birch twigs to provide support—this is much easier than constructing frames with netting.

**4.** Harvest the peas when the pods fill out. Peas picked younger are much sweeter and completely delicious, although you get a much smaller harvest.

like to feast on pea seeds. After sowing, lay a piece of chicken wire over the soil to deter birds and rodents, or dip the seeds in seaweed fertilizer before planting to make them unpalatable to rodents.

Mildew is another common problem, especially in the autumn or dry periods, best avoided by sowing resistant varieties. It looks like a fine white powder or dust that starts at the tips of the leaves and will eventually cover the whole plant.

Pea moth can be a problem in your vegetable garden. To avoid the problem, sow only early and late as the pea moth lays its eggs on the flowers of plants that will produce midsummer, and the maggots then hatch and burrow their way into the pods. Alternatively, drape an insect barrier mesh over your crop once it comes into flower. If you find you are badly affected by pea moth, move your peas as far away as you can the following year, as the moth pupates in the soil.

## Green Beans (French Beans)

Green beans (French beans) are the gourmet's alternative to the runner bean. They are inclined to be more tender, more flavorful, and have the enormous benefit of being much easier to prepare. They are a little fussier than runner beans to grow, but not much. Climbing varieties are best as they give a bigger harvest for the space they occupy and produce for longer than the dwarf varieties, which can be useful in pots or in windy sites. Green bean (French bean) cultivars are available with purple and yellow pods, too.

### VARIETIES TO TRY

- **'Cobra'** is a climbing green bean (French bean) cultivar that produces a profusion of long, tender, stringless, pale pods with a good flavor right through to the autumn. It has a pretty purple flower, too.
- **'Blue Lake'** is an older, reliable climbing variety that can be eaten whole or left on the plant, so the seeds ripen to be used as haricots.
- **'Purple King'** beans are a rich purple color while growing but, perhaps disappointingly, the color fades on cooking. Great flavor.

### PLANT OR SEED
Seed.

At this stage, young bean plants can be killed overnight by slugs, so a plastic bottle cloche is a good idea. Once they get a little bigger, the odd nibble won't matter so much.

### SPACING AND PLANTING
Plant seeds 2"–4" (5.1–10.2cm) apart and 2" (5.1cm) deep, two at each station. Remove the weaker seedling if both germinate. If you are growing them up a cane tunnel, leave 24" (61cm) between rows.

### WHEN TO SOW
Very late spring to early summer; the plants are not frost-hardy, and the seeds need a temperature of 54°F (12°C) to germinate.

### WHEN TO HARVEST
You should start picking beans about 10–12 weeks from planting. Even if there are only a few ready, pick them to encourage the plants to produce more. If you want to use some beans as haricots, leave the pods on the plants for the beans to swell until the pods become brown and dry. This will halt the production of new pods, so use particular plants or wait until late in the season. It is easier to let this process take place on the plant naturally, but if the ripe pods are likely to suffer in very wet or frosty weather, the pods can be dried inside.

### HOW MANY?
Plant in 6½'–10' (2–3m) rows.

These 'Purple King' beans have a stunningly rich color that sadly fades when cooked.

### REPEAT SOWING

Sow another batch about six to eight weeks after the first. To make life simpler, if the first planting is spaced a little more widely, the second batch can be planted among the first using the same support.

### IDEAL CONDITIONS

Good, rich soil with plenty of organic matter.

### MAINTENANCE

Climbing beans need a framework or support to climb—canes, obelisks, or netting are fine. They will spiral around anything as they head skyward. Mulch around the plants once they are up to keep weeds down and preserve moisture—grass cuttings or newspaper will do.

### WHEN TO WATER

Water when flowering starts if the weather is very dry to increase yields.

### COMMON PROBLEMS AND SOLUTIONS

Slugs are one of the biggest problems with green beans (French beans). To prevent the seedlings from being completely eaten, plant each pair of seeds and immediately put a plastic bottle cloche over them, pushed well into the soil, to protect them.

The other likely hazard is being in too much of a hurry to get the seeds into the ground—they really don't like cold, damp conditions, and even if they come up, the plants can rot.

## Borlotti Beans

Borlotti bean plants yield pods splashed with crimson and great-tasting beans that make it worth growing just a few if you have the space. The growing requirements for borlotti beans are much like those for green beans (French beans). 'Borlotto Lingua di Fuoco,' or 'Fire Tongue', is the most common variety.

The bright red flowers and dappled red pods of the borlotti bean make a colorful splash in your vegetable garden.

# Runner Beans

Fully formed 'Celebration' pods.

One of the easiest vegetables to grow and one of the most likely crops to overplant, the runner bean will reliably produce an abundant crop and sprout colorful flowers. If you have too many, you can always freeze them. Runner beans are a very rewarding plant for the novice.

## VARIETIES TO TRY

- **'Celebration'** is an early-maturing cultivar that produces a heavy crop of smooth, tasty beans and has the added appeal of pretty salmon-pink flowers. It is also resistant to rust.
- **'Red Rum'** also matures early and promises a high yield of particularly fine-flavored beans. If you have trouble getting your bean flowers to set, this variety is worth trying, as its flowers set extremely well, even in poor conditions. It is also resistant to Halo blight.

## PLANT OR SEED?
Seed.

## SPACING AND PLANTING
Direct sow 2" (5.1cm) deep and about 6"–9" (15.2–22.9cm) apart. Use two seeds at each station in case one fails to germinate and pull out one seedling if two grow. If growing beans up the traditional tunnel of sloping canes, allow at least 12" (30.5cm) between rows.

## WHEN TO SOW
Runner beans need fairly warm soil to germinate, so wait until all risk of frosts have passed, probably in late spring.

## WHEN TO HARVEST
You will probably harvest your first beans about 10–12 weeks from sowing. Regular picking encourages more pods to form.

## HOW MANY?
Plant an 8' (2.4m) double row and see how it goes.

## REPEAT SOWING
Possible but beware of overplanting.

## IDEAL CONDITIONS
Beans are a hungry crop; they need very rich soil with plenty of organic matter. Some gardeners labor all through the winter at filling a trench with waste in the spot they plan to grow their beans. This is not necessary if your soil is in good condition, just add plenty of organic material on planting. They will thrive on new beds created by deep-layer mulching.

## MAINTENANCE
Runners need a framework to grow up. Traditionally, this is provided by two rows of 6½' (2m) canes or hazel rods about 12"–24" (30.5–61cm) apart sloping toward each other and tied at the top to a horizontal cane. Any type of obelisk will suffice. Pinch out the tips of the plants when they reach the top of the supports, and mulch around the plants with compost or grass clippings to suppress weeds and keep in moisture. The most important thing is to keep picking. If you only visit your vegetable garden once a week, pick some beans slightly early to avoid them becoming old and unpalatable and to ensure that the production of new pods is not suppressed.

## WHEN TO WATER

Runner beans are thirsty, so water well throughout the season.

## COMMON PROBLEMS AND SOLUTIONS

Runners are a robust crop and there is little to worry about.

Failure to set, where the flowers fail to develop into pods, is one of the most common problems. If this seems to be an issue, step up the watering and mulch the bed to keep in moisture. This should help the pods form. It may be caused by a lack of pollinating insects, so in subsequent years, add more companion planting to your plot or sow a few sweet peas among the beans (if you try this, take care not to harvest and eat the sweet pea pods).

Halo blight is something to look out for; this causes a pale ring on the leaves with a darker spot at its center. If you catch it early, you can pinch off the affected leaves and destroy them, otherwise it can spread to the whole plant, eventually killing it. The alternative is to grow a resistant cultivar like 'Red Rum'.

Tendrils of 'Celebration' growing up a rope.

# Fava Beans (Broad Beans)

Almost ready for harvest, these perfect pods of 'Aquadulce Claudia' will each contain about six or seven perfect beans.

The humble fava bean (broad bean) is one of the earliest known cultivated crops; it earns its place in the vegetable patch today as it is the earliest of the beans to be ready for picking. Pick them while they are small and tender as the older the beans, the starchier they become. Being one of the earliest vegetable crops of the season, it is well worth making space for a row, even if you just make the one sowing. There are plenty of other beans that will produce later in the season.

## VARIETIES TO TRY

- **'Aquadulce Claudia'** produces reliable, fantastic harvests of long pods. Reputed to be the best for autumn planting for early harvests.
- **'The Sutton'** is a more compact, dwarf variety that can be planted with less space between rows. It can be sown in autumn or spring. Good for windy sites.

## PLANT OR SEED?
Seed.

## SPACING AND PLANTING
Sow in double rows with 4" (10.2cm) between seeds, 12" (30.5cm) between rows, and 24" (61cm) between double rows, 2" (5.1cm) deep or in staggered rows with 6" (15.2cm) between each seed.

## WHEN TO SOW
There are two planting periods for fava beans (broad beans): one in autumn to early winter, the other in early spring through to the beginning of summer. Planting in the autumn makes for sturdy plants that are less attractive to blackfly. The young plants are pretty tough, surviving down to 14°F (-10°C) if the seed doesn't rot in the ground or get devoured by hungry rodents before it germinates. Plant in early spring and the plants get going faster. Later summer sowings are more prone to aphid attack and yields can be affected, so perhaps attempt just one or two sowings in spring when aphids are less troublesome.

A fine wire mesh pinned over newly planted bean seeds should prevent rodents getting to the seed before it germinates.

## WHEN TO HARVEST
The beans are ready when you can just see them through the pod, about 16 weeks from a spring planting.

## HOW MANY?
In very good conditions, a row of beans will produce 2lb. (1kg) per meter, so a couple of 6 ½' (2m) rows should be enough.

## REPEAT SOWING
Possible, but sowing late autumn or winter for the following spring can create issues.

## IDEAL CONDITIONS
Fava beans give their best in deep, rich soils, but they will grow in poorer soils.

## MAINTENANCE
There is really little to do with these rugged beans other than provide support for tall varieties in an exposed spot by creating a cage around them with posts and string or canes. Once the harvest is finished, chop the tops off and leave the roots with the nitrogen-fixing nodules in the soil to benefit the plant that follows—the timing and nitrogen should suit brassicas.

## WHEN TO WATER
Water in prolonged dry periods.

## COMMON PROBLEMS AND SOLUTIONS
**Blackfly** is the biggest problem afflicting fava beans—they suck sap from the plant and cause it to weaken. The blackfly is drawn to the young sappy growth at the growing tips, so once the plant is in flower these tips can be pinched out to discourage the blackfly and serendipitously encourage pods to form.

**Chocolate spot** is a fungal disease that causes brown patches on the leaves of the plants. It can be prevented by improving drainage and ensuring plants are not too close together so air can circulate. Plants will continue to produce beans through a mild attack.

# Roots and Tubers

Root vegetables and tubers can be simple to grow and versatile to cook with, but are more importantly simpler to store for long periods. The types noted in this section offer an abundant and steady supply of nutrients throughout the growing season and beyond.

## Potatoes

Homegrown potatoes have many cultivars to choose from with something to suit all tastes, with different textures and skin colors to try—firm, waxy salad potatoes, fluffy ones that are great for mashing, and potatoes that will grow enormous for baking.

Potatoes fall into three categories depending on when they are ready to harvest: "first early" ready in June and July, "second early" ready for the table in July and August, and main crop potatoes, which follow on and can be stored through to the next spring. If you are short on time and space, it really isn't worth growing main crop potatoes—an early crop is a real treat and the flavors are exceptional. Main crop potatoes will occupy a lot of space when you could be growing other things, the homegrown taste is not as pronounced, and potatoes later in the season are inexpensive in the stores. Try to

Root vegetables and tubers are always a hearty option to pack nutrients into any meal.

make space for at least a first early and, if you can, a second early variety.

### VARIETIES TO TRY—FIRST EARLY

- **'Swift'** is the earliest potato of all, sometimes ready just seven weeks from planting.
- **'Winston'** is a reliable producer with a great flavor. It is also versatile—it is a tasty new potato when dug early, but any left in the ground for a while bulk up into great baking potatoes.
- **'Accent'** is slug resistant and provides a very good yield. Great both boiled and roasted.

### VARIETIES TO TRY—SECOND EARLY

- **'Kestrel'** looks great with smooth tubers and patches of pinky purple. It has a good flavor and, perhaps best of all, it is resistant to slug damage. This makes them an excellent choice where slugs ravage the garden.
- **'Charlotte'** is a lovely, large salad potato with a waxy texture and an excellent flavor that is well worth growing. Unfortunately, the yields are not as good as 'Kestrel'.
- **'Edzell Blue'** sports a purple or navy-blue skin, making it fun to grow.

The 'Kestrel' variety is resistant to slug damage and provides good-looking potatoes with plenty of tubers on each root.

There is nothing quite as satisfying as unearthing the multitude of tubers that form underground.

## "CHITTING" POTATOES

"Seed potatoes" are just potatoes you buy and plant to get more potatoes. Before the seed potatoes are planted, they should be encouraged to produce shoots—this is known as chitting. Chitting involves placing the rose end (the end with lots of eyes) up in a cool, light, frost-free place so they can develop shoots. People often use egg cartons for this—any container that will hold the seed potatoes upright will do. Leave them there for two or three weeks until the shoots or "chits" are ⅝"–1" (1.6–2.5cm) long. Then they're ready for planting.

## PLANT OR SEED?

Potatoes are grown from seed potatoes, which ideally should be at least the size of a hen's egg and come from a reputable supplier to ensure they are disease-free.

## SPACING AND PLANTING

Plant first early potatoes about 4" (10.2cm) deep and 12" (30.5cm) apart with 18" (45.7cm) between rows. Second earlies and maincrop potatoes need a bit more space at 16" (40.6cm) apart. The easiest way to plant is to scoop out a hole with a trowel (rather than dig a trench), drop in the seed potato with the shoots pointing upward, and cover with soil, being careful not to damage the brittle shoots as you cover them. Rub off any downward-facing shoots before planting. To get the spacing right, you can lay all the seed potatoes out on the bed, and then work your way along the row when planting.

## WHEN TO PLANT

Early to mid-spring, as early as possible. A good empirical indication of when to plant potatoes is when the grass and weeds start showing signs of growth. If a late frost is forecast, earth up the shoots, or drape a piece of horticultural fleece over the bed to protect the young shoots. However, planting too early can mean tubers rot in the ground before they can grow.

## WHEN TO HARVEST

Early cultivars can be ready in as little as 60 to 70 days from planting, but generally they are harvested when they finish flowering before the haulms (the stems and leaves) have died back. Dig them as you need them but go carefully. This is not just to avoid waste, but any tubers left in the ground will sprout the following year with your vegetables.

## REPEAT SOWING

A continuous supply is ensured by growing first and second early varieties and a main crop if required.

## IDEAL CONDITIONS

Potatoes are easy-going and are often used as a crop on newly cleared ground, because the process of earthing up and the bushy plants keep weeds down while the tubers open up the soil. A good soil rich with organic matter will yield the best crops, as potatoes are a very hungry crop. They do well in new deep-layer mulch beds.

## MAINTENANCE

Potatoes grown in the traditional way need earthing up—this simply means drawing the soil up around the plant to bury the shoots a few times as it grows. This prevents the potatoes coming to the surface and going green. Earthing up can also protect young shoots from late frosts. Earth up when the plants are about 6" (15.2cm) high, or sooner if frosts are predicted, and again when there is another good 6" (15.2cm) of growth showing.

## SHORTCUTS

- A handy time-saving trick is to grow potatoes through black plastic sheeting. This serves many purposes; if it is put down a few weeks before planting, it will warm the soil and encourage early production, and it will suppress the weeds and avoid the need to earth up the potatoes. The downside is that it looks unattractive. The plastic is staked out over the soil and held down by burying the edges, or with planks or stones, and the potatoes are then planted through holes in the plastic.
- An alternative is to grow potatoes under a mulch of straw and grass cuttings. This has the same advantages, perhaps looks a little more attractive, and can be used to clear new ground. A generous layer of compost is spread over the bed, and the potatoes are set out on top. The potatoes are then covered with a thick duvet of straw. This can be topped up with grass cuttings as the potatoes grow. This method of growing potatoes can even be employed

# PLANTING POTATOES

**1.** Lay out the chitted seed potatoes on the soil to ensure they are well spaced, preventing the last few from having to be squeezed in.

**2.** Some people like to dig a trench to plant potatoes in, but it is easier to scoop out a small hole for each that is about 4" (10.2cm) deep.

**3.** Place the seed potato in the hole with the chits facing up.

**4.** Once the young plants are established, they should be "earthed up," whereby the soil is dragged over the plant to leave just a little growth showing.

on a previously uncultivated area by cutting back any grass or weeds before the manure is spread and proceeding as above. To harvest the potatoes, just peel back the mulch of straw.

## WHEN TO WATER

Earlies only need thorough watering every two weeks, if rainfall is not sufficient, to get the best yield possible. To make them produce earlier, only water when the tubers are formed, around about when they flower—the crop will be early but small.

## COMMON PROBLEMS AND SOLUTIONS

There are several things that might threaten your potato crop, but many viruses can be avoided by buying good-quality certified seed potatoes. Saving your own spuds to plant the following year can lead to lower productivity and an increase in disease. If you want to try it, save seeds from one year to the next, then buy seed potatoes in the third year.

**Blight** is a fungal disease that breaks out in cool, damp summers. The first signs are brown patches on the leaves and fungal rings on the underside of these patches; eventually the plants die back and can smell putrid. The best solution is to remove and destroy the tops, dig up the potatoes, and use them only if they are unaffected. Don't be tempted to put any of the foliage or potatoes on the compost heap, as you will just be storing up the problem to release it into the garden when you spread the compost. If blight is common in your area, grow blight-resistant varieties, such as 'Milva', 'Orla', 'Karlena', 'Spunta', and the main crop 'Sarpo Mira'.

**Scab** causes small corky patches to appear on the skin of the potatoes. This is not a real problem since the potatoes are perfectly edible once peeled, but it can be a sign that your soil is drying out and could do with more organic matter.

**Keeled slugs** that live below the soil surface will eat into potatoes, causing rot to set in. If you have a problem with slugs, sow the marvelous slug-resistant variety 'Kestrel'.

Potatoes are one of the crops that are often untouched by deer, rabbits, and badgers presumably because of the toxicity of the foliage.

# Carrots

Globe carrots are a good solution in shallow or stony soils. They are popular with children, too.

Freshly dug, young, gloriously crisp, juicy carrots give crunch and color to salads, are delicious steamed and even carefully roasted, but frankly they are so much better raw than cooked. Carrots are a little more exacting than the potatoes and runner beans of the vegetable world, but they are by no means challenging.

## VARIETIES TO TRY

- **'Purple Haze'** produces shockingly purple, good-sized carrots that keep their color even when cooked. Cut in rings, they have a purple band with an orange core. The color really appeals to children, and it's a little-known fact that at one time all carrots were purple.
- **'Paris Market'** is a globe-type carrot; it produces roundish roots that are excellent for snacking on once they reach the size of large marbles. This is another favorite among children because of its unusual shape. Its short root is an advantage in stony or heavy soils.
- **'Autumn King 2'** is a solid, reliable cultivar with a rounded end. It is not as sweet and tender as some but stores well.
- **'Maestro'** is resistant to carrot flies and has good-quality roots.

## PLANT OR SEED?

Seed.

## SPACING AND PLANTING

Direct sow seed in furrows in soil worked to a fine tilth or a seed compost furrow. Sow seeds in furrows ⅜" (1cm) deep and about 8"–10" (20.3–25.4cm) apart, less for globe cultivars. Sow as thinly as possible in straight lines—this is tough because the seeds are tiny but being careful early on means you won't need to thin out seedlings later. The carrots inevitably come up in irregular knots and clusters, but they push each other out of the way, and as soon as they are large enough to be eaten, some can be carefully taken from each group and the rest left to grow on. Not thinning out saves time and seeds, but it also gives the carrot fly one less chance to detect your carrots.

## WHEN TO SOW

Early spring through to midsummer, depending on the variety.

## WHEN TO HARVEST

Start harvesting as soon as they are large enough to be useful. Remove small carrots along the row, leaving those remaining more room to grow. Covered in a mulch of straw or a layer of fleece, carrots can be left in the ground through reasonably cold winters and harvested as needed.

Straight from the ground to the table—freshly pulled carrots retain all their crunch, flavor, and nutrients.

## HOW MANY?

6½'–10' (2–3m) rows every three or four weeks until mid- to late summer.

## REPEAT SOWING

To keep up a supply of carrots, you need to keep sowing them from early spring to mid- to late summer every three weeks (about five or six batches). The final sowing should be a variety that will last well in the ground in milder areas until needed in autumn or winter, or that stores well, such as 'Autumn King 2'.

## IDEAL CONDITIONS

Carrots do best in warm, dryish ground, and carrots in dry ground should be sweeter. To form perfect, long taproots, carrots need to swell without constraints, so stony, heavy soils may produce stunted or misshapen roots. There are two ways to tackle this problem: the easiest and least time-consuming is to grow short rooted or globe varieties that won't be affected by the heavy soil. The other requires more work in modifying your soil to suit the carrots; if you prize long, slender-rooted varieties, then work some sharp sand into the bed just before planting. If you are working in raised beds, you should have already escaped these difficulties. Sowing carrots into a bed that has been recently mulched with compost or manure results in "forking" or "fanging," meaning that the roots twist and become deformed, forming two or three taproots instead of one.

## MAINTENANCE

Carrots won't grow well with competition from weeds, so hoe regularly. Carrots arranged in neat, straight rows make hoeing much easier.

## WHEN TO WATER

In very dry spells, thoroughly drench every two weeks. Heavy rain or watering after a dry spell can cause the roots to split.

## COMMON PROBLEMS AND SOLUTIONS

**Carrot fly** is probably the biggest potential threat to your carrot crop. This is a small fly that is attracted to growing carrots by smell. They lay eggs in the soil near the top of the carrots, and the maggots burrow into the soil and

The best way to retain all the healthy nutrients when cooking carrots is to boil them whole.

into the tasty taproot, leaving a mess of fine tunnels. To protect your crop from carrot flies, sow seed thinly and never thin out the seedlings. The scent generated by thinning out will really draw in the carrot fly. A physical barrier of fine insect barrier mesh will prevent them getting to the carrots, as will a vertically strung fence of mesh around the bed around 20" (50.8cm) high—carrot flies are not strong flyers and cannot fly over this. However, this type of protection can become an obstruction to gardening and is time consuming to erect and remove for harvesting, so experiment with keeping things simple. Every time you sow a row of carrots, sow a row of spring onions of equal length in the center of the gap between rows, or plant carrots between rows of garlic and onions. So far, this has proved incredibly effective and resulted in perfect carrots every time. However, if you are in a badly affected area and a physical barrier doesn't appeal, you could try one of the resistant varieties, like 'Maestro', although the resistance is only partial.

**Bolting** may be a problem in extreme drought. Remove the bolting plant immediately as it may give off hormones encouraging others to bolt, too.

## Radishes

The radish is the ultimate catch crop. It is not worth planning where to grow it as it can be slotted in among other slow-growing crops, such as cabbages, and will be ready to harvest while they are still in their infancy—a sensible way to make the best use of your growing space. Radishes are easy to grow and will obligingly produce their tasty roots with little attention from you. A good, crisp radish adds a peppery note and splash of color to summer salads.

### VARIETIES TO TRY
- **'French Breakfast'** has elongated, cylindrical roots with a white tip and a mild flavor.
- **'Cherry Belle'** has good, crisp flesh and, as you might expect, is round and red like a cherry. This is an early variety.
- **'Il Candela Di Fuoco'** is an Italian radish that produces long, tapered roots a bit like a carrot. Red-skinned with white crisp flesh, they are amazingly quick to mature.

## PLANT OR SEED?
Seed.

## SPACING AND PLANTING
Direct sow thinly in furrows ⅜" (1cm) deep and 6" (15.2cm) apart. Squeeze rows in along the edges of beds, in between other vegetables, or wherever there is a small space. The seed can be broadcast.

## WHEN TO SOW
Sow from early spring to early autumn.

## WHEN TO HARVEST
Probably within four weeks of sowing, three if conditions are good. As soon as the roots are large enough for the table, pull at intervals along the row so others can fill out.

## HOW MANY?
One row a yard (meter) or two long every two to three weeks should be ample. Better to plant a few and harvest them while young and crisp, as old radishes get woody and pithy and are not good to eat.

## REPEAT SOWING
If you want a continuous supply, sow every two to three weeks.

The fabulous color and peppery taste of radishes make repeat sowing throughout the summer worthwhile.

'French Breakfast' radishes are crisp, mild, and best eaten when young.

## IDEAL CONDITIONS
Good, rich, well-drained soil.

## MAINTENANCE
If sown too thickly, they can be thinned once the seedlings are large enough, but it is easier to sow thinly and leave them to jostle for space.

## WHEN TO WATER
Too much water will give all top and no bottom with lush leaves and no tasty root, so limit watering to once a week in dry spells.

## COMMON PROBLEMS AND SOLUTIONS
**Flea beetle** is one of the few problems affecting radishes; they pepper the leaves with tiny holes. Established plants will survive and as it is only the root you are after it is not a problem. Small seedlings, however, could be killed. Draping a piece of horticultural fleece over the plants will easily thwart flea beetle.

# Beets (Beetroot)

'Boltardy' is a reliable beet (beetroot), but this doesn't mean compromising on taste as its flesh is sweet and smooth.

This is an easy root vegetable, and not only do you get delicious roots that can be boiled, roasted, or enjoyed cold in salads, but also the young leaves taste great, too. Unlike other root crops, beets (beetroot) will grow better if your soil is a little on the thin side, as long as it doesn't dry out. Homegrown beets (beetroot) harvested when small (about the size of a squash ball) have an earthy flavor. Preparation can be a little messy but is much easier if you cook the beets (beetroot) first, then peel them, and always twist the leaves off to limit "bleeding." Growing your own gives you the chance to experiment with yellow and white varieties seldom available in the stores. Beets are a great beginner's vegetable crop.

## VARIETIES TO TRY
- **'Boltardy'** reliably produces sumptuously colored spherical roots. It has the advantage of being resistant to bolting and can be sown earlier than any other variety.
- **'Burpee's Golden'** is a fantastic beet (beetroot); its flesh is a remarkable sunshine gold color that is little diminished by cooking.

## PLANT OR SEED?
Plug plants are less work. Direct sowing works well as the seeds are in clusters and easy to handle, but they have to be soaked overnight before sowing.

## SPACING AND PLANTING
Leave 3¼" (8.3cm) between clusters of plants. Each plug of compost will have a cluster of small plants—don't separate them; plant them as they are and leave the roots to develop as a cluster.

## WHEN TO PLANT
Mid-spring to midsummer. Young plants need protecting from frost, so just fling a length of horticultural fleece over them if cold weather is forecast.

## WHEN TO HARVEST
Start harvesting when the roots are large enough to use.

## REPEAT SOWING
If you buy plugs, you could start harvesting small, taking roots at intervals along the row and leaving others to grow on, but accept that by mid- to late summer your beets (beetroot) will be finished. The alternative is to

The flesh of your beets (beetroot) should be tender, and most are best enjoyed before they get too large and become woody.

grow from seed and sow every three or four weeks until midsummer—it depends how much you love beets (beetroot). You could split the difference by planting a batch of plugs in mid-spring and then a row of seeds about four weeks later if you have space.

## IDEAL CONDITIONS
Beets (beetroot) thrive in a well-drained, moist soil and an open, sunny bed.

## MAINTENANCE
Add a thick layer of mulch between the rows every couple of weeks.

## WHEN TO WATER
Beets (beetroot) really do need regular watering to prevent the soil drying out, because if the soil dries out, they will bolt. A good soaking every couple of weeks should do the trick.

## COMMON PROBLEMS AND SOLUTIONS
**Bolting** (producing flower heads) is the most common problem with beets (beetroot). They will bolt if planted too early and if the soil is too cold or if the soil dries out. Planting when the soil has warmed a little in mid-spring and keeping the plants well-watered should prevent bolting. The best defense is to grow the popular cultivar 'Boltardy', which is resistant to bolting and can be planted earlier than any other beets (beetroot).

# Jerusalem Artichokes

Jerusalem artichokes are just as versatile to cook as potatoes and are easier to grow.

Even simpler to grow than potatoes, Jerusalem artichokes are often forgotten but well worth growing. They form tubers under the ground like potatoes but have top growth that can grow between 5' (1.5m) and 10' (3m) tall with sunflower-like blooms. They will grow just about anywhere, even in partial shade, and are harvested in the lean period in the kitchen garden. They are versatile, too—they can be boiled, baked, and roasted or used to make a thick, warming winter soup. They do take up a fair amount of space, and the height of their top growth can cast a shadow over other beds, but the yield you get for the virtually zero attention required earns them a place if you have a large garden. They can also be grown as a windbreak.

## VARIETIES TO TRY
**'Fuseau'** has smooth-skinned tubers that are much easier to prepare than the knobbier cultivars.

## PLANT OR SEED?
Tubers.

Tubers of Jerusalem artichoke 'Fuseau' are smoother than most varieties and so are much easier to prepare.

## SPACING AND PLANTING

Plant the tubers 4"–6" (10.2–15.2cm) deep in rows 12" (30.5cm) apart.

## WHEN TO PLANT

Plant tubers in early spring.

## WHEN TO HARVEST

Start harvesting in early winter and dig them as you need them. Make sure you remove every tuber, not only because it is a shame to miss out on any of your harvest, but also because any tubers left will grow in the following year, probably most inconveniently during another crop. Some people treat them as a perennial in the garden and save time and expense by deliberately leaving a tuber or so from each plant.

## HOW MANY?

Each tuber you plant should yield about eight to ten more.

## REPEAT SOWING

No.

## IDEAL CONDITIONS

Jerusalem artichokes are wonderfully undemanding and will grow in most soils and even in slight shade.

## MAINTENANCE

Earthing up the plants when they are about 12" (30.5cm) tall can help keep the plants stable. Some gardeners advise cutting back growth to about 5' (1.5m) tall in midsummer to concentrate the plant's resources on producing tubers, but it doesn't seem to be necessary. Cut back stems in the autumn when they begin to go yellow; leave about 12" (30.5cm) of stalk so you know where they are. Leave the cut stems on the soil to protect the tubers from frost.

## WHEN TO WATER

In prolonged dry periods.

## COMMON PROBLEMS AND SOLUTIONS

**Slugs** are probably the most likely problem, nibbling into the tubers underground. It is impossible to protect them, so the slugs must be kept under control.

# Brassicas

Brassicas, such as broccoli, cauliflower, and cabbage, are robust vegetables that thrive in cooler weather. They're nutrient-rich and add color and texture in a wide range of dishes. The varieties in this section are all dependable and resilient.

## Cabbage

There are many varieties of cabbage that occupy growing space and mature at different times of the year. It can be hard to find room for them through the summer when the garden is full to the point of bursting, but cultivars planted in late summer or early autumn that produce crisp, sweet spring cabbages when little else is ready are very worthwhile for growing. If you want cabbage all year round, however, the hardiest varieties of homegrown cabbage will tolerate temperatures to around 14°F (-10°C).

### VARIETIES TO TRY—SPRING
'**Spring Hero**' produces a large, crisp, round head that will stand well.

### VARIETIES TO TRY—SUMMER
- '**Kilaxy**' is a great variety for gardens with a clubroot problem as it has good resistance. It produces a firm, round head ready in late summer that will stand into the autumn.
- '**Hispi**' is a pointed cultivar that is very fast-growing and versatile.
- '**Red Jewel**' is a very fast-growing red cabbage that delivers early sweet, dense hearts that will stand well.

### VARIETIES TO TRY—WINTER
'**Tundra**' is the hardiest of all. Perfect for cold areas, this extremely crinkled savoy-type cabbage will stand through very hard winters. The only snag is that each cabbage will have occupied about 18" (45.7cm) square of your plot for probably seven or eight months, several of them being prime growing time.

### PLANT OR SEED?
Plants. You will only need a few plants, so it makes sense to buy just the right number.

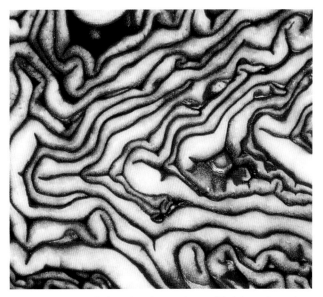
Cabbage is a versatile brassica that can be used to bring color and lightness to your dishes.

### SPACING AND PLANTING
The spacing of cabbage plants will directly affect the size of the head each plant produces. If a greater quantity of smaller cabbages would suit your needs, then plant closer together. Spring and summer cabbages should be planted about 12" (30.5cm) apart. Winter varieties need more space, about 16"–18" (40.6–45.7cm) apart. Cabbages have a shallow root system, so they need firm soil, planted a little more deeply than they were originally grown, and to be firmed in well when they are planted. Firm the roots in with your heel—it seems brutal for such small plants, but it pays!

### WHEN TO PLANT
- Spring cabbages in late summer.
- Summer cabbages in early to mid-spring.
- Winter cabbages in late spring.

### WHEN TO HARVEST
Spring cabbages will be ready to harvest the following spring, and they can be used as spring greens before the hearts form. Summer cabbages are fast-growing and are ready from midsummer, but they are not hardy and should be harvested before winter. Winter varieties are slow-growing and do not mature until late autumn or winter, and they should stand through the winter.

# PLANTING CABBAGES

1. Plant young cabbage plants a little more deeply than they were in the containers and firm them in well.

2. Fit a collar of cardboard, carpet, or a purpose-made collar from a garden center around the plant stem to prevent damage from cabbage root flies.

3. Add a covering of fine mesh or a homemade chicken wire cloche to prevent butterflies laying their eggs on the cabbages and hungry caterpillars ravaging your crop.

4. Plant a fast-growing crop between slow-to-mature cabbages to use the space efficiently. Here beets (beetroot) (to be harvested as baby beets) are being grown in the gaps, but radishes and spring onions would also work well.

Winter savoy-type cabbages, such as 'Tundra', form tightly packed heads of pale, crinkled leaves.

## HOW MANY?

Ten to twelve of any season's cabbage will probably be ample, but it is a simple crop to calculate.

## REPEAT SOWING

A supply at different times of year is ensured by planting different varieties.

## IDEAL CONDITIONS

All cabbages will do best in rich soil with plenty of organic matter. They much prefer alkaline conditions, so if you have an acid soil, lime the soil before planting.

## MAINTENANCE

Protect from pests and keep the weeds down. Mulch around spring varieties early in the year when you mulch the whole garden to give them a boost. They can be mulched with paper or grass cuttings at any time to suppress weeds.

## WHEN TO WATER

Water young plants regularly until they are established, as well as in dry periods. Spring cabbages need little watering as they grow through the colder and wetter months of the year, but summer cabbages need a regular watering to achieve lots of leaves and a good heart.

## COMMON PROBLEMS AND SOLUTIONS

**Caterpillars and birds** are likely to be the biggest threat to cabbages, as with any brassica crop. They can be protected with mesh or chicken wire cloches.

**Clubroot** is a fungal disease that distorts the root system of brassicas, limiting their growth and causing leaves to wilt and turn brown. If you suspect clubroot is a problem, dig up a plant and look at the roots. Unfortunately, if it is clubroot all the plants must be lifted and destroyed. Leave it as long as possible before planting any brassicas in that spot, as once it is in the soil clubroot persists for perhaps 20 years, far longer than any rotation system. Liming the soil can help, along with choosing a good clubroot-resistant variety, such as 'Kilaxy'.

**Cabbage root flies** lay its eggs at soil level by the stem of the cabbage plant, and the larvae hatch and feed on the roots of the plants. A small disk of cardboard, carpet, or a purpose-made collar from the garden center fitted closely around the stem of the plant can prevent the cabbage root fly getting near the stem.

## Broccoli and Calabrese

These plants are similar and often confused. Calabrese is often sold as broccoli in supermarkets, but the difference is that broccoli, or more accurately sprouting broccoli, essentially produces through the winter in milder climates and produces a number of edible shoots. Although, broccoli has some faster-maturing new varieties, such as 'Bordeaux', that could produce in as little as 10–15 weeks from planting. Calabrese produces a single central head, and will produce side shoots once this is harvested, and matures in the summer. They are both sown at a similar time, but the sprouting broccoli occupies the ground for longer, is a much larger plant, and will therefore probably need staking. It is, however, easier to grow than calabrese. Both produce flower heads that have to be picked before they open.

This purple sprouting broccoli looks just as good in the vegetable patch as it does on the dinner table.

## VARIETIES TO TRY

- Calabrese **'Trixie'** is a compact plant that is resistant to clubroot.
- Calabrese **'Iron Man'** is a resilient variety, ready to harvest from midsummer. Resistant to crown rot, Fusarium, and downy mildew, plus it stands well in the garden.
- Sprouting broccoli **'Claret'** has a very attractive dark red color.
- Sprouting broccoli **'Bordeaux'** is a very early broccoli, producing sprouts from late summer through to autumn.

## PLANT OR SEED?

Plants.

## SPACING AND PLANTING

About 12" (30.5cm) between plants. If you have an acid soil, lime it before planting. Use a collar to prevent cabbage root flies.

## WHEN TO PLANT

Both broccoli and calabrese can be transplanted outside in mid- to late spring.

## WHEN TO HARVEST

Calabrese should be ready to harvest from mid- to late summer, while sprouting broccoli is harvested in the winter months.

## HOW MANY?

Ten to twelve plants should give a worthwhile yield.

## REPEAT SOWING

No.

## IDEAL CONDITIONS

Very rich, fertile soil with plenty of organic matter—the nitrogen levels in the previous season's legume bed can give all brassica crops a boost.

## MAINTENANCE

Broccoli will need staking through the winter—the plants can reach 3' (91cm) high and have relatively shallow roots. Protect from pests and diseases.

## WHEN TO WATER

Water transplants until they are established but avoid over-watering broccoli as its growth has to be tough enough to make it through the winter, and fleshy growth may rot. Calabrese needs to be kept moist throughout the growing season.

## COMMON PROBLEMS AND SOLUTIONS

Same as for Cabbage (see page 223).

# Kale

Butterflies either can't or won't lay their eggs on the intricately frilly leaves of 'Redbor' kale, which saves the effort of trying to keep them off.

Kale is one of the hardiest winter vegetables and the easiest, least-fussy brassica to grow, delivering a multitude of dark crinkled leaves through the leanest time in the vegetable garden. It is versatile, too, and some varieties can be used as cut-and-come-again salad leaves. The craggy plants are in fact quite ornamental, especially when ennobled by sparkling frost. Kale is more straightforward than other brassicas that produce in milder climates through the winter, such as broccoli and Brussels sprouts, as it produces for months in return for the absolute minimum of care. It is also more popular and versatile.

## VARIETIES TO TRY
- **'Black Tuscany'** or **'Cavolo Nero'** has narrow dark leaves. It looks good, tastes great, and better still can be grown as a cut-and-come-again salad crop. As it is an upright variety it takes up less space than others.
- **'Redbor'** is a colorful, frilly kale that is very decorative and has a strong flavor. It is very hardy and has good resistance to pests and diseases.

## PLANT OR SEED?
Either plant or seed. Seed sown directly into the ground has always germinated reliably and grown easily.

## SPACING AND PLANTING
Plants you intend to harvest over winter need to be between 12" (30.5cm) and 24" (61cm) apart depending on the variety.

## WHEN TO PLANT
Seeds in spring and plants in summer.

## WHEN TO HARVEST
You can take some young leaves for salads and stir-fries, but the main period of harvest is late autumn and winter. Pick a few leaves from each plant each time. The seemingly spent plants should produce another batch of tender leaves in the spring before running to seed.

## HOW MANY?
Ten to fifteen plants will deliver a good harvest.

## REPEAT SOWING
No.

## IDEAL CONDITIONS
Most brassicas prefer a good, rich soil, and while kale will grow in poorer conditions, it will do better in soil with plenty of organic matter.

## MAINTENANCE
There is really nothing to be done except keeping the weeds down by hoeing or mulching and protecting the kale from marauding pests.

## WHEN TO WATER
Once the plants are established, water only in prolonged periods of very dry weather. Too much water could potentially make growth too soft to withstand the rigors of winter.

## COMMON PROBLEMS AND SOLUTIONS
To keep the **caterpillars** of cabbage white butterflies from ravaging the leaves, **flea beetles** from eating additional tiny holes, and **pigeons** having a feast, too, the kale needs to be protected with fleece or fine mesh. Mesh is probably the best in the heat of summer as fleece can raise the temperature and humidity.

# Stems and Bulbs

Stem and bulb vegetables come back year after year. Most have unique initial requirements, but the extra early effort pays off, leaving you with hardy plants that provide flavors and textures achievable with nothing else.

## Asparagus

The slim shoots of crisp, young asparagus are a gourmet's delight and one of the real treats of spring. As a perennial, it will occupy a fair chunk of space all year round for just a few weeks of production, and you have to resist harvesting any spears in their first season. Depending on the vigor of the variety you decide to grow, you may even want to take only a few in the second. So, asparagus requires space, patience, and a really good start; clearing out all perennial weeds is essential along with good, rich soil. All that said, once a bed is up and running, it should provide amazing asparagus for 10–20 years in return for being kept weed-free and covered with a good layer of mulch in the spring. So, there is a fair bit of work to getting asparagus established, but if you get it right, it should be smooth sailing from then on.

Purple asparagus has an appealing color and usually a sweeter flavor than green varieties.

### VARIETIES TO TRY

- **'Pacific 2000'** is sweet tasting and provides a bumper harvest. This mid-season, green variety is a reliable choice.
- **'Stewarts Purple'** is a new variety that is much sweeter than green cultivars. The purple color makes the spears even more appealing, and it even keeps its color when lightly cooked.

### PLANT OR SEED?

Buy one-year-old crowns as these are the root system of an asparagus plant.

### SPACING AND PLANTING

It is best to have a dedicated asparagus bed built for the purpose if you can. The crowns need to be about 12" (30.5cm) apart, and they can be arranged in a staggered double row. If you have more than one row, leave 18" (45.7cm) between double rows. Soak the crowns in water for about an hour before planting.

### WHEN TO PLANT

Early spring.

You don't need an asparagus steamer to enjoy this seasonal treat. Simply drizzle the spears with olive oil and roast them on low heat for 15–20 minutes.

# PLANTING ASPARAGUS

**1.** To plant the crowns, dig a trench about 8" (20.3cm) deep and just wide enough for the crowns. Put a layer of garden compost in the bottom, and then build up a ridge of soil along the trench to sit the crowns on so that the buds will be at soil level.

**2.** Arrange the crowns 12" (30.5cm) apart, and spread the roots out down the sides of the ridge.

**3.** When all the crowns are in position, backfill the trench with soil and mulch the whole bed with a layer of garden compost.

## WHEN TO HARVEST

You should be able to take a light harvest in the spring of the following year after planting. Cut the spears about ¾" (1.9cm) below soil level with a knife when they are about 6" (15.2cm) tall. Once plants are established, you can keep taking spears for about six weeks, then leave the spears to develop into tall, feathery ferns, allowing the plants to regenerate.

## HOW MANY?

Twelve crowns should keep a family going. Each crown should produce about 10–12 spears in the harvest period. This will occupy about a 13' (4m) row or a 3' x 6½' (91cm x 2m) bed.

## REPEAT SOWING

To extend the harvest, plant two varieties, an early and a mid-season.

## IDEAL CONDITIONS

Asparagus needs a well-drained soil to flourish—there is no point sticking it in heavy soil and hoping for the best. If you are working in flat beds in heavy soil, building a raised bed is the best solution. It also needs plenty of organic matter in the soil. Late frosts can also be a problem as the spears are tender.

## MAINTENANCE

Mulch once a year in the spring. The ferny top growth may need supporting to keep it from breaking in the wind and keep it tidy. When the foliage begins to die in the autumn, cut it down to just above soil level and put it on the compost heap.

## WHEN TO WATER

In the first year, keep the crowns well-watered in dry conditions.

## COMMON PROBLEMS AND SOLUTIONS

**Slugs** can damage the emerging spears—if they are a severe problem, you could consider mulching the bed with sharp grit.

**Weak and spindly spears** can be caused by a number of factors, such as picking too heavily, too soon, or for too long, or a lack of nutrients in the soil.

**Asparagus beetle** is a common pest. It is easy to spot as it boasts black-and-yellow stripes, and its caterpillar is grayish. Both can be removed by hand along with the clumps of black eggs. If asparagus beetles are a problem, destroy the foliage at the end of the season rather than composting it.

## Rhubarb

Growing rhubarb takes almost no effort for a big pay-off.

Rhubarb comes so early in the year, especially if it's forced. If you like rhubarb, then you really should grow it because it requires little work in the garden.

## VARIETIES TO TRY

- **'Timperley Early'** is one of the earliest varieties. It is good for forcing and its stems remain tender until late in the season.
- **'Red Champagne'** is a mid-season variety that delivers a hefty vegetable of rich red stems.

## PLANT OR SEED?

Bare-root crowns or potted plants.

## SPACING AND PLANTING

Allow each plant about 11' (3.4m) square and ensure there is plenty of organic matter in the soil.

Rhubarb is among the best of the early garden crops. The early harvest and light, bright flavor really get you in the mood for the rest of the gardening season.

A well-fed rhubarb plant should yield a delicious crop of stems for about ten years.

## WHEN TO PLANT

Rhubarb is usually planted as dormant crowns in autumn or late winter. Pot-grown plants are available in garden centers later in the year if you miss the dormant period.

## WHEN TO HARVEST

- Stalks cannot be pulled from newly planted crowns. The plants need the first year to get established. In the second year, forced plants can be ready from late winter to very early spring. You can keep harvesting until mid- to late summer. Never completely strip a plant—always leave about half the stems each time to allow the plant to regenerate. Stop harvesting around midsummer so the crown can recover; by this time, there are plenty of other things ready for harvest and the stalks become coarser and less tasty.
- The stems should always be pulled by holding the stem close to the base and pulling away from the crown while twisting slightly. Try not to dislodge forming stems.

## HOW MANY?

Two or three crowns provide enough rhubarb for most families.

## REPEAT SOWING

No, but some cultivars produce slightly earlier than others.

## IDEAL CONDITIONS

Rhubarb is not difficult as long as there is plenty of organic matter in the soil.

## MAINTENANCE

- Mulch well as part of the annual mulching with well-rotted manure if you can, as this really gives the plants a boost. If none is available, use garden compost.
- For an early crop, rhubarb can be forced—this means covering the crown with a large up-turned garbage pail, chimney pot, or purpose-made terra-cotta forcing jar. The forcer can be stuffed with straw and put in position in late winter. The forced stems are pale, tender, and delicate and can be harvested weeks earlier than they would be otherwise. Forced plants should be given the rest of the season to recover, and the same plant should not be forced two years running.
- If the crown produces a flower spike (this will look very different to the leaf stems), remove it as close to the base as possible. Established plants will survive a few weeds until they can be dealt with.

## WHEN TO WATER

Only once established in extended periods of dry weather.

## COMMON PROBLEMS AND SOLUTIONS

There is very little to worry about with rhubarb, except that old plants will gradually lose their vigor and should be replaced with new ones in a different location.

# Celeriac

Not the most beautiful of vegetables but one of the easiest to grow in the low-maintenance vegetable garden, as long as you have enough space.

It seems you either love the pungent combination of celery and fennel flavors of celeriac, or you hate it. It is terrific used raw in salads, makes a good mash, works well in hearty winter soups and casseroles, and even roasts beautifully. The only downside is the length of time it is in the ground, from late spring (when planted as a plug) through the autumn and winter.

## VARIETIES TO TRY
'**Brilliant**' produces less knobby roots than other varieties, and these don't seem to become pithy. Its flesh does not discolor.

## PLANT OR SEED?
Plants. Seed germination is sometimes erratic.

## SPACING AND PLANTING
About 12" (30.5cm) apart each way.

## WHEN TO PLANT
Mid- to late spring.

## WHEN TO HARVEST
You probably won't need to harvest celeriac until mid-autumn. There is so much else on offer in the garden, the roots will happily stay in the ground all winter in mild areas, or they can be protected from heavy frosts with a mulch of straw or dug and stored in a cool place. They should keep for months.

## HOW MANY?
Twelve plants should take most people through the winter, that's one a week for twelve weeks, taking just over 11' (3.4m) square of space. If you are a fan and have the space, indulge yourself with more.

## REPEAT SOWING
No.

## IDEAL CONDITIONS
Good, rich soil will make for good-sized roots.

## MAINTENANCE
To help retain moisture and thwart weeds, mulch with garden compost or straw between the plants. Removing the lower leaves will encourage the roots to swell, and the results have been fine.

## WHEN TO WATER
A good deluge once a fortnight if the weather is dry.

## COMMON PROBLEMS AND SOLUTIONS
It is usually rare to have a problem with this vegetable.

In all except the coldest areas, celeriac can be left in the ground until needed. A useful vegetable to fill the lean winter period.

# Fruiting Vegetables

Fruiting vegetables are the stars of summer, thriving most often in warm weather. Choosing the right varieties will give you a vibrant and abundant crop for creating culinary masterpieces all season long.

## Tomatoes

'Tumbler' produces a profusion of sweet bite-sized cherry tomatoes, which are always popular with children.

As the low-maintenance vegetable garden doesn't extend to managing a greenhouse, gardeners in a cold climate will struggle to grow good tomatoes outdoors. However, in regions with enough sun, there are varieties that can be grown successfully. These fall into two categories: cordon (tall) and bush tomatoes. Cordon tomatoes require a lot of time spent staking, tying-in, and pinching out the side shoots. They are generally much more demanding and exacting than bush varieties which need none of these ministrations. For this reason, stick to growing less demanding bush varieties as these produce masses of smaller fruit on low plants and demand much less time. As a rule, the larger the fruit, the more sun they will need to ripen.

### VARIETIES TO TRY

- **'Tumbler'** is a trailing bush variety that produces lots of succulent cherry tomatoes. Plant them near the corners of raised beds so the plants can trail over the side. They will also grow well in pots and hanging baskets, although they need a little extra care.
- **'Tumbling Tom Yellow'** is a very compact plant, and this and its fellow 'Tumbling Tom Red' produce a good crop of cherry-sized tomatoes, the yellow being a little less sweet than the red.
- **'Red Alert'** is an earlier equally fruitful variety.

### PLANT OR SEED?
Plants.

### SPACING AND PLANTING
Leave about 18" (45.7cm) between bush plants.

### WHEN TO PLANT
After the last frost.

### WHEN TO HARVEST
Pick the fruits as they ripen.

Plant young tomato plants at the same level they were in their pots. If the weather is cold, protect them with a layer of fleece.

Trailing plants, such as 'Tumbler' and 'Tumbling Tom', can be planted so that they spill out over the edge of raised beds.

It is reassuring to know that your homegrown tomato is packed with vitamin C and antioxidants as well as flavor.

## HOW MANY?
Three or four plants.

## REPEAT SOWING
No.

## IDEAL CONDITIONS
Tomatoes do best in a warm, sunny, and sheltered spot in good soil with plenty of organic matter.

## MAINTENANCE
Bush tomatoes are very easy to grow—all they require is a liquid feed with a high potash organic fertilizer once a week once they are flowering. If your soil is good, getting a little slipshod with the feeding doesn't seem to do too much harm.

## WHEN TO WATER
Young plants need regular watering until they are established, and then two or three times a week when the plants are in flower and the fruits are forming. There is a tendency to water tomato plants a great deal, and while this certainly swells the fruit, too much water can dilute the delicious flavor of the ripe fruits, robbing them of their sweetness.

## COMMON PROBLEMS AND SOLUTIONS
Fortunately, tomatoes grown outdoors suffer from far fewer problems than those grown under glass.

**Blight** is the most likely problem with outdoor tomatoes. This is the same disease that afflicts potatoes, and it is most likely to be a problem in cool, wet summers. Plants develop brown patches on the leaves and discolored patches on the fruits. There is little that can be done once a plant is badly affected, and the fruit and foliage have to be removed and destroyed. There are some cultivars that show resistance to blight, such as 'Fantasio,' which are worth trying if blight is a recurrent problem in your area.

**Blossom end rot** is a black patch at the base of the fruit; this is a symptom of erratic watering. It is fortunately uncommon in plants grown in the ground.

In a cool or short summer, you may be left with a great number of green fruits, and you can help the last few fruits to ripen by removing some of the foliage to let more light get to the fruits. If this fails, green tomatoes can be put in a brown paper bag with a banana in a cool place to ripen. Alternatively, pickle them or make chutney.

Plant marigolds among tomato plants to deter insect pests.

# Peppers and Chilies

Chilies are a fantastic way to spice up food. For a milder effect, remove the seeds before cooking. Always take care not to touch your face or eyes when preparing chilies.

If you are growing in a cool climate and aiming for the best harvest possible from your vegetable garden, peppers are probably not for you. A good outdoor harvest really does need Mediterranean conditions, and even if you go to a great deal of trouble and fuss with cloches, the yield will probably not be good. Chilies, however, are a different matter as they are more tolerant of changes in temperature despite requiring a warm spot. Just one or two good-sized plants could deliver all the chilies you will need for the year. They are easily dried once ripe and will last if kept in a cool, dry place. In some places, chilies are called chili peppers or hot peppers, creating some labeling confusion. Regardless, peppers, chilies, chili peppers, and hot peppers are essentially grown in the same manner.

## VARIETIES TO TRY
- **'Apache'** is a compact variety of chili with medium strength and plump, round-ended fruits. Can be grown in pots.
- **'Bell Boy'** is a popular variety of pepper, ripening to give red fruit.
- **'Big Banana'** is an unusual pepper cultivar with long, tapered fruit.

## PLANT OR SEED?
Plants.

## SPACING AND PLANTING
Allow about 18" (45.7cm) between plants.

## WHEN TO PLANT
Early summer if the weather is warm.

## WHEN TO HARVEST
Peppers can be harvested green or left to ripen to orange, red, or black depending on the cultivar. If you leave the peppers to ripen, then the harvest will be smaller as the plants will stop producing new fruits. Take care when harvesting chilies; wear gloves, snip them from the plant, and avoid any juice contacting your skin.

## HOW MANY?
One or two plants for chilies, five or six for peppers.

## REPEAT SOWING
No.

## IDEAL CONDITIONS
Good, rich soil in a very warm, sheltered, sunny spot.

## MAINTENANCE
There is little to do except feed once every couple of weeks with tomato food once in flower. If you decide to grow peppers in a cool climate, protect them with polycarbonate cloches in cool weather. At the end of the growing season, snip all chilies from the plant and lay them out to dry. You can move the plant to a frost-free spot and let the chilies dry on the plant. Store the dried chilies in an airtight container.

## WHEN TO WATER
Water very sparingly, especially if the weather is cool.

## COMMON PROBLEMS AND SOLUTIONS
If the weather is cold and cloudy, the fruits may fail to develop.

**Aphids** (greenfly) are a common problem and can weaken young plants. They can be removed by hand, but mature plants should withstand a minor infestation. Companion planting (see page 116) may help.

# Eggplants (Aubergines)

The eggplant (aubergine) plant produces one of the prettiest flowers on the vegetable plot.

Eggplants are even more of a struggle to grow outdoors in a temperate climate than peppers. They are tropical in origin and so require sustained heat to flourish, but if you have this, then they are fairly straightforward to grow. Unless you garden in a reliably warm spot, the harvest is probably not going to justify the work you have to put in to grow them outside.

## VARIETIES TO TRY
- **'Moneymaker'** is the most commonly available plant, producing long purple-black fruits.
- **'Ova'** produces interesting white fruits.

## PLANT OR SEED?
Plants. Start with large, well-established plants in colder areas to give the best chance of a harvest.

## SPACING AND PLANTING
Leave about 24" (61cm) between plants.

## WHEN TO PLANT
Summer.

## WHEN TO HARVEST
The fruits are ready as soon as they are fully colored.

## HOW MANY?
Each plant will probably yield three fruits, which isn't a great deal, so plan accordingly.

## REPEAT SOWING
No.

## IDEAL CONDITIONS
Rich, moist soil.

## MAINTENANCE
Feed the plants once a week with high potash organic fertilizer once flowering begins. To encourage the plants to become bushy, the growing tip can be removed once the plants are 12" (30.5cm) tall.

## WHEN TO WATER
Eggplants require plenty of water all through the season.

## COMMON PROBLEMS AND SOLUTIONS
As for Tomatoes (see page 234).

Eggplants are a relative of the tomato but are much more difficult to grow in temperate climates without protection.

# Zucchinis (Courgettes) and Summer Squash (Marrows)

Picked young and sliced thinly, zucchinis (courgettes) are a good addition to summer salads.

Given enough water and compost, zucchinis are effortless to grow. Homegrown zucchinis are usually available in such profusion that they can be picked while still young, sweet, and delicious, and are nothing like some of the pithy, oversized tasteless examples from the supermarket. They are a staple of so many dishes yet are equally delicious sliced thinly in salads or simply stir-fried in butter. Even the magnificent yellow trumpet flowers are edible. A really rewarding plant.

## VARIETIES TO TRY

- **'One Ball'** produces shining, round, yellow zucchinis with creamy, sweet flesh. 'One Ball' is a bit of a novelty but still pulls its weight, giving a good harvest and having a good shape for stuffing.
- **'Orelia'** is another golden-colored cultivar. It has a very vigorous habit and produces an amazingly good yield of tasty zucchinis.
- **'El Greco'** has the advantage of producing early. It produces an open, erect plant that makes picking

easy and a profusion of mid-green, excellently flavored zucchinis.

- **'Defender'** is another reliable early green variety of zucchini worth trying, especially as it has some resistance to mosaic virus and downy mildew.

## PLANT OR SEED?

Zucchinis are reasonably easy when sown directly into the soil, but it is still easier to buy plants as you will only need three or four.

## SPACING AND PLANTING

Each plant really does need some room—11' (3.4m) square or just under—but for that space and very little work, you will get an abundance, if not a glut, of zucchinis. Plant the young plants with plenty of compost on a small mound and mulch around them with compost.

## WHEN TO PLANT

Late spring.

## WHEN TO HARVEST

Eight to ten weeks from planting. Pick the zucchinis when they are still young and tender at about 4"–5" (10.2–12.7cm) long and keep picking to ensure a continued supply. If you are a weekend gardener or seldom able to visit your garden, then picking the fruits

It is almost miraculous how rapidly 'El Greco' can produce more fruits.

The 'One Ball' is a bit of a novelty and adds color and interest to the vegetable garden.

young is a must, as in a week a small tender fruit can become oversized and old.

## HOW MANY?
Two to four plants should be ample, which will take 6½'–10' (2–3m) of your growing space all through the summer. If you will be away from your plot for a couple of weeks, remove all the fruits and flowers—it seems harsh, but this will ensure you have a crop to come home to.

## REPEAT SOWING
No.

## IDEAL CONDITIONS
A plentiful supply of organic matter and water is the key to success with zucchinis and summer squash. From the start, they need plenty of nutrition to generate those enormous, coarse leaves that provide the energy to keep the fruits coming. A space-saving tip is to try planting zucchinis and summer squash on the compost heap as they will thrive in the rich, moist environment.

## MAINTENANCE
Beyond mulching and watering there is little else to do except feeding once a week once fruiting has started. Young plants may need protecting from slugs and snails with a bottle cloche. Once the plants are established, they can tolerate a little competition from weeds until these can be dealt with.

## WHEN TO WATER
Water regularly to keep the soil moist.

## COMMON PROBLEMS AND SOLUTIONS
**Mosaic virus**, or more correctly cucumber mosaic virus (CMV), appears as small yellow patches on the leaves that spread to give the mosaic pattern. The leaves then crinkle, and the plants fail to thrive and produce few fruits. The plants are best removed and destroyed. The virus is common in the garden and spread by aphids or knives used for harvesting, so there is little that can be done to defend your crop or treat it once it is infected. Growing resistant varieties, such as 'Defender', is the best solution.

**Powdery mildew** is less serious and usually strikes during the autumn. A white powder appears on the leaves, and the plants tend to lose their vitality and production slows. Badly affected leaves can be removed, and the plants can be perked up with some lavish watering and a liquid feed if you aren't doing so already.

'One Ball' is an unusual, round summer squash with a particularly sweet flesh.

# Pumpkins and Winter Squashes

Reducing the number of fruits on each plant will increase the likelihood of achieving good-sized pumpkins.

These plants require a great deal of space. Their stems roam across the soil and throw up enormous, crinkled leaves, but this prodigious growth means they are immensely satisfying to grow, and the flowers are edible, too. Fiery orange pumpkins are stunningly ornamental. A neat space-saving technique is to grow your squashes under your sweet corn as neither will interfere with the growth of the other, and you get two crops from one bed. This is the Native American Three Sisters planting strategy, in which beans, sweet corn, and squashes were grown together to really amp up the soil nutrients and get the most out of a small space. The squashes' large leaves also help to suppress weeds. Squashes can be trained up obelisks or other supports as a space-saving strategy, but even so in a small vegetable garden, large pumpkins will probably be impractical and in cooler regions they can be unreliable.

## VARIETIES TO TRY

- **'Racer'** produces plenty of large, perfectly shaped Halloween pumpkins.
- **'Jack of All Trades'** is another great pumpkin for carving, with each plant producing plenty of large, orange fruits.
- **'Cobnut'** is a variety of butternut squash that is tasty and sweet when roasted. It is a fast-maturing variety, which is helpful in cooler areas.

## PLANT OR SEED?
Plants.

## SPACING AND PLANTING
As pumpkin and squash cultivars vary enormously, refer to the instructions for the particular variety you are growing.

## WHEN TO PLANT
Late spring.

## WHEN TO HARVEST
Early autumn.

## REPEAT SOWING
No.

## IDEAL CONDITIONS
Rich, moist soil in a sunny spot.

## MAINTENANCE
Nothing beyond regular watering. Cut away leaves at the end of the season to allow fruits to ripen and gather before first frosts.

## WHEN TO WATER
Pumpkins have good root systems and so need less water than you might expect but keep the soil moist.

## HOW MANY?
Pumpkin and squash cultivars vary enormously in the size and shapes of the fruit they produce, so it is hard to be prescriptive. They take up plenty of space, too. If you love pumpkin and have plenty of space, try three or four plants, otherwise start with one or two.

## COMMON PROBLEMS AND SOLUTIONS
**Powdery mildew** is a possible threat (see Zucchinis [Courgettes] and Summer Squash [Marrows] on page 238).

**Slugs and snails** can devour young plants, so protect plants with plastic bottle cloches.

To be grown well, pumpkins and squashes need to be left on the plant until the skin hardens, then cut leaving a long stalk and left in the sun until they sound hollow when tapped.

# Artichokes

Pick the flower buds just before they open.

The statuesque globe artichoke has much to recommend it to the time-poor gardener. It is a perennial, and given a sunny spot should carry on producing tasty buds for four or five years with little attention. Artichokes generally start producing in early summer, which can be a lean time in the vegetable garden, and they're a real gourmet treat. The downside is that each plant will permanently occupy about 11' (3.4m) square of space and the yield for the space occupied is not immense. However, if you have the room and really enjoy eating them, they are easy to grow and can be treated just like any herbaceous perennial.

## VARIETIES TO TRY

- **'Green Globe'** is perhaps the most commonly available variety, but not perhaps the tastiest. It produces large green buds and is reasonably hardy.
- **'Purple Globe'** is hardier than 'Green Globe' and produces similarly large buds with fleshy bases to its scales.
- **'Violetto di Chioggia'** is very beautiful and would be an asset in any flower border, but it may be difficult to find. It is very early, producing smaller buds with dark purple scales.

## PLANT OR SEED?

For a quick start, buy established plants of named cultivars in pots from the garden center or by mail order. They can be grown from seed or supplied as rooted offsets.

## SPACING AND PLANTING

Consider that the plants will be about 5' (1.5m) tall with large, arching, silvery leaves and so likely to cast shade over neighboring beds.

## WHEN TO PLANT

Late winter.

## WHEN TO HARVEST

Early summer.

## HOW MANY?

Space might be a factor, but usually three plants.

## REPEAT SOWING

Plant varieties that produce at different times if you have space.

Technically not a fruit but a flower bud, the artichoke is probably more fuss to eat than it is to grow.

## IDEAL CONDITIONS

Globe artichokes thrive in a well-drained, rich soil in an open, sunny environment. Dig in some well-rotted manure when planting and on heavier, poorly drained soils add grit.

## MAINTENANCE

A good layer of compost around the plants during the annual mulch will build up the plants and improve harvests. If they are in a windy spot provide some support—a simple cane should do—to prevent the brittle stems from breaking. At the end of the season when the leaves wither, cut back the foliage, and in frost-prone areas, protect the crown with straw or horticultural fleece.

## WHEN TO WATER

In prolonged periods without rainfall.

## COMMON PROBLEMS AND SOLUTIONS

**Blackfly** is the most likely problem that congregates on the shoots and buds. The best treatment is to dislodge them with a strong jet of water before the infestation gets too great.

# Cucumbers

Homegrown outdoor cucumbers are slightly different to greenhouse varieties. They tend to be shorter and rough-skinned, but they taste every bit as good, and thankfully the outdoor varieties are much easier to manage than their glasshouse relatives. Cucumbers do best when grown up an obelisk or some form of support and so take up little growing space. Once they are established, they produce fruits at an astonishing rate. Even outdoor varieties, however, need a warm and sheltered location to succeed. Do note that it is not worth trying indoor varieties outside as they are rarely a success.

## VARIETIES TO TRY

- **'Burpless Tasty Green'** is as tasty as its name promises and has no bitterness. It does well even in poor summers.
- **'Green Fingers'** produces masses of small cucumbers with a good flavor. One cucumber is just about an individual portion, and these are very popular with children. Resistant to powdery mildew.

## PLANT OR SEED?

Plants.

## SPACING AND PLANTING

Space the plants about 24" (61cm) apart. Draw up the soil into a mound and plant the young plant on the top. Handle the young plants with care as they are brittle and resent the disturbance of being transplanted. Mulch around the plants.

## WHEN TO PLANT

In early summer when all risk of frost has passed.

Cucumbers can be trained up any support or left to scramble through plants at ground level.

## WHEN TO HARVEST

Pick fruits as they form as soon as they fill out. Very young fruits may not be the best tasting, while very old plants will have tough skin and pronounced seeds. Always cut the cucumber from the plant as the stems are brittle and likely to break.

## HOW MANY?

Two or three plants.

## REPEAT SOWING

No.

## IDEAL CONDITIONS

Very rich, moist soil in a warm spot. Cucumbers won't do well in a cold, windy location.

## MAINTENANCE

Thick layers of mulch will help to keep the soil warm and retain moisture. Planting through a sheet mulch of black plastic can help keep the roots warm and suppress weeds. The plants can suffer a slight check in growth after planting but should recover and grow strongly.

## WHEN TO WATER

At least twice a week, copiously once growing strongly.

## COMMON PROBLEMS AND SOLUTIONS

**Slugs** will attack young plants, so use plastic bottle cloches to protect them.

**Mildew** often coats the leaves toward the end of the summer; remove the affected leaves and destroy them and the plant should continue to produce.

**Cucumber mosaic virus** can also be a problem (see under Zucchinis [Courgettes] and Summer Squash [Marrows] on page 238).

# Sweet Corn

Grow the right varieties, and you will never have tasted sweet corn so sweet, tender, and delicious. Most sweet corn varieties are now termed "supersweet" (the sweetest) or "sugar-enhanced," and they contain far more sugars than the regular varieties. The yield for the growing space they occupy is not the best, but it is reasonable, and the cobs, cooked just minutes after picking, are so unlike anything you can buy they are well worth growing. As soon as a cob is picked the sugars start turning into starch, so the supermarket will never be able to match the taste. The cobs tend to all ripen at once unless you carefully stagger repeat sowing. Cold weather can also prevent ripening, and the supersweet cultivars do need warmer conditions to do well.

## VARIETIES TO TRY

- **'Lark'** is a tendersweet variety—it is sweet like the supersweets but even more tender and easier to digest. The cobs are not large, but the taste is indescribably good.
- **'Earlibird'** is a supersweet cultivar that produces lovely, neat cobs earlier than any other supersweet.

Statuesque sweet corn plants are wonderfully decorative and don't look out of place among the flowers for cutting.

This cob is not quite ripe—its tassel, or silk, has not turned brown yet.

### PLANT OR SEED?

Growing from small plants is recommended, but handle them carefully as sweet corn resent root disturbance.

### SPACING AND PLANTING

- Plant 14" (35.6cm) apart in each direction in blocks rather than rows. Sweet corn is wind-pollinated and planting in a block gives the best chance of good pollination. Position the plants so they are a little deeper than they were in the pots to encourage adventitious roots and to keep them stable. In warm areas, direct sowing is possible but only when the soil temperature has really warmed up in early summer.
- Sweet corn is one of the vegetables that can be planted through a sheet of black plastic to cut back on the need for weeding and to keep the roots warm. Mulching well and underplanting with squashes will help to keep weeds down, too.

### WHEN TO PLANT

Late spring to early summer after the risk of frost has passed.

### WHEN TO HARVEST

Mid- to late summer. Once the silks or tassels on the cobs begin to turn brown, the sweet corn is probably ripe. To check if sweet corn is ripe and ready for picking, carefully peel back the green outer covering and the filaments and push your nail into the kernels. If the juice is milky, then the cob is ripe. Twist the ripe cob off, leaving the second to ripen.

### HOW MANY?

Sixteen plants should yield around 32 cobs, requiring a block of growing space of just over 16" (40.6cm) square.

### REPEAT SOWING

Possible if you have enough room and the temperatures are adequate. Often late plantings won't ripen because the autumn weather is not warm enough.

### IDEAL CONDITIONS

Sweet corn needs good soil with plenty of organic matter. If you can put them in last season's pea bed, they will enjoy the nitrogen left in the soil by the peas.

### MAINTENANCE

In windy areas, earth can be piled up around the stems to keep them stable. Once established, they are tall enough not to be smothered by a few weeds, but it is much smarter to cut down on weeding around sweet corn plants by applying a good mulch and planting small squashes or zucchinis between the plants. The two crops will grow happily together, and the mulch and the tough, spreading leaves of the squash or zucchinis will suppress weeds. You also get two crops out of one space.

### WHEN TO WATER

Sweet corn plants need plenty of water, especially as the cobs are swelling.

### COMMON PROBLEMS AND SOLUTIONS

**Underdeveloped cobs** or bald patches on the cobs caused by poor pollination are the most common problems with sweet corn.

**Slugs and birds** can also be a problem, and sweet corn is one of the young plants you can try to plant out with a plastic bottle cloche to protect the tender leaves. The plants also enjoy the extra warmth they offer. The same bottles can be used to protect the ripening cobs from squirrels later in the season if they are a problem.

# Allium Family

The allium family is the cornerstone of flavorful cooking and an essential part of any garden. The vegetables all have bold flavors. Because they're so aromatic and undemanding, they're also beneficial when used as companion plantings.

## Onions

Once planted, all a row of onions requires is occasional hoeing to keep weeds from swamping them, and that's it. Their undemanding nature and their status as a basic in the kitchen make them a natural choice for those wanting to get the maximum out of their vegetable garden with little effort. They can be planted in spring or autumn, and for those juggling crops on a small plot, autumn sowing makes sense as the onions will occupy the space over the winter when there are fewer demands. As you begin to harvest them in June, zucchinis and summer squash can then fill the gap, making economical use of growing space.

### VARIETIES TO TRY
- **'Red Delicious'** is a large, sweet red onion that matures early when planted in the spring.
- **'Radar'** is an autumn-planting variety that has a mild flavor and a strong resistance to bolting.

'Hercules' is reputed to be an excellent keeper.

Onion sets are small, immature onion bulbs that are harvested early for replanting. They get things started much more quickly than seeds.

- **'Hercules'** produces a yellow, round-shaped bulb that keeps well and is suitable for spring planting.
- **'Senshyu Yellow'** is planted in the autumn for an early harvest the following summer. The tops can be used in the same way as chives.

### PLANT OR SEED?
Onions are most straightforward when grown from sets—these are small, partially grown onions where the growth has been arrested, leaving them ready to spring into life once planted. Growing from seed is possible but not worthwhile for the busy gardener.

### SPACING AND PLANTING
Plant sets by pushing them gently into the soil so they sit just below the surface. In heavy soils, you may need to use a trowel to avoid damaging the set. If birds are a problem in your garden, snip off the papery tip so they can't drag the set out of the soil. If you want the biggest onions you can get, plant them 4" (10.2cm) apart, and if you would like a few smaller onions, plant some 2" (5.1cm) apart, cramming more into the space. Leave 8" (20.3cm) between rows.

## WHEN TO PLANT
Overwintering varieties are planted in early autumn, and main crop onions in mid- to late spring.

## WHEN TO HARVEST
You can begin taking a few autumn-planted onions in early summer, while the rest of the crop can be lifted when the tops turn yellow and fall over, usually in midsummer. Gently ease each onion out of the ground and leave them in the sun, a sheltered porch, or shed to

The easiest way to grow onions is from sets.

Snip the tip from the set and push it into the ground so it is just visible. Use a dibble in hard ground.

allow the skins to harden. Store them by tying them in bunches, hanging them in a net sack, or making strings and hanging them in a cool, airy place.

## HOW MANY?
Your onion yield is easy to predict—you plant 50 sets, and you should get 50 onions, although the sizes may vary. Sets are often sold by weight and 50 sets weighs about 7 oz. (198.4g). Growing 50 large onions requires one 16' (4.9m) row. Just calculate how many onions you use in a week and go from there.

## REPEAT SOWING
No.

## MAINTENANCE
Onions won't grow well if there is competition from weeds, so once every couple of weeks quickly hoe between the rows slicing young weed plants from their roots. A time-saving solution is to grow onions through a sheet mulch of black plastic.

## WHEN TO WATER
Onions really don't need watering unless the weather is exceptionally dry, as they develop a deep root system, and it seems regular watering has little effect on their production. In fact, too much water at the end of the growing period can be detrimental as the onions won't keep as well.

## COMMON PROBLEMS AND SOLUTIONS
**White rot** causes onion leaves to become yellow and fluffy and white mold with black spots to form around the bulb. This is a fungal disease with fruiting bodies that can persist in the soil, infecting any member of the allium family. Unfortunately, this is one of the rare vegetable garden problems with no solution, but with care the problem can be contained and avoided in subsequent years. Any infected onions must be destroyed and not composted. Leave it as long as possible before growing onions or leeks in the affected bed as the disease can persist in the soil for up to eight years.

**Bolting** (onions producing a flower spike) can be a proble. If you come across this, try growing heat-resistant

Lifted onions need to be left in the sun or a warm place to allow the skins to harden.

varieties. These are more expensive but have a reduced instance of bolting.

Mildew can also be a problem, causing a white fungal growth to appear on the leaves. Affected leaves should be removed and destroyed, but the bulbs should still be usable, although they will probably not store well.

## Shallots

As blissfully easy to grow as onions, shallots have a special flavor and sweetness, although they tend to be expensive and harder to find in stores. In most respects, they are managed in the same way as onions, but each set you plant will grow into a cluster of shallots all about the same size. For each set you plant, you should harvest at least five or six shallots.

### VARIETIES TO TRY

- 'Jermor' produces long, thin bulbs with a copper-colored skin, pinky flesh, and a superb flavor, and can keep remarkably well.
- 'Delvad' gives a good yield of round bulbs, eight to ten per cluster. It has tasty, pinkish flesh.

### PLANT OR SEED?

Sets. If you get the chance to choose your own, small ones are less likely to bolt.

### SPACING AND PLANTING

They can be spaced at 6" (15.2cm) apart with 8" (20.3cm) between rows or 4" (10.2cm) apart with 12" (30.5cm) between rows. Push them into the soil so

This healthy clump of 'Jermor' (shown both from above and close in on the bulbs) miraculously delivers eight shallots for the one set planted. All the gardener has to do is hoe a few times.

the tops are just level with the surface of the soil. As with onions, snip off the papery tip to prevent birds from unearthing the set. If you find sets on the surface, just poke them back in.

## WHEN TO PLANT
Winter or early to mid-spring.

## WHEN TO HARVEST
As soon as they look large enough, you can start taking a few for cooking. Then when the foliage yellows and dies back, lift the clumps of shallots, and leave them to dry off in the sun or in a dry, airy space. They can be stored in trays, netting sacks, or tied into bunches in a frost-free, dry place.

## HOW MANY?
Each shallot will give a harvest of about five or six more, so 30 sets should yield about 150 shallots, which is probably plenty. It is helpful to know that 2 lbs. (1kg) of sets equals about 100 sets.

## REPEAT SOWING
No.

## IDEAL CONDITIONS
Good, fertile soil.

## MAINTENANCE
Shallots will not do well if they are competing with weeds, so hoe between the rows every couple of weeks.

## WHEN TO WATER
Water in extremely dry weather.

## COMMON PROBLEMS AND SOLUTIONS
Very trouble-free. Although they are susceptible to the same conditions as onions, they have the reputation of being more robust and problem-free.

# Garlic

These ample cloves should produce good-size bulbs when planted.

If you regularly cook with garlic and enjoy its pungent flavor, then it is a must-have in your vegetable garden, not only because you can feast on wonderfully flavorsome garlic and experiment with the tastes of different varieties, but also because it is incredibly low maintenance. Like most of the allium family, hoeing is the only task to keep up with once they are planted (until harvesting). Garlic also makes a great companion plant as its strong smell confounds pests in search of other vegetables. You will need to dry and store your vegetable, but this is no hardship—they can be tied into small bundles (fancy braiding is nice but not obligatory) and kept in a dry, not-too-cool place (too cool encourages them to sprout). Garlic is a great vegetable crop for beginners as long as the site is suitable.

## VARIETIES TO TRY
There are varieties suited to planting in autumn that will keep about four months from harvest, and spring-planting varieties that will keep for a couple of months longer.
- **'Germidour'** is a mild-flavored French variety suitable for autumn planting.

## CAN'T I JUST PLANT GARLIC FROM THE SUPERMARKET?

You can, but chances are it's been imported so won't be a variety that grows well in your climate. There is also a greater risk of viruses and nematodes infecting the crop, and you won't know what you are growing or how long it will keep. It's much better to buy from a garden center or check out a specialty supplier—you'll also get a much wider choice of varieties that way.

- **'Marco'** is planted in autumn and is said to keep for a year. It has a very fine, punchy flavor.
- **'Cristo'** produces large, strongly flavored bulbs and can be planted in autumn or spring, plus it has the advantage of a long storage period.

### PLANT OR SEED?

Cloves broken from a bulb of garlic. Bigger cloves produce bigger bulbs, and some of the smaller ones toward the center of the bulb may not be worth planting.

### SPACING AND PLANTING

Leave about 6" (15.2cm) between cloves and 12" (30.2cm) between rows. Push them into the soil flat end first so the point is just below the surface of the soil. If you want to grow them in a block, plant the cloves 6" (15.2cm) apart in staggered rows.

### WHEN TO PLANT

Autumn or spring.

### WHEN TO HARVEST

The bulbs should be fully formed by midsummer—harvest them when the leaves fade or they may sprout new leaves. If you are impatient, you can enjoy green or wet garlic sooner, whenever the bulbs look large enough.

### HOW MANY?

Each bulb of garlic you buy should yield about ten cloves that are worth planting, and each clove planted should produce a plump bulb of garlic. Three bulbs are probably a good amount to begin with.

### IDEAL CONDITIONS

Garlic likes heat and well-drained soil—if you can put them in the sunniest spot. They don't need much organic matter to be added to the soil.

### MAINTENANCE

Hoe once every couple of weeks to keep the weeds down.

### WHEN TO WATER

Only in very dry spells.

Plant in late autumn and by early summer. Astonishingly, the single clove will become a plump bulb ready for eating.

Each clove is planted flat side down with its papery tip uppermost.

## COMMON PROBLEMS AND SOLUTIONS

**Bolting** (producing a flower spike) can be a problem, usually caused by bad weather conditions. Remove the flower spike and the bulb will still be edible (and the flower spikes are, too). Use the bulbs that bolt first.

**Rust** is a threat to all the allium family. This is not too much of a problem, although the bulbs produced will be smaller than usual and the foliage must be destroyed rather than composted. If you have a crop blighted by rust, leave it as long as possible before growing a member of the allium family in that spot again. Rust can be a symptom of poor drainage, so it is worth investigating if you suspect there may be an underlying problem.

## Leeks

The magnificent leek has many virtues: it is a cinch to grow, is ready for harvest at the leanest time in the vegetable garden, will stand through a tough winter with no extra care, its blue-green leaves look stunning through the winter, and it has a very special homegrown taste. Freshly harvested leeks are crisper and juicier than the ones in the supermarket, and if you have worked organically, they won't have been subjected to the wide range of sprays often used to get a commercial crop. Leeks really do earn their place in the vegetable garden and are a very good crop for the novice vegetable grower.

### VARIETIES TO TRY

- **'Pancho'** is the variety to choose if you were growing just one variety of leek, as it matures quickly but will happily stand in the bed awaiting harvest until midwinter and possibly beyond. It has a good flavor and texture.
- **'Toledo'** is a good partner for 'Pancho,' as it matures later, from late autumn, and will stand through to spring. It has dark blue leaves that look majestic in your winter garden and is valuable as it is resistant to bolting.
- **'Musselburgh'** is an extremely robust leek that will stand a really hard winter, so it's worth trying in really cold areas. It matures late from early winter and will stand through to spring.
- **'Atal'** is a variety of baby leek. They don't have to be transplanted and mature in just 10–12 weeks to about

Unlike other varieties, grow these remarkably resilient 'Atal' baby leeks from seed.

the size of a spring onion. Useful in salads or stir-fries, they also grow well in containers.

### PLANT OR SEED?

Plants. Leeks are traditionally sown in a seed bed and then transplanted when they are about as thick as a pencil, but by ordering young plants you step in at the point they are transplanted. If you have the choice, as a rule, bigger transplants will produce bigger leeks.

### SPACING AND PLANTING

- Generally, leeks are grown 6". (15.2cm) apart, but this can be reduced to 4" (10.2cm) in rows 12" (30.2cm) apart. However, if you plan on enjoying some of your crop when they are young and succulent, then you can plant some at just half that distance apart and harvest every other one while they are small, leaving the bulk of the crop to grow on to maturity.
- The small leek plants are planted slightly differently to other plug plants. The leek plants may look a little droopy after planting, but they will soon perk up and the holes will fill naturally with soil over time.

# PLANTING LEEKS

1. Make a 6" (15.2cm) deep hole with a dibble.

2. Drop in one leek plant, ensuring that it makes it to the bottom of the hole.

3. The plants may look a little droopy after planting but don't panic as they will soon stand up.

4. Over time, the holes will fill naturally with soil.

The arching leaves of 'Pancho' look superb among the early autumn nasturtiums.

## WHEN TO PLANT
Late spring.

## WHEN TO HARVEST
You can start using a few leeks as soon as they reach a usable size (being that of the baby leeks sold at a premium in supermarkets), but beware of taking too many this young as you will get a lot more leek for your money later in the season. Also, in the summer there is plenty to choose from in the vegetable garden, while the leek is one of the stalwarts of the vegetable patch in winter.

## HOW MANY?
It is simple to calculate the harvest for leeks—unless you are extremely unlucky, for each leek you plant you should pull one leek harvesting over a four- or five-month period. Fifty would be worthwhile, but 150 may not be too many for a family of leek lovers if you have the space.

## IDEAL CONDITIONS
They are unfussy and good soil is sufficient, but they do not do well in compacted soil.

## MAINTENANCE
A truly easy vegetable crop where all there is to do is keep the weeds down with a few minutes of hoeing every week or two.

## WHEN TO WATER
Only in extremely dry periods.

## COMMON PROBLEMS AND SOLUTIONS
**Rust** is the most common problem afflicting leeks—bright, orangey brown patches that appear on the leaves. Eventually, the leaves turn yellow and wilt. The best thing is to salvage what you can, cutting the leeks before the problem is too bad. Normally, the white part is unaffected and can still be eaten. The rust-spotted leaves should be destroyed, not composted. If rust does strike, remember not to grow onions, leeks, garlic, or shallots on that spot for as long as possible.

# Spring Onions

Fast-growing spring or salad onions are essential, not only because they give a punchy bite to salads and stir-fries, but also because they are a great companion for carrots in the battle against carrot flies. They are quick to reach a usable size and some varieties can be left to grow on into full-sized onions, so there is no hurry or pressure to harvest the onions. There are even varieties that will stand through cold winters.

## VARIETIES TO TRY
- **'White Lisbon Winter Hardy'** is a strong-growing variety that will stand through the winter.
- **'Red Beard'** can be ready to harvest in 12–14 weeks and is a beautiful red color. If left in the ground, they can be grown on to form bulb onions.

## PLANT OR SEED?
Seed.

Spring onions are a great way to edge an ornamental bed.

Spring onions are easy to grow—a rewarding addition to any vegetable garden.

## SPACING AND PLANTING

Sow seed into furrows ½" (1.3cm) deep, leaving about 6" (15.2cm) between rows. Sprinkle the seed finely along the furrow. There is no need to thin out the onions as they will make their own space.

## WHEN TO PLANT

A short row of spring onions can be slotted in anywhere around the garden, but they are best when planted side by side with carrots to deter carrot flies. Plant from early spring through to midsummer. Plant whenever you plant carrots.

## WHEN TO HARVEST

As soon as the onion is of a usable size, or sooner if you have planted far too thickly. The tops can be used like chives.

## HOW MANY?

A 6½' (2m) row every three or four weeks, or synchronize with carrots.

## IDEAL CONDITIONS

Very unfussy; reasonable soil will give a reasonable crop.

## WHEN TO WATER

Water in very dry weather.

## COMMON PROBLEMS AND SOLUTIONS

Nothing much should trouble your crop of spring onions.

Taking a few small onions as soon as they are usable creates space for those remaining to grow larger.

# CHAPTER 7
# Sowing and Planting, Growing, and Harvesting

Propagation is where all gardening starts. With vegetables and herbs, the plants will be started into growth by one of four methods. Fruit trees are a slightly different matter: most trees are bought either as one-year-old single-stemmed plants, known as "whips," or as partially trained trees. Soft fruits can also be propagated to bulk up stocks or simply to replace old and unproductive plants. Each method of propagation is covered here in great detail, so that successful initial production of crops should be a mere formality. From there, this section details the growth of the plants through to the final harvest.

## Sowing Seeds

Seed sowing is the most commonly used method of propagation for vegetables and many herbs, as it is cheap and, in most cases, very successful. The primary consideration before sowing seed is whether the seed is viable. It is not always cost-effective to use fresh seed each year, as some seed packets contain enough seed

Cardboard egg cartons work well for chitting potatoes (see page 214).

to keep a family supplied in that particular vegetable for several years. The seeds usually come in a paper outer packet. In some cases, the seeds are sealed within a foil packet inside. In most cases, this foil packet will keep the seeds fresh for more than one season. By the end of the growing season, you may have seeds, such as radishes, lettuce, carrots, any of the brassicas, leeks, and so on left over. If so, fold the end of the foil packet to reseal the seeds inside, place the packet back into its original paper packet (so that you know what the seeds are), and then put it away in a cool place until required the following year. Keep the seeds for only one extra year before discarding them, as germination becomes less reliable after that point. The most unreliable vegetable variety from seed is undoubtedly parsnips, with the seed only being viable if it is fresh, so these cannot be kept for more than the season in which they were bought.

Apart from correctly sowing the seed, the most important job is to label everything—otherwise, things can get very confusing. Put as much information on the label as you can, with the plant type and variety on one side and the date sown and a code for the seed company marked on the reverse. It may never be used, but you may find it useful to follow the crop from sowing date to harvest for future reference. Also, as far as the seed company is concerned, if there is poor germination one year with seeds from the same company, it is worthwhile information to have.

### Sourcing Seeds

Seeds are remarkable—they contain not only an embryonic new plant but almost everything it needs to get through the first few days of life. There are few things more fascinating and satisfying than sowing a row of vegetables, and then catching that first glimpse of fragile green shoots breaking through the soil a few days later.

## DECODING THE PACKET

Some of the descriptions on seed packets can be confusing. Here are a few terms used to describe seed types.

- **Cultivar:** Meaning "cultivated variety," a plant that has been created or selected and maintained by gardeners. Often simply referred to as a "variety," which is a strain of a plant species with the same characteristics, such as leaf shape, size, color, or growth rate. The part of a plant name set inside single quote marks, such as Tomato 'Tom Thumb', identifies the cultivar.
- **F1 hybrids:** Seeds from a deliberate cross between two varieties. They may be expensive but produce uniform crops. Seeds collected from these plants won't produce the same type of plant, so don't save them.
- **Open-pollinated:** Seeds from plants that have been fertilized naturally. They can produce the same, "true" plant as the parent plant if fertilized by the same variety.
- **Pelleted:** Small, oddly-shaped seeds covered with an inert claylike material to make them easier to handle.
- **Treated:** These seeds are pretreated with a fungicide to prevent disease. They are dyed to identify them as chemically treated.

An empty seed packet is a quick way to remind yourself of what you have planted in a certain space.

Most (but not all) common garden vegetables are grown from seeds. Nurseries and garden centers usually have a good selection of seeds in the spring, but for the best choice of cultivars and varieties, order seeds from one of the many mail-order suppliers. Their catalogs usually start arriving in the mail in early fall, and the earlier you place your order, the more likely you will get your pick of the vegetables you want. Alternatively, many interesting seeds are sold online. Don't be tempted by glossy pictures to buy seeds that are unsuitable for your climate.

## Seed Preparation
Some seed requires special treatment before it can be sown. Two good examples of this are parsley and potatoes. Parsley germinates at a much faster rate and more evenly if it is treated with boiling water first. The boiling will break the built-in dormancy of the seed, allowing it to germinate in two to three days. The seeds can be put into a dish, the water poured onto them, drained, and the seeds left to dry before sowing, or they can be sown, and

## COLLECTING SEED
Collecting and storing your own seed is simple with peas and beans because a few pods can be left on the plants to dry at the end of the season and gathered before the damper weather comes. The seed can be stored in brown envelopes or paper bags in a cool, dark place with the cultivar names written on. Other plants are less straightforward; vegetables such as carrots, for example, require you to allow some carrots to flower and set seed. Saving a few potatoes for the following year's crop is possible, but you run the risk of a buildup of viruses or disease. Saving a few Jerusalem artichokes makes sense, and to save time, they can be treated like perennials by just throwing a few tubers back when you harvest. It is also worth remembering that the seed of an F1 hybrid will not come true; that is, the plants will not share the characteristics of the parents.

Beans are the easiest seed to collect. They are large, easy to handle, and come packed in neat pods. You can grow beans for their seed pods, but some other plants, such as carrots and onions, have to be allowed to run to seed before any can be collected.

the water very carefully poured over them in situ. The problem with the second method is that if too much water is poured too quickly, most of the seed will be washed to the outer extremities of the seed tray.

Although called seed potatoes, they are not strictly seed; however, potatoes perform much better if "chitted" before sowing. To chit the potatoes, place them on a tray with individual compartments (an egg carton works well to hold the potatoes in place); for each potato, the end with the most eyes should point upward. Place your tray(s) in a light, warm place to initiate growth, for example, under greenhouse benches. Small shoots will begin to grow out from the eyes, at which point you can plant the potatoes. This method of starting their growth before planting means that, after planting, the potatoes will just keep growing and give a more rapid return than if planted without chitting.

## Soil Preparation

It is worth spending the time in preparing the soil so that seeds germinate well, to maximize the potential of all crops. If you have a heavy or clay soil, it is a good idea first to cover the area required for sowing with a piece of plastic. This prevents the soil from becoming too wet to work, while also warming it up to give those early crops a head start. As a lot of vegetable seeds are quite small, they are unable to push through large clods of soil or a capped soil surface. This means that the most important

Large robust seeds such as these runner beans can simply be pushed into the soil.

part of preparing a seedbed is to ensure a fine tilth at the end. First, the soil needs to be tilled. If it is part of a crop rotation, then there is no need to add any extra organic matter.

Prepare the soil for growing vegetables by digging in advance, ideally over winter. Once the soil has been dug and the larger clods broken up with a fork, the whole area needs to be raked to leave a level area consisting of fine soil particles. For most crops, add pelleted chicken manure prior to raking; this provides ample food for the growing crop. If it is still too early to sow seeds into the soil, then cover the area with plastic.

In the spring as the soil starts to dry, finish the seedbed by breaking down the surface into a fine crumbly tilth, using a fork and rake. If the soil is not sticky, you can tread the soil at this stage, which breaks the clods and gently firms the surface. Apply a general balanced fertilizer in a ratio of 2 ounces per square yard (60 grams per square meter) or use an organic alternative, then do a final raking. Remove excess stones, remaining clods, and any weeds. The surface should be fine and crumbly but not dusty. Such preparation is basic to virtually all vegetables mentioned in this book. Ideally, prepare your seedbed well in advance of sowing, and leave it empty to allow the first crop of weeds to germinate so you can then hoe them off before seed sowing.

Pencil bean seeds can be sown by pushing them into the soil. Sow a couple at each spot in case one seed fails to germinate.

## A SHORTCUT TO A FINE TILTH

Packets of small seeds will undoubtedly suggest that the soil be worked to a fine tilth before sowing, meaning a soil that is fine and free from large lumps. This makes sense as small seeds can be washed through a lumpy soil, and therefore, need to be surrounded by warm, damp soil to germinate successfully. They will be far more successful in putting down roots and throwing up shoots if they don't encounter large, hard clods or dry cavities. However, achieving a fine tilth is not always easy. Even if you pull aside the most recent layer of mulch, the soil may still look inhospitable, especially if it is still new to cultivation. To solve this, draw out a furrow three or four times the depth required, fill it with an organic seed compost or mole hills if you have them, sow the seeds as above, and then fill the furrow with the same compost. (Moles are a nuisance, but mole hills contain fine soil, perfect for seeds.) Effectively, what you have done is plant your seeds in a container of perfect compost, one that their roots can grow straight out of into fertile soil when they are ready.

Larger seeds, such as beans and zucchinis, can be planted by simply pushing them gently into the ground to the right depth. Packets normally recommend planting two seeds at each spot to allow for any seeds that fail to germinate. The weakest seedling at each station can then be removed, leaving the more robust plant to grow. Pull out the weakling gently so as not to damage the remaining plant.

Tiny kale seeds need good contact with the soil to germinate well, so use the shortcut to a fine tilth by creating a channel of potting compost and pulling back the rough mulch so you are sowing them in a perfect growing medium.

You can also cover the area with straw, just be sure to use enough straw that the thickness eliminates the light.

Most seeds are sown in a drill, which is a narrow V-shaped shallow channel. Traditionally, this is made by running a draw hoe alongside a tightly stretched garden line. You may find it easier to use a straight edge, such as a plank, and to scratch out a drill using a stick or bamboo cane. The depth of the drill is very important, as seeds should be sown at a depth of no more than twice their diameter, which is very shallow for small seeds, often less than ½" (1.3cm).

Sow seeds very thinly, bearing in mind the eventual spacing required. For example, lettuces should be thinned to about 12" (30.5cm) and parsnips to about 6" (15.2cm). If the seeds are large enough, you can individually sow at the final spacing, allowing a couple of seeds at each station. If both grow, remove one seedling later. After sowing, gently rake the soil back into the drill to cover the seed. If conditions are dry, you can run water along the drill before sowing, but it is not good to water after sowing, as this can pan the soil down and inhibit germination.

## Sowing Directly into the Garden

In a low-maintenance vegetable garden, it's easiest to use only seeds that can be sown directly into the soil where they are to germinate and grow without much

## STALE SEEDBED METHOD

This is a very useful technique if the next crop to be sown is a slow-maturing type, such as parsnips, where the annual weeds will grow more rapidly than the crop, smothering it before it has a chance to mature. If you are plagued with annual weeds, the stale seedbed method can also be used to help resolve the problem before any crop is planted. There are two basic methods that can be employed to obtain the same result.

The **first method** is to prepare the area to be sown about three to four weeks before it is required, then leave it so that the annual weeds can grow. As soon as there is a good flush of weeds, use a hoe to cut off the tops and put these tops on the compost heap. As they have not had a chance to flower and seed, this should greatly reduce any further germination of annual weeds, allowing the crop to germinate and grow without unwanted competition.

The **second method** is to cover the ground with a sheet of black plastic about six to eight weeks before use. The soil underneath will be heated, encouraging the weeds to grow, and they will subsequently die due to the lack of light. Use this method more in the early part of the growing season, as the plastic also warms the ground in anticipation of the crop when it is sown, and the crop therefore gets a good start. As the season progresses and the weather improves, the benefit of warming the soil for the crop diminishes.

Potatoes, directly sown in a shallow furrow.

fuss. It is the most commonly used method since it involves no expensive materials. It is limited by climatic conditions, however, as most vegetable varieties can be sown outside only once the temperatures have increased for germination and to ensure the soft seedling tops are not burnt off by severe frosts. Direct sowing starts in early to mid-spring and carries on right through until early fall, depending on the type of vegetable. Always check the seed packet for instructions—you can sow some varieties early in the season, but for others, you will need to wait until the soil gets warm. Smaller seeds are planted into narrow furrows that are created using the corner of a hoe or rake or a bit of cane.

For seeds to grow well, the soil needs to be broken down into fine, even crumbs. Digging beds in fall will allow winter frost to break down lumps and make the soil easier to work. However, before sowing, you will need to turn the soil over once again with a fork, and then use a rake to break up any lumps and to smooth the surface until level. Wait until the soil is reasonably dry and crumbly before you prepare it for sowing, because wet soil won't break down to a fine enough texture.

Most small seeds like carrots, radishes, and salad leaves are sown in shallow furrows created by dragging a hoe, a trowel, or your hand through the soil. For the beginner gardener, make sure to keep your row straight. Seedlings in orderly, poker-straight rows are easy to hoe, and the invading weeds are easily spotted. It looks neat, too. To keep plants in line, use a cane, a garden line, or a homemade board marked with centimeter or inch measurements to help with spacing.

For seeds requiring a furrow, first mark out your furrows to about the right depth. Each vegetable or herb variety will have a depth at which it needs to be sown—usually between ½" and 1" (1.3 and 2.5cm) deep. Gently water the furrow with a watering can with a fine rose if the soil is dry. It is important to water the bottom of the furrow at this stage to avoid watering overhead initially; watering first prevents the soil surface from "capping" (becoming crusty and almost impenetrable to the germinating seed) while still giving the seed the moisture it requires for germination. Then sprinkle the seeds thinly along the furrow—don't shake them from the packet as the likelihood is that hundreds of seeds will land in the same spot. Instead, pour a few seeds into one

## TIPS FOR SOWING IN ROWS AND TRENCHES

- When sowing short rows, it is sometimes easier to make a furrow by laying the handle of the rake on the soil surface and treading on it lightly to make a shallow depression.
- Most vegetables are best sown in straight rows, not because they look neat but to make it easier to control weeds and take care of the plants.
- The depth of your furrow depends on the size of the seeds being sown; aim to cover seeds to about their own depth in soil.
- In dry conditions, water the bottom of the furrow before sowing, using a gentle dribble of water.
- In general, avoid overcrowding the seeds because crowded seedlings will not develop well, and you will have extra work in thinning them out later.
- You can carefully tap larger seeds straight out of the packet—creasing the open edge of the packet to form a funnel shape will make this easier. Alternatively, take pinches of seeds and sprinkle them thinly along the furrow.
- You can sow some seeds, such as peas and bush bean seeds, in double rows a few inches apart. Leave wider paths between the furrows to make more room for picking. Use a hoe with a 4"–6" (10.2–15.2cm) blade and keep the depth of the furrow even so all the seeds emerge at the same time. (This technique can also be used for radishes, scallions, and other vegetables that grow close together; just thin them out as they grow.)
- Large seeds, such as beans or zucchini, are easy to handle, so you can space them individually. However, you should sow a few extra in case some of the seeds fail to germinate, which often happens.

### Fluid Sowing

Fluid sowing is a method that can be used with seeds that have been pregerminated (see page 270), and it is one that is not restricted to parsnips—you can use it on any crop that requires thinning. This system can be used for most smaller-seeded vegetable varieties and will provide an even sowing of seeds that yields an earlier crop because the seeds will grow much quicker. Once the radicle (small root) is seen on most of the seeds, it is time to sow.

You can buy a special kit, but it is cheaper and just as effective to use a clear plastic freezer bag and fungicide-free wallpaper paste. The wallpaper paste is mixed, and the seeds stirred into it so that they are well dispersed. The seeded paste is then poured into the plastic bag. Once a furrow has been prepared outside, one corner of the bag is cut, and the paste is squeezed out along the length of the furrow. It is rather like squeezing icing out of an icing bag onto a cake.

Once the line of paste has been dispensed, the furrow is refilled with soil and watered. Do not let the soil dry out for the first few days, as this may cause the paste to harden and therefore not allow the seed to grow out of it.

## SOWING INTO CONTAINERS: WHICH CONTAINER TO USE?

What kind of container you use depends on the number of plants you want and how long they will stay indoors before being planted outside. There are two basic types of containers to consider:

- **Seed-starting trays** (see page 265) have individual compartments joined together, making it easier for you to water a number of plants at the same time. However, they are shallow, so seedlings run out of room for their roots quickly.
- **Plug trays or larger pot trays** (see page 268) have larger separate spaces that can usually be replanted as single units. For a small number of plants, such as a few tomatoes, sow seeds in 3½" (8.9cm) pots. These are deeper than trays, so the seedlings do not need repotting as quickly. You can attach a plastic propagator top to both trays and pots, which will keep warmth and humidity high to encourage germination.

hand and sprinkle into the furrow with the other, a pinch at a time. Finally, gently shuffle the soil on the edge back over the furrow and gently firm it. Remember to put in a label right away. Always label each end of the row so that if one is lost or pulled out by birds, you still have a record of what was sown. If you only sow a part row, leaving space for a repeat sowing, stick a marker where the first planting finishes.

Sow one to three seeds into the indentations you've made in each cell.

## Sowing into Seed-Starting Trays

Sowing into seed-starting trays means that crops can be started earlier and raised in a greenhouse, under a cold frame, or on a windowsill before they are sown directly into the ground at the appropriate time. This means you can start when the weather is still to cool, and the soil is too wet. It also makes maximum use of the available space. You can start raising the next batch of plants so that they are ready to replace an existing crop after it

is harvested. Starting seeds in containers can be more economical. Because indoor seedlings are easier to look after, you are more likely to raise the maximum number of healthy plants from expensive seeds. In addition, when a small number of plants is needed, it is often easier to look after them in their early stages if they are sown in containers. Regardless of what size seed tray you are using, the sowing method is the same.

Before you start, ensure that the seed tray is clean; if it has been used previously, pests and diseases can be carried from crop to crop on soil or plant debris. First, overfill the seed tray with soil—make sure that there are no lumps by rubbing the soil between your hands as you fill. Then, slightly lift each end of the seed tray and drop them back down two or three times to settle the soil into the tray. Using a firming board, level the soil off at the top of the tray, and then press the firming board down onto the soil gently, just enough to compress it a little.

Always water the soil well with a watering can with a rose attachment before sowing, as this prevents the seed from being washed to the sides of the tray (as would

Large seeds are easy to sow into individual compartments.

**Above:** Seed-starting kits come with a transparent plastic propagator top, which helps seeds germinate.

**Left:** Seeds planted in the right conditions will soon emerge as healthy young seedlings.

happen if you watered after sowing). Allow the water to drain before sowing. The seed can then be sown thinly and evenly across the surface of the soil.

You might find it easier to sow the seed from the slightly cupped palm of your hand. This cupping makes a nice groove right in the center of the hand and, when you tap your hand gently, the seed is channeled at an even pace down the groove and onto the soil surface, creating a nice, even seed spacing. It is far easier to control seeds using this method than sowing directly from the packet or sowing by gently letting seed fall from between your finger and thumb. The seed can then be covered with a thin layer of vermiculite.

Using a small pot to do this job works very well. Vermiculite is recommended because it allows light to reach the seed, eventually breaks down in the soil, and does not form a hard crust on the surface as peat does. The seed tray can then be put into a propagator with artificial heat, set on greenhouse benches under a cold frame, or placed on a windowsill until the seed germinates. The unheated seeds will germinate, albeit more slowly than the artificially heated ones.

Handle seedlings gently when transplanting, not by the stems as shown here.

You can also cover the newly sown trays with a plastic propagator top or a sheet of glass, and then—except for celery and some types of lettuce, which need more light—lay a sheet of newspaper on top. This covering keeps in both warmth and moisture to create the humid atmosphere seeds need for germination to take place. Put the container in an evenly warm spot, and keep the soil mix just moist. As soon as the first seedlings start to emerge, remove the newspaper layer and move the container to a position with good lighting, such as near a window. Water the soil mix carefully when the seedlings appear—it is easy to knock them over with a strong jet of water.

### TRANSPLANTING FROM SEED-STARTING TRAYS

Once you've sown your seeds into trays and they have germinated and produced their first true leaves, the seedlings are large enough to handle and are ready to be transplanted. This is the process of moving the seedlings from the seed tray either into cells or small pots so that they can continue to grow. It is a delicate process because the seedlings can be damaged very easily at this stage, and

## BRASSICA SEEDBED

Because all brassicas move very well, it is more economic to grow them into the seedling stage and then transplant them into their final positions. For a faster crop, it is advisable to sow them into a cold frame. The idea is to sow the amount required thinly but evenly into short furrows inside the cold frame and then leave them to germinate. Once they reach a height of 3" (7.6cm), the seedlings should be touching each other in one continuous row. They can then be lifted and carefully separated.

Brassicas can suffer a check in growth from lack of water soon after transplanting. To give them the best start possible, place them into a small water-filled trench once lifted from the seedbed. They can be left there for a couple of hours while they take up any water they require; as an added bonus, their roots will be covered with a film of wet soil that aids establishment. They will still require a good watering after transplanting.

seedlings with little to no root damage will grow much faster than damaged ones.

The principle is to remove the seedling from the soil in the seed tray, causing as little damage to the roots as possible, transferring it to a larger container. It is possible to buy special tools for teasing out the seedlings from the soil or you can use a dibble, but a short piece of cane or a pencil does the job more than adequately. Hold the seedling by the old seed leaves only and gently ease the roots out of the soil. Either move the seedlings to another tray, spacing them farther apart, or repot them individually. Once the seed tray is empty, the soil can go straight onto the compost heap.

## Sowing into Plug Trays

Sowing into plug trays is a different procedure from sowing into seed trays because it involves sowing into many individual cells that collectively make up the plug tray. When propagating vegetables or herbs, use trays with at least fifty-four cells, but no smaller; otherwise, the plants will begin to starve before they are big enough to plant. As with seed trays, overfill the plug tray with soil, tap each end to consolidate the soil, and level off any excess at the top using your hand. Next, make a small indentation in the soil in each cell for the seeds to be dropped into, leaving enough room to cover the seeds with vermiculite. Once you've prepared every cell, you can sow the seeds into these indentations, aiming to place one to three seeds in each cell.

You can also cover the newly sown trays with a plastic propagator top or a sheet of glass, and then—except for celery and some types of lettuce, which need more light—lay a sheet of newspaper on top. This covering keeps in both warmth and moisture to create the humid atmosphere seeds need for germination to take place. Put the container in an evenly warm spot, and keep the soil mix just moist. As soon as the first seedlings start to emerge, remove the newspaper layer and move the container to a position with good lighting, such as near a window. Water the soil mix carefully when the seedlings appear—it is easy to knock them over with a strong jet of water.

After the seeds have germinated and the seedlings have reached the first true leaf stage, you'll remove the weaker seedlings to leave one seedling per cell. A key aspect of growing in plug trays is that you can repot or plant the plugs (the mini plants) directly from the plug tray without the need for transplanting. This eliminates the potential for root damage, and therefore, keeps the young plants growing at their maximum rate.

Sowing in plug trays is not suitable for all vegetables and herbs. This system is used primarily for varieties that germinate readily because a lot of space and soil is taken up if the seeds fail. It is also possible to transplant seedlings from a seed tray into plug trays to avoid wasting soil. These plants would then be planted directly from the plug tray.

With vegetables such as leeks, onions, carrots, beets (beetroot), kohlrabi, and turnips, you can use these plugs for the multisowing method. This is an excellent way of producing young, tender, and quick crops in limited space and thus is ideally suited to the bed system. You fill the tray and make indentations in the same manner as previously described, but you drop between five and seven seeds into each cell and do not thin the seedlings. You then plant the plugs in their little clumps, and, as they mature, each one will push the others out of its way.

With beets (beetroot), for example, you harvest the roots when they reach golf-ball size; you can either pull them individually, harvest them as needed, or harvest the whole clump at one time. With the latter, you can get a crop of young and tender beets in a very short time that is equivalent to each root of the much slower-to-mature individual roots of main-crop beets.

## Sowing into Pots and Tubes

The two previous sowing methods are perfectly adequate for smaller seeds, but the larger types need larger containers. Seeds of melons, cucumbers, zucchini, summer squash (marrows), and some companion plants are better sown into 3" (7.6cm) pots or tubes. You can purchase pots made from various materials or make them yourself, while the tubes are generally either made of "whalehide" (cardboard coated in bitumen) or homemade from several sheets of recycled newspaper. Newspaper is fine to use in an organic garden as long as it has only black print, and it makes very cheap pots and tubes. Overfill the pot or tube with soil, tap on the potting bench, and then level off the soil. You can then push the seed into the soil and water the whole thing.

Having room to grow produces strong, sturdy plants.

You can sow fast-maturing summer vegetables for pots and tubs, such as baby leaf salad greens and radishes, directly into the containers in which they will grow until harvesting.

You can plant pots made of compressed coir (as shown here), newspaper, and whalehide as complete units, and they will break down in the soil.

# PREGERMINATING DIFFICULT SEEDS

Pregerminating is a widely used and simple technique for parsnip seeds, as they are notoriously poor germinators. Pregerminating the seed eliminates the problems associated with erratic germination where a row will contain parts that have a seedling every 1" (2.5cm) and then 24"–36" (61–91.4cm) with no seedlings germinated at all. As parsnips also move very poorly, it is not feasible to lift seedlings and replant them in the gaps. Getting the seed started inside first provides the opportunity to see which seed is viable and will continue to grow. The part-germinated seed can then be sown at their required spacing for an even crop. Place the seed onto a piece of moist tissue paper (which must be kept moist while waiting for the seed to begin germinating). It is better if the seeds are given a bit of gentle heat, as this will help to get an even germination. You do not want to leave the seeds to germinate too far, as inevitable damage will be caused when they are handled during sowing.

Germinating seed before sowing encourages consistency in the crop.

## Sowing onto Tissue Paper and into Jars

Sowing onto tissue paper and into jars probably gives you the easiest and quickest return of all sowing methods. The seeds of both mustard and cress will germinate on moist paper towels placed in the bottom of a seed tray. It is important to keep the paper towels moist; these seeds germinate perfectly happily in less than a week, either in the greenhouse or on a windowsill. Mung beans are very nutritious and can be grown in either a jar or a bowl. They need to be soaked for about twelve hours, drained, and then put into their growing containers in a warm room, but not in direct sunlight. Fill the jar with water every day and drain to rinse the beans. Depending on how much root you want on your beans, they can be harvested from as little as two days after their initial soaking, up to about a week.

## Station Sowing

Station sowing is a technique used with pregerminated seed or for varieties that do not germinate well, such as parsnip. If using pregerminated seed, place it at the final spacing for the crop so that no thinning is required—the seed is 99.9 percent certain to keep growing. This method is used with vegetables that germinate poorly to ensure a good, even spacing of the vegetable. Make a furrow, as for direct sowing, and sow two or three seeds at the final crop spacing and cover them as usual. The likelihood is that at least one seed will germinate at each station, giving a perfectly spaced vegetable. If more than one seed germinates, thin the weaker plants, leaving the strongest to grow.

## Sowing into a Gutter

This simple technique is used primarily for peas but can also be used with other crops. It is an excellent way to start peas off early that takes up little or no space in the greenhouse. Use this method instead of sowing straight outside if you have problems with mice removing and eating directly sown seeds. A length of gutter is filled with soil and leveled off. Use two pots at each end of the gutter to stop the soil from falling out.

The seeds are sown in succession, with the next length of gutter sown once the seedlings in the first reach a height of 2" (5.1cm). They can be hardened off (see page 272) and then transplanted once the plants have reached

Sanitize and recycle plastic trays and cups for seed starting.

3" (7.6cm) high. When they are ready to be planted, you make a furrow with a hoe, place one end of the gutter in the far end of the furrow, and then, as you move the gutter backward, the rooted peas will slide effortlessly into the prepared furrow.

## Thinning

There are not many gardeners that either have a precision sowing machine or have mastered the art of sowing by hand to such a degree that they can be absolutely precise. Therefore, most vegetable varieties sown directly into the ground will need to be thinned at some stage. The thinning process involves leaving the crop until the seedlings are of a manageable size but not too big. Any unwanted seedlings are generally pulled out by hand.

Most pulled-out seedlings cannot be used for anything and will wilt very quickly, so they generally end up on the compost heap. Some crops, however, are thinned at a point where they can be used. With beets, radishes, mini vegetables, parsnips, kohlrabi, Florence fennel, scallions, and early carrot varieties, the whole crop is left in situ and the larger plants pulled as soon as they are of a size where they are useful. This continues as the crop matures and will ultimately leave enough space for the remainder of the plants to grow on into a useful size.

# Planting Seedlings

Transplanting is the process of putting plants and trees into the ground when not raised in their final position. Pot- and cell-raised vegetable and herb plants need to be transplanted into the ground with the top of the soil of their original container buried just below soil level. Soil-raised vegetables (such as brassicas), divided herbs, and fruit trees all need to have the new soil level at the same height as it was in their previous position. Burying vegetables, herbs, and fruits too deeply can cause them to rot, while not transplanting deeply enough can cause plants and trees to dry out.

## Hardening Off

Hardening off is a vital procedure for all plants that have been started inside. If a plant is removed from a very warm environment and placed into a much more exposed and colder one, its growth rate could stop or slow down dramatically. Plants raised inside therefore need to be acclimatized to the outside conditions gradually. For greenhouse-raised plants, this means moving them into a cold frame or tunnel for a few days before planting; those raised in a cold frame need to be well ventilated prior to planting for a similar effect.

Thinning a crop means removing seedlings by hand.

Hardening off is a requirement for transferring plants into new climates.

## How and When to Plant

Before planting in the ground, ensure that your plant has recently been watered. Dig out a small hole to fit the plant root ball, pop in the plant, check that the soil level is the same as in the original container, and then gently push the soil around the root ball. Use a watering can with a fine rose to water it. There are a few exceptions: young leeks are dropped into a hole made with a dibble (see page 252); sweet corn needs to be planted slightly deeper than in their original pots to encourage rooting; zucchinis and pumpkins can be planted up to the level of their seed leaves (the first pair of leaves the plant grows); and brassicas need to be planted deeply and really firmed in well, perhaps with your heel, to thrive. Use a line or board to keep rows straight and easy to weed. Keep the young plants watered if the weather is dry, and protect them with cloches or fleece if the weather is cold until they are established. If you can, choose to plant out on a gray day so the plants lose less moisture.

Young plants take only a few moments to get into the ground—but take care not to damage their root systems.

# Spacing and Seasonal Planning

Every seed packet and plant label will have recommendations for spacing between plants and between rows of plants. Spacing crops is important to ensure that each plant gets enough light, nutrients, and water to grow well and to allow easy weeding between plants and rows. It follows that in fertile, well-drained, moisture-retentive soil (such as in well-maintained raised beds), plants can thrive with less space than in poorer, dry soils and provide the best possible harvest from the area you cultivate. Using growing space effectively is like packing the plants in the most efficient way, and staggering plants in neighboring rows usually creates a tight, economical fit.

The distance at which one plant grows from another can influence its size. This can be useful as you may want to grow a large number of smaller onions rather than fewer larger ones, or you may want to work other vegetables into the space. Closer spacing can also help to keep the beds covered, leaving less space for weeds. Leafy plants, such as zucchinis, will cover the ground,

preventing weeds from growing. So spacing does not have to be as rigid as you may imagine. The range of spacing for each vegetable is suggested in the Plant Profiles beginning on page 194, but don't be afraid to use common sense and experiment within reason to adapt the spacing to the practicalities of your beds.

## Catch Crops

Beyond packing plants effectively, it makes sense to generate as much harvest as you can from the space available. Growing a fast-maturing crop among a slower-growing crop gives two or perhaps three harvests out of one area without compromising on the quality of either. The fast-growing crop is known as a "catch crop." Radishes, beets, salad leaves, spring onions, and lettuces all make good catch crops. Filling the space also allows less room for weeds to grow.

## Succession Planting

Continuity is important, and you should aim to produce vegetables that you can continue to harvest over many weeks, maybe the whole summer. The classic mistake is to grow too much of one thing. With most crops, this will mean making a number of sowings at different stages so

Containers can double your growing space.

that the vegetables mature at different intervals. With some crops, you will also need to use early, mid- and late-season varieties that mature at different times. Succession also involves the continued use of the space in a vegetable garden. For example, when a crop of spring cabbage has been harvested in late spring, the ground can be cleared and cultivated ready to take a row of celery that will mature later in the summer.

It is important for a vegetable gardener to be ready to pop in seeds or plants of a second or third crop as soon as they have harvested the first or second planting. It is essential to know that certain cool season vegetables need a month longer to mature than the speedy kinds, so pay close attention to "days to maturity" for each kind of vegetable. In areas with a short growing season, you can leave about one-quarter of the garden open during spring because some spring vegetables might not mature quickly enough to allow timely planting of long-season, warmth-loving annuals.

## Intercropping/Interplanting

Intercropping/interplanting is quite simply making the best of limited space by juggling one crop between another. For example, sweet corn, which is slow-growing and will not be mature until the end of summer, would be planted at least 18" (45.7cm) apart. It is possible to grow a crop of lettuce between the sweet corn, which is finished by mid-summer. Sometimes this will mean planting or sowing the quick crop first, and leaving space for the later main crop, which is planted in between. Avoid planting crops too closely together, which would risk spoiling one of the vegetable crops.

A few kinds of small, quick-growing vegetables are suitable for growing between larger, longer-season vegetables and small fruits. Foremost among these are

Young leaves can be difficult to identify, so make sure you label each row of vegetables to help you remember what you planted where.

leaf lettuce, mustard greens, onion sets, radishes, spinach, and Swiss chard. A few kinds of annual herbs can also be wedged in between the hulking plants of large vegetables: cilantro, summer savory, parsley, and dwarf basils, such as 'Spicy Globe', are good examples. Don't get carried away and try to interplant vegetables, such as beans or cabbage. Their plants are vigorous enough to compete strongly with nearby large vegetables. Interplanting is a good use for excess seedlings you have pried out of rows of direct-seeded vegetables. Seedlings that are "pulled out by the ears" rather than dug out seldom survive transplanting.

### COOL-SEASON CROPS FROM SEEDS

Many cool-season crops are needed in such quantities that starting from plants is unnecessarily expensive. Among the cool-season crops that are best started by

Quick-growing radishes are cool-season crops that are best started by direct-seeding.

direct-seeding in early spring are beets, chard, cilantro, kohlrabi, lettuce, mustard greens, green peas, radishes, spinach, and snap peas.

Direct-seeding of cool-season crops past a short window of time in the spring is virtually useless. Hot weather and long days will cause cool-season crops to either shoot up heads of flowers and go to seed or become too bitter to eat. This is why experienced gardeners prepare garden beds in the fall. They only have to rake them lightly to get them ready for spring seeding. Late summer is the preferred time to direct-seed second plantings of greens and root crops. Endive and escarole grow especially well when fall-planted, as well as collard greens and turnips.

### COOL-SEASON CROPS FROM SEEDLINGS

The cool-season crops that are customarily set out as seedlings in the spring and again in late summer are broccoli, cabbage, and cauliflower. Cool-season crops transplanted in very early spring need protection from hard frosts. Experienced gardeners know to shelter their plants using plastic milk jugs with their bottoms cut off and their caps removed, or with spun-bonded acrylic floating row covers.

In the South and at low elevations in the West, gardens pass quickly from winter to summer with virtually no cool spring weather. In these zones, cool-season crops are best planted during late summer or early fall, in time for them to come to near-maturity before the onset of short, wet, winter days.

In recent years, shipping costs have raised the price of potatoes so drastically that it has become more cost-effective to grow them in home gardens. Potatoes are a cool-season crop, and are usually started in early spring from "seed pieces." These are cut from whole, disease-free "seed potatoes" purchased at garden centers or ordered by mail.

When you divide a seed potato into pieces, each piece should have an "eye," which is a juvenile sprout. Dusting the freshly cut seed piece with powdered sulfur—which you can purchase in small bags at your local garden center—helps prevent the pieces from rotting before the sprouts emerge from the ground.

### DIRECT-SEEDING OF FROST-TENDER CROPS

You will get better results by direct-seeding the following frost-tender crops: beans, cantaloupes, cucumbers, honeydew and Crenshaw melons, okra, squash, southern

# MORE TIPS ON EFFICIENT VEGETABLE GROWING

Many kinds of vegetables are considered efficient because they occupy the soil for only a short period of time. Most of these are planted early in the spring (fall where winters are mild) and mature within a span of two months. Chinese cabbage, lettuce, mustard greens, peas, bunching onions, radishes, and spinach are usually direct seeded. A second crop of these cool-loving vegetables (except for peas) can be planted in mid-to-late summer for fall maturity.

Gardeners in the South typically wait until around mid-August before planting turnips, mustard, spinach, and collard greens. There, these frost-hardy, highly nutritious crops mature quickly and yield a lot of food for the space occupied. In the South and warm Southwest, green peas and snap peas can be planted in late summer for fall and winter harvesting. Elsewhere, fall frosts kill pea vines before the pods can mature.

### Plant compact varieties of vining, spreading vegetables

Some kinds of vegetables spread so widely that they take up a lot of space and thus are not appropriate for small gardens. However, you can buy "compact" varieties of most vining vegetables. Whereas standard varieties of pumpkins, hard-shelled winter-keeper squash, cantaloupes, watermelons, cucumbers, and sweet potatoes can form runners 8' to 12' (2.4 to 3.7m) in length, compact varieties of these crops spread, on average, only half as far.

### A Bit More Guidance on Onions

Like potatoes, the price of onions has risen at the market. Fortunately, this heavy-yielding crop has become one of the most efficient you can grow. Onions are cool-season vegetables, planted in early spring over most of the country, late summer in the Deep South. Really big, sweet, slicing onions are grown from seedlings. Onion sets, on the other hand, are small bulbs produced from seeds that are genetically programmed to mature at rather small sizes. Onion sets are best used to produce green onions, also called scallions, which can be planted quite early.

Before you plant, know that different varieties of hybrid onions form large bulbs at different maturity dates. They are sold as "short-day," "long-day," and "intermediate-day" varieties, respectively. To grow them, you must start from well-grown seedlings. You can order onion seedlings from specialty growers at 60 to 100 seedlings per bunch.

This compact variety of cucumber is suitable for growing in a smaller garden.

Big, sweet slicing onions are grown from seedlings, not sets.

Special seed potatoes are readied for planting.

peas, sweet corn, and watermelons. Seeds of these vegetables and fruits should be sown one to three weeks after the frost-free date for your area. They mature from mid-summer on. Carefully observe the "distances apart" instructions on the seed packets, and thin the plants accordingly. Too-close spacing will stunt the plants.

The warm-season, frost-tender vegetables and fruits that are customarily planted as seedlings soon after the average frost-free date are eggplant, peppers, sweet potatoes, and tomatoes. Sweet potato seedlings, commonly called "slips," are produced from sprouting roots. The sprouts draw on the nutrients stored in the fleshy root to form fibrous root systems and are sold by the bunch as well as in individual pots. Ornamental sweet potatoes—the ones with purple, chartreuse, or varicolored foliage—can form large roots, but they are not of eating quality.

# Time to Maturity

The vegetables (and herbs and fruits) featured in in the Plant Profiles chapter starting on page 194 have been chosen because they are all easy to grow. Also, they won't make you wait for months before you can enjoy your harvest.

A vegetable's growing speed is not determined by how long it takes them to reach maturity, but by how long they must grow before you can start using them, which is not necessarily the same thing. Leeks, for example, take a long time to reach full size. They are traditionally sown in early to mid-spring, and they are not ready for harvesting until winter or even the following spring. However, you do not have to follow these traditional methods. Baby leeks are mild, sweet, and delicious, and they can be enjoyed within a few weeks of sowing, from midsummer onward. They may not be as large as fully grown, mature plants, but they are just as delicious and enjoyable.

Think like the manager of a small business when planning a food garden. Will you get back in value as much as you invest in time and effort? Probably not, if your garden is less than 500' (152.4m) square, or 20' x

25' (6.1 x 7.6m) in size. (Try picturing two small bedrooms side by side for a better idea of these dimensions.) This is not to say that small gardens are not worth your time and effort. They deliver many emotional and physical benefits, in addition to truly fresh and flavorful vegetables. Perhaps just as important is that a small garden is easier to manage.

When you step up the size of your vegetable patch—to 1,000' (305m) square or larger—you can begin to quantify true cost savings. It is then possible to grow many kinds of vegetables for less than you would pay per pound at the supermarket. Make no mistake, though: when you plant a large food garden, you become a farmer, and farming of vegetables means work, some of it during all types of weather.

How much of a given vegetable or fruit you should plant depends upon how and when it will be consumed. Will the vegetables go straight from the garden to your table, or do you plan to freeze or preserve some of your bounty for later use? With a number of types, such as tomatoes, zucchini, and cabbage, you can do both. But other vegetables, such as lettuce and radishes, can only be eaten fresh. You also have to consider whether you will be vacationing during summer harvest season. What a waste if your tomato, corn, and pepper yields ripen for picking when you are away!

Because the length of the rows you'll need to plant is best learned from experience, count on your first year or two of gardening to produce "feast or famine" results. You can help matters by reviewing vegetable garden plans on the internet (the Hume Seeds website is one good source). Many sites offer guidelines on how much of each kind of vegetable to grow for a family of four. This will give you a good starting point.

## Average Days to Maturity

Choose efficient kinds of vegetables to get the biggest bang for your buck. "Efficient" vegetables are those that produce the maximum amount of food within a given area and time. The "average days to maturity" will be listed on all seed packets and is included in the description of each variety in seed catalogs. This gives you a rough estimate of the days required for a crop to mature from direct-seeding (planting seeds straight from the packet) into garden rows or beds. Average days to maturity can range from 27 days for early-maturing

Keep your seed packets as they contain necessary information like the average days to maturity or days to harvest.

Eggplant is one of the most efficient crops in a vegetable garden since you can harvest fruit from each plant for a longer period of time.

radish varieties to 110 days for certain hard-shelled squash. When you set out (transplant) seedlings rather than seed, you cut an average of eight weeks off the posted maturity date. If you garden in hardiness zone 3, 4, or 5, you have a relatively short frost-free growing season. Because of this, the average-days-to-maturity information is a critical factor in choosing varieties for your garden.

Whether it's the fruit of a plant or the plant itself that's eaten is another factor in its efficiency, as are the number of pickings you can make. Tomatoes, peppers, okra, eggplant, and ever-bearing strawberries are among the most efficient crops because you can pick their fruit over an extended period. Cabbage, collards, kale, and Swiss chard are efficient because you can either eat the entire plant or harvest bottom leaves and stems as they mature. Sweet corn is not efficient. Once you have pulled an ear or two from a stalk, that's it. However, the flavor of fresh-picked corn makes up for its inefficiency.

## Days to Harvest

Many seed packets and catalogs provide a number for each variety that represents how many days it will take from sowing (or sometimes from transplanting) until the crop is ready for harvest. Treat these estimates with caution. The actual length of time it takes to grow the plant can vary considerably between regions and between gardens. The climate, seasonal weather, soil type, amount of fertilizer, and many other factors will affect the speed of growth. Sometimes, the number varies from catalog to catalog for the same variety. This may reflect each catalog company's experience of growing in different regions.

The "days to harvest" number on the packet also may not consider that you can harvest some vegetables, such as baby salad greens, at an earlier, immature stage. Fortunately, more companies are now giving maturity dates for "baby" vegetables, where appropriate.

Despite the inconsistencies, "days to harvest" or "days to maturity" is a useful guide to differences between varieties. In one catalog, for example, the radish 'French Breakfast' is described as maturing in 25 to 30 days, while the radish 'Black Spanish Round' matures in 60 days. Even if these numbers are not exact when it comes to growing these radishes in your own garden, it's obvious which variety you should choose if speed is important.

# Growing and Care

Watering is perhaps the most important element of the garden under your control. Make sure to keep track of your rainfall. An inexpensive rain gauge is a great investment. In the Northeast, you'll typically get one good soaking storm per week during the summer, and that's perfect. If a week goes by without one, it's time to water—but not twenty minutes a night every night for a week; you'd be watering at the worst time of day and promoting shallow root growth.

When you need to provide supplemental water, you should try to do so like nature would—a long, slow soaking that delivers 1" (2.5cm) of water, once a week. An inch doesn't sound like much, but it amounts to at least a full night of heavy rain.

The best time to water is in the morning, which can begin overnight if it takes a couple of hours for your irrigation system to deliver that inch of water—as long as you end the watering just as the morning sun begins to dry the plants. Don't water in the evening and stop before the sun rises; a plant that stays wet overnight will

A rain gauge is essential to prevent overwatering and underwatering. It's a must-have.

## MEASURE MOISTNESS BEFORE YOU WATER

Let's say you've lost track of all rainfall, and you don't know when it last rained. Put a stick that will show wetness (like a paint stirrer) down into the soil a couple of inches. If you can see moistness, don't water; the roots are still wet. But, if you push it down to a depth of 6" (15.2cm) or so and still see only dry soil, go ahead and water. Don't water just because the surface of the soil is dry! The top 1" (2.5cm) or so of a garden can dry out fast, but it doesn't count; it's the moisture down at the root zone that matters.

Also be sure not to water just because the leaves of a plant are wilting, and it *looks* like it needs water. Especially if it's the middle of a hot and sunny day (that plant will probably perk right back up at sunset), or you've been pouring a bucketful on the poor plant every day for the past month, rain or shine (that plant will never perk up again—because overwatered plants look exactly like plants that need water).

be an unhappy plant—especially a tomato plant. This is also true for lawns, lilacs, roses, and dogwoods—they all respond dramatically to wet evenings.

If you use a sprinkler and are uncertain how long it takes your particular sprinkler to deliver 1" (2.5cm) of water, it's easy to test and find out. Arrange a couple of rain gauges, tin cans, or small containers throughout the area to be watered, and then time how long it takes them to fill up to 1" (2.5cm). That's how long you want your sprinkler to water. Use a timer if the necessary timing would require you to get up and turn it on at 3:30 in the morning.

Some people just love to water their landscape every evening, because that's when the neighbors are out watching. But nighttime watering of any kind invites disease, and frequent short watering at any time of the day or night leads to plants with shallow roots. And constant watering that never allows roots to ever dry out completely will just drown your plants.

In a typical summer, with typical rain, you shouldn't have to water much, if at all—especially if you've got a

## WATERING BASICS

Apply about 1" (2.5cm) of water a week, preferably delivered all at once, slowly and right at the root zone, and ending just as the sun rises in the early morning.

Really—that's it. And it's true for almost every plant: tomatoes, flowers, lawns, trees, etc. One inch (2.5cm) a week "from you or the sky," as the saying goes.

Watering that wets the plants should only be done in the early morning, never in the evening.

nice moisture-conserving mulch around the base of (but not touching) your plants to keep moisture in the soil. However, some gardens will dry out faster than others. These include:

- Gardens in full sun
- Gardens with un-mulched soil
- Gardens with sandy soil
- Gardens in a blisteringly hot climate
- Gardens in any climate during a blisteringly hot, dry season

Pay attention to conditions and be prepared to deviate from suggested watering patterns if the weather is chaotic or unusual.

## Water Application Options

If you want to leave a hose dripping away at the base of each of your plants for an hour or so, and then move it to the next one, that will work fine. It is better for the plants than a sprinkler, but a sprinkler set up high in the middle of a garden can take care of everything at once.

The best way to water is with soaker hoses: specialized hoses that you lay on the surface of the soil and cover with mulch. The hoses either release small amounts of water through little pinholes or sweat the water out. They

waste zero water, apply it at the slow rate plants love, and (unlike a sprinkler) only apply water where you want and do not water weeds.

Soaker hoses are especially worth looking into if you live in a traditionally dry climate, pay for your water, or sometimes face water restrictions. (They can see the sprinkler spinning around; they can't see hoses sweating under your mulch!) Alternatively, use a rotating sprinkler up on a big pole in the center of the garden for when you need it. It does a great job of wetting everything down, especially early in the morning.

## Watering Time

The exact amount of time and effort you need to spend watering or setting your irrigation system to water will depend on your local conditions, particularly how moisture-retentive you have managed to make your soil and the vagaries of the weather in any particular year. In general, however, once plants are established, they require watering less often than might be expected, and a great deal of time can be saved by knowing when your watering will significantly increase the harvest a crop produces. Watering frugally encourages plants to develop a good root system, sending roots deep into the soil in search of water, and this in turn makes them better able to gather moisture and nutrients from the soil, rendering them less reliant on being watered and more drought tolerant.

In a low-maintenance plot, less work is the aim, so well-thought-out watering pays off. Overwatering can affect the taste of some crops, literally diluting the taste, and possibly makes them more susceptible to diseases and encourages slugs and snails. Too much water can also compact the soil and wash away the nutrients you have worked hard to get into the soil. Often a good soaking just once a week is enough for most crops, if at all. It is hard to be dogmatic as many factors will affect the need to water, but here are some guidelines:

- Recently transplanted young plants and newly emerged seedlings will need to be watered, especially in very warm weather, until they are established.
- A good deluge once a week or every ten days, depending on the weather conditions, should be sufficient for most vegetables. This is preferable to watering more frequently in small amounts as this encourages surface rooting, which in turn makes plants more reliant on watering. Most plants draw water from the top 12" (30.5cm) of soil, so aim to keep that moist. The surface may look dry but that is irrelevant to your vegetables—the condition of the soil several inches down is what matters.

- Focus on watering when it really counts. Some plants, such as leafy brassicas, spinach, and salad leaves, need a steady supply of water, while others will produce a much heavier crop if they are watered at the key time, usually when they are flowering and fruits are being produced. Also, water any wilting plants, as this is a sign that moisture levels are low.
- It is better to water very early in the morning rather than at night or in the heat of the day. Water applied in the heat of the day will be likely to evaporate before it does any good or will scorch the leaves, and watering at night engenders the kind of damp environment that encourages slugs and snails and can cause molds.
- Water the soil, not the plant, as delicate leaves can be damaged or rot if blasted with a watering can or sprinkler. Use a fine rose on a watering can or drip or spray delivery nozzles on an irrigation system to avoid washing away the soil and prevent the water from running off rather than seeping into the soil.
- If it rains enough, there is no need to water, but light showers in warm or windy weather may not actually be enough to really wet the soil.

Soaker hoses, which release small amounts of water into the ground via little holes without wetting plant leaves, are a great way to water.

- Watering with rainwater is best for the plants, the environment, and your pocket if you are on a water meter. A few simple rain barrels under downspouts from the house, garage, or shed roofs will collect sufficient rainwater for watering, although increasingly complex rainwater harvesting systems are available with below-ground tanks to service the needs of the garden and some parts of the house. Submersible pumps are available for rain barrels that can be connected to an irrigation system. Gray water collected from the house should not be used in the vegetable patch as it is likely to contain residues of cleaning products.

## WHEN AND HOW MUCH TO WATER COMMON VEGETABLES

The lists here are a general guide for which vegetables require a lot of water, which require minimal amounts of water, and which require more careful timing for watering. These are general guidelines based around the average climate and average plants, so remember to evaluate your watering needs based on the conditions in your garden and the health of your own plants.

### Plants Needing Plenty of Water

- Zucchinis
- Squash
- Pumpkins
- Runner beans
- Salad leaves and lettuces
- Cucumbers

### Plants to Water at Key Times When Fruits Are Swelling

- Fava beans (broad beans)
- Peas
- Green beans
- Raspberries
- Strawberries
- Tomatoes

### Plants That Seldom Need Watering

- Carrots
- Beets and most root crops
- Onions
- Shallots
- Garlic
- Rhubarb
- Jerusalem artichokes
- Artichokes

# Crop Rotation in Practice

Not growing the same crop in the same bed each year is common sense. Each crop removes a slightly different set of nutrients from the soil, and repeatedly growing the same crop in the same area would deplete the special mix of nutrients that crop requires. Pests and diseases associated with the crop will build up in the soil and become an intractable problem. So, it is logical to leave it as long as possible before growing a crop or closely related crops in the same bed. Some gardeners find that three years works well, others four. If you have a real problem with a particular disease, leave it as long as you can before returning the same crop to that bed.

This is one of the areas in which keeping a good notebook or set of plans recording what you've grown where over several seasons will be helpful, especially if you use catch crops and attractive patterns that can be difficult to remember. Get your previous plans out when you put in orders for plants and seeds and make a new plan for the upcoming year, ensuring that you have enough space for everything in a different spot from where it grew previously.

There are a whole host of rules that you can follow, with crops divided into groups and the order in which they should follow each other set out. The rules are all very sensible and have sound horticultural reasons behind them, but the likelihood is that in reality it will be hard to adhere to them for a number of reasons. Firstly, the exact growing space required by one group may not be identical to that required by the group that follows, and you may want to grow more cabbages than peas, or maybe no cabbages at all. Secondly, crops such as runner beans and Jerusalem artichokes can only occupy certain spots in the garden to avoid casting a shadow over other beds. And thirdly, you may just not have enough space for the system to work. A small plot has little space between beds and so diseases and pests might easily travel. Some diseases, such as clubroot, persist in the soil for tens of years so can't be outmaneuvered!

Having said all that, here are the pared-down rules to aspire to. Grouped for a three-year rotation, crops follow each other in numerical order. A four-year rotation would subdivide the groups even further.

- **Group 1**—Roots, such as carrots, leeks, onions, beets (beetroot), and shallots.
- **Group 2**—Podded and fruiting vegetables, such as peas, beans, zucchinis (courgettes), cucumbers, pumpkins, and sweet corn.
- **Group 3**—Brassicas, such as broccoli, cabbages, kale, and radishes.
- **Other crops can be slotted in anywhere.**

A major advantage of rotation is that the character of one crop can be used to benefit the next. Podded vegetables fix nitrogen into the soil via nodules on their roots, so if you leave these in the soil, the brassicas that follow benefit from this and can draw on that reserve of nitrogen to produce a profusion of robust leaves. It then follows that root crops requiring less nitrogen can be planted in the next rotation after the brassicas. Also, crops such as potatoes can shade out weeds, so the following year those beds should have less of a weed problem and will suit onions and carrots. Crop rotation is at the very heart of low-maintenance vegetable gardening, particularly if you are choosing to grow organically, and a bit of time spent planning will reward you for years to come.

---

### THE BASICS

Leave as long as possible before growing the same crop and all related crops in the same location. This avoids a buildup of pests and diseases and the partial erosion of fertility.

---

# Never Let Weeds Get Out of Hand

You will have to deal with some weeds throughout every growing season. They will sprout from seeds that blow in on the wind or that lurk in the soil. The trick is to dig weeds out of beds and aisles before they go to seed or spread a network of perennial roots. But keep in mind that every time you disturb the soil, you expose a few more dormant weed seeds. Take a dandelion digger with you on your weed safaris. With its small, V-pointed, long-shank blade, you can cut roots deep in the soil and pull the weed out with little disturbance. Throw weeds into your compost pile. If you leave them where they were pulled, they may take root and regrow. The day following a rain or deep irrigation is ideal for weeding.

If you pull, dig out, or hoe weeds as soon as you see them, and don't allow them to go to seed, you will soon reduce the number that sprout in your garden. While weeds among your vegetables might attract beneficial insects, weeds compete strongly with vegetables for plant nutrients and soil moisture.

## Minimize Weeds from the Get-Go

Your first year of gardening can determine how much time you will spend weeding over the next several years. You need to start by eliminating as many weed and grass seeds and roots of perennial grasses as possible. If you also modify your soil with an organic soil conditioner, you will help to minimize weeds and sprouting grasses for several years. The few that do germinate or sprout can be hoed or pulled out of the crumbly soil with little difficulty. See Combating Weeds starting on page 184 for more details on preventing weeds before you plant.

On the other hand, if you merely dig up the soil, sod and all, and throw in some seeds, you will encourage grass clumps and the sprouting of weed seeds that have been lying dormant for many years. This will make it extremely difficult to thin out crops of vegetables that produce small, slow-growing seedlings because they will be hard to distinguish from the weeds.

For many years, the commonly accepted method for reducing aggressive perennial grasses and weeds was to spray with a glyphosate weed and grass killer. Now,

Rid your garden of weeds when they are still small.

## PLANTS THAT ACT LIKE WEEDS

You are asking for trouble if you grow any flavor of mint or any species of fennel or garlic chives in your garden soil. Fennel is such a robust, free-seeding plant that it has been declared an invasive weed in some states. Garlic chives are just as determined and will persist as a weed for years after you dig out and discard the original plants.

Robust plants, such as mint, can act like invasive weeds, popping up for years in your garden soil. The best defense is to keep these plants contained in pots or half-barrels.

# CONTROLLING WEEDS WITHOUT CHEMICALS

If you choose not to use herbicides to control weeds:

1. Use a spade to remove the top 2" (5.1cm) of soil or sod.
2. Till or spade the scalped soil to "spade depth" (8" to 9" [20.3 to 22.9cm] deep).
3. Irrigate the soil, and wait three weeks for weed seeds or perennial roots to sprout.
4. Rake the garden more or less level, watching for and removing fleshy roots of perennial grasses and weeds. Discard stones and sticks.
5. Spread soil conditioner and fertilizer and work them into the top 6" (15.2cm) of soil. Wait for three weeks. Rake the soil more or less level.
6. Shovel soil from the aisles onto the beds to raise their level. Smooth and level the beds using an iron rake. This will eliminate many of the weed seedlings.
7. Check the aisles for sufficient slope, and spread mulch over walkways.
8. Begin planting your crops.
9. If you did not spray with herbicide, you will need to watch for sprigs of Bermuda grass and other perennial weeds and dig them out promptly. Simply pulling them out will usually leave enough roots to resprout.

Lettuce and corn mulched with black plastic grow weed free.

because research is throwing doubt on the safety of many herbicides, organic gardeners opt instead to remove the top 2" (5.1cm) of soil or turf where weed seeds and perennial roots are concentrated. Fortunately, you will find many uses for this extra soil, such as filling low spots.

Another way to deal with weeds is to cover the worked-up soil with a sheet of plastic anchored around the edges. This is touted as a way to sterilize soil, thus killing weed seeds and roots. The problem is that the heat that collects beneath the plastic tends to rise and move to the top of the slope, leaving lower areas of the garden without its benefits.

A somewhat unattractive alternative is covering tilled soil with used carpet for about a month during warm weather. You can also spade soil rather than pulverizing it with a power tiller. Keep one spade that is lightweight with a standard-size blade, one that has a small blade for setting out perennials, and a third that has a steel handle and a heavy-duty blade for prying out rocks and stumps.

# Picking and Harvesting

It makes good sense to harvest crops as soon as they are ready. Doing so prolongs the picking season and reduces the stress on the plants. Fruits that drop on the ground should either be salvaged or put in the compost pile, as should chopped prunings.

The degree of grooming required depends on how visible your garden is from windows in the house or from the street, how much free time you have, and whether you are a fastidious person by nature. Routine, periodic grooming takes less time than playing catch-up with a weed crop or garden that has gotten out of hand.

## Harvest Time

It's that moment that rewards all your hard work—the moment when you proudly carry your first crops of the season to the kitchen. With fast-maturing vegetables, you won't have to wait too long for that moment to arrive. You don't always have to wait until a crop is mature.

### PICK WHEN LARGE ENOUGH

The quickest crops to harvest are sprouting seeds. Just a few days after they have started to grow, they will be ready to eat. When they have grown enough to provide a meal, it will just be a case of giving them a quick rinse before eating.

You can also harvest baby leaf greens as soon as they are large enough to make picking them worthwhile. You can either pick a few leaves at a time from each of several plants of different varieties or cut a number of plants all at once. Leave a stump about 1"–2" (2.5–5.1cm) tall, and it will resprout to provide another harvest after a couple of weeks. You might even get three or more cuttings from the same plant.

Many plants provide the tastiest, most tender crops if they are picked while young. Marble-size new potatoes have a wonderful flavor, and nothing is sweeter than a tiny baby carrot. However, the total weight of your

You can usually tell when berries, such as blueberries, are ripe by the color. The deeper the color, the sweeter the berry.

Some vegetables, such as squash, continue to grow quickly once they are ready to harvest. Make sure you inspect and harvest plants regularly before they mature too much.

A pair of sharp scissors is ideal for cutting baby leaf greens quickly.

harvest will be higher if you let the plants grow until they are bulkier. You may prefer to let them grow just a little larger to get a better return for the amount of space the plants have taken up—and for the effort you have put in.

### PICK WHEN RIPE

Some vegetables need to be left until they are fully developed to be worth eating. Tomatoes, for example, have the best flavor when the fruit is left on the plants until they are completely ripe. If they are picked while still slightly green, they will eventually ripen even off the plant. However, they do not taste as sweet as those that ripen on the vine. You should also let blueberries and strawberries ripen before picking them.

### PICK IN BETWEEN

Several crops need to develop to a midway stage, but you can harvest them before they reach full maturity. Peas, for example, need time to flower and develop pods, but you can pick the pods well before the peas inside are mature. Harvest them when the pods are plump, smooth, and green, with the peas inside visible when the pod is held up to the light. The peas should be small enough to be separate and not touching within the pod. If the pods are left on the

Pick pea pods before they become limp by the late afternoon to ensure that new flowers—and a new crop—will keep developing.

plants until they become dry and parchmentlike, with the peas crammed tightly together inside, they will be mealy and starchy instead of tender and sweet.

Pick beans while they are still young enough to snap crisply in half. Zucchini and summer squash are best harvested while the flower is still attached to the vegetable.

Harvest peppers and chilies at several stages. You can enjoy the immature, green vegetable as soon as it is large enough, but if you leave it on the plant, it will change in color and flavor as it approaches ripeness, becoming sweeter (peppers) or hotter (chilies).

## Harvest Basics

Making sure you pick your crops in the right way will enable you to enjoy them at their best. Using the correct harvesting techniques can also help to ensure that the plants keep producing for as long as possible.

### CHOOSE THE RIGHT TIME OF DAY

The best time to pick most crops is early in the morning, when they contain the most moisture. On hot, sunny days, some crops, such as lettuce and zucchini, can become limp and flabby by the late afternoon or early evening, and they will not be as tasty, or keep as well, if they are picked then.

A large border fork will enable you to harvest several potatoes at a time—but be careful not to spear them.

### CUTTING

A sharp knife is valuable for harvesting many crops. If you pull up lettuce by hand, you will often bring up the root as well. Not only will this disturb the roots of the neighboring plants in the row, but it will also shower their heads with soil. It's much better to slice the lettuce off cleanly at the base with a knife.

Use a sharp knife for picking other leafy crops, such as spinach, too, because pulling leaves away by hand can often loosen the plants in the soil. For baby leaves, a pair of sharp kitchen scissors does the job well.

### PLUCKING

Handle ripe "fruits," such as tomatoes, gently so that you don't bruise them, cupping them in the palm of your hand instead of pinching them with your fingers. Break the stem of tomatoes at the swollen knuckle on the stem so that the spiderlike calyx remains attached to the fruit. You should also pick strawberries complete with their frilly calyx. These fruits will usually keep better if the calyx is still attached.

Pull peas and beans from the plants as they are ready, but be careful that you don't tug too hard and pull the whole plant up by the root, especially in light soil. Hold onto the plant stem with one hand while you pick the pods with the other.

### DIGGING

Lift root crops, such as potatoes, carrots, and beets, and rootlike stems, such as onions and kohlrabi, from the soil. In light, loose soil that contains plenty of organic matter, you can simply pull these vegetables up by hand, but more often it is advisable to use a garden fork—either a hand fork or a full-size border fork, depending on the crop. Drive the fork into the soil a few inches away from the row and lever up the roots carefully. When digging potatoes, remember that the tubers spread widely. If you dig too close to the plant stem, you will probably bring up the fork and find a potato impaled on every prong. The best time to pick most crops is early in the morning, when they contain the most moisture.

### KEEP THEM CROPPING

A plant's purpose is usually to grow, flower, and produce ripe seeds to perpetuate itself. Once it has achieved that, its job is done, and it will stop cropping. If you want

When plucking fruit, be sure to gently lift and twist—if it's ripe, there won't be any resistance.

to keep vegetables such as peas, beans, and zucchini producing food for a long period, do not let their seeds mature. This will force the plant into producing more and more seeds to try to achieve its aim. Always pick these kinds of vegetables as soon as they are ready for eating, so they never get a chance to mature fully.

## Harvesting Fruits

The storage life of all fruits will depend primarily on whether or not the fruit was initially picked correctly; incorrectly harvested fruits will deteriorate very quickly. The storage of the fruit can be short term, where they are placed in a fruit bowl for eating quickly, or long term, for fruits placed in storage to be eaten over a period of months. No fruit picked from a tree can cope with being handled roughly, so a gentle approach is required.

To check whether the fruits are ready for harvest, select a fruit and lift it, usually with a cupped hand, then either continue to lift gently or lift gently while twisting slightly.

If the fruit is ready, it will come away from the tree easily, but if it shows resistance to these actions, it is not fully ripe and should be left in place.

When the fruits are ready to be picked, harvesting should be carried out with a container, such as a basket, bucket, or something similar that has a soft bottom to it. If the container has a hard or rough bottom, line it with a cloth or towel so that the fruits have a soft base on which to sit. Once you have removed the fruits from the tree, place them carefully in the container and, once the bottom layer has been completed, place any subsequent fruits on top of each other with extra care. If fruits are dropped onto each other, even from a low height, they will bruise, shortening their storage time. When the container is full, take out the fruits with exactly the same care used to pick and place them in in the first place. It may seem like overkill to be so careful, but it will make an enormous difference in the time during which they are ideal for eating or storing.

# CHAPTER 8
# Storing and Using Your Produce

Whether you simply have too many of one type of vegetable to eat at once, or whether you want to store some so that you can enjoy them at a later date, you need to know the best ways to keep your produce in prime condition. How you store your produce is crucial, as it will extend the time during which you can your vegetables, fruits, and herbs. The primary aim is to ensure that these stored vegetables will be on hand during the winter months when the availability of fresh produce is not at its highest, thereby providing a greater choice for mealtimes. Most fruits, vegetables, and herbs will store better using traditional methods than in the more modern chest freezer, although some crops can be frozen.

The most important point to note about storing vegetables, fruits, and herbs is to store only perfectly healthy produce. Each item should be carefully checked before being stored. Any produce with blemishes or mechanical damage, or showing signs of rotting, needs to be eaten immediately or discarded rather than stored, as it will potentially rot and affect perfectly healthy crops in the process.

Some vegetables stay in the best condition if left on the plants until needed. This is true for hardy fall and winter crops, such as leeks and beets. However, many crops need to be picked while at their peak and will spoil if left too long. Pick these as soon as they are ready.

Vegetables and fruits are at their best when eaten as soon as possible after picking. Once picked, they continue to lose moisture through evaporation, with no opportunity to replace it from the soil. Instead of being crisp and fresh, they will soon become limp, flabby, and nowhere near as appetizing. The sugar present in vegetables such as peas also begins to be transformed into starch as soon as they are harvested from the plant; in a short time, their wonderful sweetness is lost.

**CROPS SUITABLE FOR FREEZING**
- Beans
- Broccoli
- Carrots
- Herbs
- Peas
- Spinach
- Swiss chard

Select only healthy, unblemished produce for storage.

# Short-Term Storage

If it is not possible to eat crops immediately after picking, you can slow down the deterioration process. Harvest in the cool early morning so that the crops are filled with moisture. Put any damaged produce to one side so that mold cannot spread. Place newly picked produce in a cool, shady, well-ventilated place as soon as possible; rinse or spray it with fresh, cold water, if appropriate.

Slow down further moisture evaporation by placing the produce in a plastic bag or wrapping it in damp paper towels; then place it in a cool pantry or the refrigerator vegetable crisper drawer. Most vegetables will remain in good condition for several days like this. Leave vegetables such as beans whole instead of preparing them ahead of time. Once cut up, they deteriorate more rapidly.

# Long-Term Storage

If you intend to keep your produce for longer than a few days—so that you can enjoy some of this summer's surplus next winter, for example—there are several methods you can use to store it.

**Frozen:** One way to store surplus fruits and vegetables is by freezing, which usually keeps them in good condition. Not all crops freeze well—tomatoes and zucchini, for example, turn mushy. However, turn them into a cooked dish, such as ratatouille, and even they will freeze successfully. You can extend the useful life of many frozen vegetables by blanching them briefly in boiling water before freezing, which improves their long-term color and texture.

**Dried:** Drying is an age-old method of storage and is good for vegetables such as shelling beans, tomatoes, herbs, and chilies. A warm, well-ventilated place is necessary for drying. The modern method is to use a food dehydrator, which does an excellent job.

## TIME-SAVER

If you have a short-term abundance of vegetables that you need to freeze, and you know you'll be eating them within a few weeks, you don't need to blanch the vegetables before freezing them.

**Pickled or preserved:** Sugar, salt, and vinegar are all great preservatives that have been used for generations. Any good recipe book will have plenty of recipes that use a wide variety of vegetables and fruits to produce a whole range of preserves—including jellies, chutneys, and pickles—to stock your pantry shelves.

# Storage Tips by Plant Type

The storage conditions for most fruits and vegetables are fairly similar in that they generally require a cool, dark place to keep for the maximum time. The coolness of storage will slow the maturing or ripening process of the produce. For longer storage, the cooler, the better, as long as it remains frost-free. If the produce does become frosted, it will generally turn into an inedible mush. Darkness also helps to reduce the maturing and ripening process. Usually, a garage or shed is ideal for storing fruits and vegetables, as long as it is free from rodents. Most produce should be stored in containers, although for large amounts of potatoes or root crops, a straw clamp (a traditional method for storing root vegetables underground) can be used. If straw is readily available, pile the crop into a heap and pack the straw over it as insulation from frost. Due to the looseness and lightness of straw, it is best kept in bales or held in place by a tarp. Move the straw and remove any produce as and when it is required.

## Onions, Shallots, and Garlic

It is important when growing onions, shallots, and garlic for storage to select the varieties you grow carefully. Some varieties do not store well, while others will store for several months. Taste is all-important to most people, but so is the supply of bulbs throughout the winter and early spring. While the taste of varieties that store well is important, it is secondary to their ability to store. The length a storing variety will last in storage is determined by the variety itself (some store longer than others) in combination with correct growing, harvesting, and drying practices prior to storing.

The most important first step is to ensure that the stems of each bulb are allowed to fall over of their own

Root vegetables can be cleaned up for easy storage. Other vegetables require freezing, drying, or pickling/preserving.

free will. Do not be tempted to bend over the stems before they are ready, as this will not enable the crop to be lifted early, dried in the sunnier weather, and stored. Trying to rush the process artificially only results in the storage life of the bulbs being shortened.

Once the stems of the onions, shallots, and garlic have fallen over, gone brown, and withered on the whole row, they are ready to be lifted. To harden the skin and extend storage time, the bulbs then need to be dried. The easiest way is to first, as the tops of the bulbs start to bend, carefully pull some of the soil away from the bulb to expose as much of it as possible to the sun and start the drying process. When they are ready to be lifted, build a very simple drying bed consisting of four posts and a piece of chicken wire. Pound in the four posts and attach the chicken wire to it with *U* nails so that it is tight, but not completely inflexible. This wire cradle should be 18"–24" (45.7–61cm) from the ground to allow good air circulation.

If the weather turns very wet and it looks as if this is likely to last for several days, the onions, shallots, and garlic need to be brought inside to complete the drying process under cover. A polyethylene tunnel is best for this, but a lean-to, shed, or similar structure will do the same job. After a couple of weeks, the bulbs will have dried enough to store. The easiest and cheapest way to store your bulbs is to request netted onion bags from a fruit and vegetable vendor at a farmers' market. Before storing in netted bags, remove and discard the brown, withered bulb tops. The produce can then be stored in a cool, dark place on slatted benches or, better still, hanging up where they will get excellent air circulation. The second way of storing is to tie them into long strands or bunches, as you'll often see in the supermarkets with garlic.

## Potatoes

This is an easy crop to store and will potentially last until February or March. Just like when they're growing, stored potatoes will turn green if exposed to light, so they need to be stored in a dark place. It is also important to use paper bags that are not coated with any waxy substances; the bag must be able to breathe so that the potatoes inside do not sweat and ultimately rot. Burlap bags are very good, but only if the potatoes are stored in complete darkness since the bags are woven and will allow light through.

Once lifted, the main-crop potatoes for storage must be left on the soil surface to dry for a day or so. It is important to remove as much of the soil from each potato as possible while harvesting. This soil not only adds weight to the bag but also potentially harbors pests—as well as being very messy when you ultimately clean the potatoes prior to cooking. The drying on the soil surface hardens the skin and extends the storage time.

Just as with onions, shallots, and garlic, there are some varieties of potato that store better than others, so you should research prior to ordering. Once the potatoes have dried, sort them into perfect tubers for storage and imperfect ones to be eaten first. Due to their different uses, always store only one variety of potato to a bag. After filling, tie the bag at the top, label it with the potato variety, and move the bag into storage. To prevent any rotting from a damp floor, stand your bags on an old wooden pallet. This will allow good air circulation around the whole bag. The bags can then be opened, and potatoes taken as required. Always remember to reseal the bag to prevent the potatoes from turning green.

## Parsnips

It has long been a belief held by gardeners that the sweetness in parsnips is obtained by the roots being subjected to a good, hard, and penetrating frost. This may or may not be the case, but the fact is that if the ground

Potatoes will turn green and become harmful if exposed to light. If this happens, be sure to remove all green parts of the potatoes prior to eating.

is frozen solid and parsnips are on the menu, there is no chance whatsoever of getting them out of the ground to eat. This is where short- and long-term storage becomes essential. Short-term storage involves digging up a few parsnips every week and storing them in a loosely filled trench, so that they can be easily harvested from there when required, even after a particularly hard frost. The method of long-term storage is identical to that for all the other root crops.

## Other Root Crops

Most of the root crops, such as carrot, beet, celeriac, rutabaga (swede), kohlrabi, turnip, scorzonera (black salsify), and salsify, can be stored for a lengthy period by using this method. Each of the crops, once harvested, needs to be cleaned of as much soil as possible without damaging the roots. This removes any harboring pests, as well as enabling the roots to be checked for damage. For all of the root types except beets, the tops should be cut off with a sharp knife as close to the top of the root as possible. If too much top growth is left on, this may potentially rot, possibly causing the rest of the root to rot from the top down. Beets, however, will "bleed" if the leaf stems are cut cleanly, limiting their storage potential. Therefore, it is best to hold the root firmly while twisting the tops until they tear, leaving approximately 1" (2.5cm) of top on the root. The leaf stems of beets do not seem to rot in storage.

Once the roots have been cleaned and the tops dealt with, the roots are ready for storing. The container used to store them can be a deep tray, wooden box, or large planter—in fact, anything that can be moved, if required, and can contain the packing material. Moist coarse sand, vermiculite (a mica-like mineral), bark, or moist soil can all be used as packing material around the roots. It is important that the packing material is kept moist (but not wet) to keep the roots cool and prevent them from drying out and becoming inedible. If the tray or box to be used is slatted or has regular holes that the packing material will fall through, line it with cardboard or newspaper.

Next, put a thin layer of packing material into the bottom of the tray, and lay out the first layer of roots. They need to be packed in as tightly as possible without touching. Place another layer of packing material over the roots, ensuring that it falls between the roots and totally

Beet leaf stems need to be left on or torn shorter rather than cut, but luckily they don't tend to rot in storage.

covers them, before repeating the laying-out process. Continue until the tray or box is full and the last layer is completely covered with the packing material. If it is a large tray or box, you should fill it where you plan to store the items because the container will probably be too heavy to move once filled with sand, soil, or bark.

For smaller amounts of roots, you can use a large pot. Cut a circle of cardboard to cover the drainage holes at the bottom of the pot, then cover it with a 4" (10.2cm) layer of packing material. Push the roots into the material so that they are standing vertically, placing as many as the pot will accommodate without touching. Fill in around and over the tops of the roots with the packing material. When storing celeriac roots, use a very large pot, up to 4' (121.9cm) in diameter, because the roots tend to be quite big.

Once you've stored each of the roots in its appropriate container, the most important job is to label the containers; otherwise, attempting to collect produce from storage becomes a mess. After labeling, store in a cool, dark place—the cooler, the better, as this will slow down the regrowth of the root tops. Also, if there is a possibility of cats gaining access to the storage area, ensure that each pot is covered with a piece of cardboard held down with a stone or brick. If you do not do this, there may be an unpleasant surprise waiting for the first person to harvest produce!

## Summer Squash (Marrows), Pumpkins, and Other Squash

The most important aspect when considering the storage life of pumpkins or squash is the toughness of the outer skin. In order to get the maximum storage time, the skin needs to be ripened and toughened in the late summer sun for several weeks. To get the best overall ripeness, stand each fruit on a brick, pot, or something similar that lifts it away from the moist ground.

Once the skin feels tough and before the first frost, cut the fruits so that 4"–6" (10.2–15.2cm) of stalk is left on the fruit. The stalk dries and hardens very quickly, protecting the neck of the fruit in storage. Then store the fruits in a cool, dry place in a position where they receive excellent air circulation; sitting on slatted shelves or an old wooden pallet would be ideal. If ripened for long enough, summer squash can last two to three months in storage, while pumpkins and winter squashes can be stored for up to nine months.

## Hot Peppers

Hopefully, by the end of the summer, your crop will be laden with an abundance of hot peppers. Harvest and either dry them on greenhouse benching or similar indoor structures for at least a couple of weeks. Once dried, store them in sealed airtight jars, where they will last for several years.

## Celery

Self-blanching celery cannot be stored outside because it is produced aboveground and will therefore succumb to frost. It can be lifted and plunged into vermiculite, soil, or bark, where it will last for two to three weeks. Blanched or trench celery, however, is buried in the ground and the tops mounded with soil, giving the plants excellent insulation against frost. These can be stored in the ground and dug up as and when required.

Dried hot peppers are long-lasting and perfect to have on hand in the kitchen.

# Index

Note: Page numbers in **bold** indicate vegetable profiles including **general information, varieties, sowing, growing, harvesting, and common problem/solutions information**.

# Photo Credits